Thirty Years
On the Road
with Gene Autry

Best Wishes
Johnny Bond

Thirty Years
On the Road
with Gene Autry

RECOLLECTIONS

by

Johnny Bond

BEVERLY AND JIM ROGERS MUSEUM OF *Lone Pine* FILM HISTORY

Published by Riverwood Press and the
Beverly and Jim Rogers Museum of Lone Pine Film History

Copyright © 2007 by Sherry Bond

General Editor: Packy Smith
Cover Design: Elizabeth Gulick
Prepress Production: Michael Bifulco
Printed by: Sheridan Books, Inc.
Typefaces: Meta and Minion

ISBN 978-1-880756-18-8

Printed in the United States of America

FIRST EDITION

10 9 8 7 6 5 4 3 2 1

Acknowledgments

Like any book of this type, an enormous amount of gratitude is owed a number of people who recognized the value of 'the Manuscript' and supported the effort to see it published after so many years.

First, to Chris Langley, the Executive Director of the Beverly and Jim Rogers Museum of Lone Pine Film History, for seeing the value of this book and agreeing to allow it to be the first title to come under the new Museum's imprint. Thanks also to Woody Wise, who helped guarantee that the book would be published with both moral and financial support.

For help with pictures, we want to thank Les Leverett, Boyd and Donna Magers, Packy Smith, Ed Phillips, Neil Summers, Danny Schwartz and the family of Johnny Bond.

Thanks to Mike Bifulco for his tireless efforts in the layout and design of the text; and thanks to Elizabeth Gulick for the design and execution of the beautiful cover.

Last and most important, thanks to Stanley Rojo. Not only did he recognize the manuscript for what it was when it was offered at auction, he graciously agreed to allow access so that the entire story could be told, just as Johnny Bond intended.

Contents

Foreword

People often ask me what I remember most about my Dad. I remember him always sitting at the typewriter . . . well, actually, I remember him sitting, standing, walking with the D-28 Martin in his hands, just casually strumming chords. I asked him why he always had the Martin with him, and he told me it was to keep his calluses up. His fret fingers had huge arthritis knots on the knuckles. They looked like they really hurt; but if they did, he never said so. He would strum that Martin while talking to mom or me, while watching TV, and even when Jimmy and Inez Wakely were over visiting, which was often.

But when he didn't have the Martin in his hands, he was at the typewriter. It was a new-fangled electric Royal . . . an amazing machine with a strike so hard the periods and asterisks would go right through the paper. He was mostly typing letters to producers (urging them to record his or his writers' songs) Chet Atkins, Owen Bradley and Don Pierce among many others.

Here is a story about one of Johnny's letters! In Nashville in 1984, a popular local vintage record shop called The Great Escape honored Dad for his accomplishments. *American Songwriter Magazine* presented the award and named Johnny Bond "the man who created the hyphenated title 'singer-songwriter'". We count that title among his highest honors, of which he received many including, the ultimate, induction into the Country Music Hall of Fame in 1999. When you read this book, you will find out just how much that would have meant to him. Roselee Maphis was one of the presenters that day, and she read a letter Dad wrote to her. He wrote the letter just to give her and husband Joe directions to our mountain cabin in Wrightwood, CA; but it was a rambling narrative that was clever, witty and hysterically funny. He ended with the line, "you can't get there from here."

Back to the typewriter, and *'TheManuscript'!!* He was documenting, or I should say reminiscing, about his remarkable association with a living legend – Gene Autry. When you read this book you will be able to feel the love he had for Gene and all those crazy characters that were a part of Gene's life – Frankie Marvin, Carl Cotner, Merle Travis, Pat Buttram, and Smiley "Frog" Burnette. This book will reveal just how much he truly revered his traveling buddies.

When he finished 'The Manuscript' he shared it with Gene . . . he quotes him in these pages as saying it would be fine for him to write about their life on the road and their long relationship, that nobody would care. But when presented with an actual manuscript, Gene said, "If you publish this book, I'll buy every copy." In other words, don't publish it. Dad was crushed. He went back and revised the manuscript, cutting it down from 600 pages to 300 pages (double-spaced Royal typewriter pages). Gene still said "No", so Dad put it away; in his office in the back room on Lincoln Street, where it remained until after he died in 1978. Dad and Gene were such close friends that he never considered publishing the book against Gene's wishes.

When his close friend, Tex Ritter, passed away suddenly and unexpectedly, Dorothy Ritter called Johnny and asked him to write *The Tex Ritter Story*. She didn't ask . . . she insisted until he said OK. Once he sat down at that typewriter and started writing, we rarely saw him anyplace else other than his back-room studio at 1001 Lincoln Street in Burbank, California . . . typing away.

The John Edwards Memorial Foundation, now located at the University of North Carolina, then at UCLA, asked him to write his autobiography. They were collecting as much as they could about the history of Western and country music and building quite an impressive collection. So he wrote an autobiographical essay that he called "Recollections," which the Foundation published under the title "Reflections". All I can say about Johnny's 'autobiography' is . . . "wow, Dad, you sure left a lot out!" Maybe that was because he was still hoping that the Gene Autry manuscript would eventually be published.

After Dad passed away, it was always in the back of my mind to publish the book. But the promise Dad made to Gene nagged at my conscience. I thought I'd wait until Gene passed away and then maybe it will be OK. Thankfully, Gene lived to a ripe old age and didn't leave us before his time. In the meantime, the manuscript was gathering dust. I did talk to the Country Music Foundation about the possibility of them publishing it and gave them a copy. A wake-up call came when a package arrived in the mail from Doug Green. It was an autographed copy of *Singing in the Saddle, The History of the Singing Cowboy*, written by Doug and published by the Country Music Foundation Press and Vanderbilt University Press. It is a comprehensive documentation of western music history and a first-class publication. We'll forgive Ranger Doug for putting that other singing cowboy on the cover!

'Call the Country Music Foundation' went on my to-do list, but I never made the call. Then two things happened almost simultaneously.

The First: I was sitting at my computer reading email when I received one from Stanley Rojo (Stanley is one of Gene's most ardent fans and collectors). It said (paraphrased), "Dear Sherry, I purchased your Dad's original manuscript off of the Internet, but it is missing Chapter 16. Could you please send that to me?" My reaction must have been the same as Dad's when Gene asked him not to publish the book (kinda like a karate punch to the solar-plexus). I cried. I mused, "I have the only copy. How can this be? I was going to publish it, and now it's on the Internet!" And then as I often do, I gave it up to Fate. I answered Stanley by sending him Chapter 16. I later learned that Dad had also given a copy to Gene, which is now in the Autry archive.

It's time for a little family discussion here. We all loved Dad very much, but we weren't collectors (oh what I would give now for one of his western shirts!). Mom gave the manuscript and many of Dad's things to a friend and fan, Gene Bear. When Gene was dying, he gave it all to another collector who also passed away suddenly. It all wound up in a warehouse, where it was auctioned off as unclaimed property. This was about 1992. Several years later, the purchaser sold it on eBay. (I'm still watching eBay for the out-takes from *The Tex Ritter Story*—the pages Dorothy Ritter made Johnny take out of his original copy!)

Stanley emailed back, "Your Chapter 16 doesn't match my pagination. It appears that I am missing than you have to fill in. I have 560 pages." My manuscript had 260. All this time. All these years, only come to find that I had the edited manuscript. Stanley now has *The Manuscript*.

Chapter 16 is a very significant chapter. It is about how Gene Autry came to record "Rudolf The Red Nosed Reindeer". The chapter contained in this book says that Ina Autry advised her husband to record the song. There is another version floating about, one I have heard for most of my life, and one that I would like to believe. When Gene rejected the lead sheet (written version) of the song that was sent to him in the mail, encouraged by Ina, Johnny went into his back room studio on Lincoln Street and made a demo of the song. Once Gene heard this recording of the song, he agreed to include it in his next recording session, time permitting.

The Second: The Call that I should have made a long time ago came instead from Packy Smith. (He had been in touch with me about a series of *Town Hall Party* DVDs he was then working on for Bear Family Records. He also has written notes for Bear Family Box sets and CDs of Tex Ritter and Gene Autry recordings, among others, including Johnny Bond.). Packy said, "Your father's manuscript must be published." If it weren't for him, you would not be holding this book in your hands. When we approached Stanley Rojo with our plan to publish the book, he too wanted the complete story to be told and graciously allowed us access to *The Manuscript*.

If it weren't for these two, you would never have had the opportunity to read Johnny Bond's colorful depiction of life on the road with Gene Autry. You never would know the intimate feelings of America's Favorite Cowboy. Packy made arrangements for The Jim and Beverly Rogers' Lone Pine Museum of Western Film History to make this the first publication under its new imprint. He also edited the original uncut manuscript and wove "Recollections" into the text to produce the book you are holding, so readers would have a deeper understanding about the author, Johnny Bond. It was decided to re-title the new work, *30 Years On The Road With Gene Autry: Recollections* by Johnny Bond

So Dear Readers, I hope you will feel I did the right thing allowing Johnny's manuscript to be published against Gene's wishes . . . Dad loved Gene, and I love Gene . . . heck, everybody loves Gene Autry! And I love my father, Johnny Bond.

Sherry Bond
Nashville, Tennessee
April, 2007

Preface

In the year of our Lord, Nineteen-Hundred-and-Forty, I went to work for the Gene Autry Organization. My job initially was to sing as part of a trio. Soon I was picking a guitar in a variety of situations. I was reading comedy and drama in the radio shows. I was criss-crossing the country on a tour bus as a member of the Gene Autry variety show. Within that show I was performing comedy with my Boss as straight man. I also wrote songs that he recorded; while I recorded for the record company he owned. These tasks plus about any other music related job in all aspects of Country and Western music within the organization. Oh, and one other thing I did: I observed while listening.

After more than thirty years of watchful observation I find myself compelled to write down and pass along many of the experiences in the hope that you, the reader, will get to know the great Star as I did. My employment with the singing Cowboy did not come to an abrupt end; in fact, I don't consider it having ever ended. Since I still receive royalties from both his publishing and record companies, I still feel connected to the Autry organization. I am proud to add that the friendship and fellowship is there, as strong as ever.

I will not reveal here what this story is; however, I do feel compelled to tell what it is not. This is NOT a Gene Autry biography. There are too many people trodding this earth much more capable, knowledgeable and qualified than I to do that. It is my hope and desire that someone will eventually do so. Neither will this tome offer any insight into Gene's uncanny ability to turn a quick million. Nor, is it an intimate spyglass prying into his personal and private life. It is simply the Gene Autry that I worked for and with, and whom I got to know as a friend about as well as anyone within his employ can possibly do.

If someone should ask me to sum up my total and unqualified opinion of the man I could do it. The word I would use was first connected to him back in 1930, as the name of one of the record labels he recorded for. It became a familiar word to his many millions of fans over the years as the name of his faithful horse. It is truly the one word that applies to Gene Autry.

Champion.

Johnny Bond
Burbank, California
1973

PART ONE
Recollections

"Life before Gene Autry"

Johnny Whitfield (Johnny's first billing) on WKY, 1935.

Although it is still listed on some road maps, there's no use trying to locate the little community of Enville anymore. It went away. It was at one time about half way between Marietta and Madill, in the extreme south central section of Oklahoma, not far from the Red River and right close to Lake Murray, which I helped dig.

When I first saw the light of day there on June 1, 1915, Enville was a bustling little frontier town of about 100 souls, most of whom barely eked out a living on their small plots of sandy loam. There was one schoolhouse, which also served as the Church and Sunday school, one cotton gin and two general stores. At the general stores one could purchase a wide assortment of items such as groceries, strawberry soda pop, licorice sticks, jaw breakers, sticky fly paper, syrup of pepsin, clothespins, binder twine, horse and mule collars, buggy whips, jelly beans, barbed wire, bailing wire, knee high rubber boots, pitch forks, saddles, blankets, Mason fruit jars, Karo syrup, overalls, pharmacy products, postage stamps, Post Toasties, Grape Nuts, garden seeds, hemp rope, Iodine, shoe laces, hard- ware for plowing and harvesting, axes, hoe handles, straw hats, spades and shovels, ladies bonnets, knitting needles and yarn, axle grease, coal oil, chewing tobacco and snuff, Bull Durham makin's, Vanilla extract, Arm & Hammer baking soda, Calumet baking powder, sacks of flour and corn meal, buckets of lard, pinto and navy beans, black-eyed peas, and just about anything else that comes under the heading: necessities for human survival.

Much of the population was Indian, since prior to the coming of Statehood in 1907, this was part of the old Chickasaw Nation, and all lived in houses that looked like ours and wore the same kind of clothes that we did. One of them, Jim McCurtain, was the Postmaster, who occupied a little corner of our General Store. (I neglected to mention that my father, Rufus Thomas Bond, operated one of the stores as well as the Cotton Gin). The Indians went to our school, but the many Blacks who lived in nearby Ran had one all to themselves.

R. T. Bond, son of Andrew Bond, had come into the Indian Territory before the turn of the Century, the entire family traveling in a covered wagon all the way from Georgia. They had settled first in central Oklahoma, opening up a dry goods store in the little town of Alex, before making the move to Enville about 1900. Preceding me were three brothers, Cecil, Howard and Rufus, and one sister, Mary. Another sister, Geraldine, came along a few years later.

Often I've been asked if any other members of the family were musically inclined. There were none, at least down through all of the relatives that I knew. Papa played the harmonica once or twice for fun, but that was about it. He didn't even own one. Music was a rare commodity in and around Enville. Home radio, as we would know it, was still a good five or more years away. A few people might have had phonographs, indeed, the Null family had a cylinder player, but we didn't get our flat record player until after we had moved to a farm/ranch two miles north of Marietta in 1917. Still, we always kept in touch with Enville and moved back into that area a year after Papa lost all of his holdings in the Panic of 1922.

Most of the transportation at that time was by horseback, buggy, or wagon and team. A one-horse buggy cost between thirty and fifty dollars, depending upon how much fringe one wanted on top. There may have been a few Model T cars, but they were few and far between. Those that did have them had all of the bumpy dirt roads pretty much to themselves.

In 1971, my wife, Dorothy, daughter, Susan and I happened to be visiting in the home State so I drove by Enville just to show them where I was born. Before I realized what had happened, I had driven right on by the place. It had changed that much. There simply was nothing there. We did spot the old storm cellar, and there was one new house, but no general stores, no schoolhouse—nothing. The cotton gin had burned down shortly after we left there and I think I expected to still see a little smoke curling skyward, but all we saw were weeds. Acres and acres of Johnson grass. I looked around for a few old Ghosts; but even they had left.

I wrote back home for some photographs of Enville in it's hey-day, but none have been forthcoming. My parents did manage to have a few snap shots taken of us when we were small. I display them herein, chiefly because they do show a small bit of Enville type background.

1917, Cyrus Whitfield Bond (Johnny, the baby) with older siblings (l to r): Cecil, Mary, Howard, and Rufus.

Where did Enville go? I can only assume that with the coming of better roads and more rapid transportation, all of the younger generation gradually moved on down the line—as I did.

At our farm/ranch north of Marietta, we had just about everything that a young lad of five could want; ponies to ride, fresh, clear, clean air, and many miles of wide open spaces to roam around in unhindered. Still, about the most fascinating thing that we had in that home was the old wind-em-up Victrola phonograph player. It played the flat, 78-rpm records as opposed to the cylinder type discs. Many years later someone asked, "Why the speed of 78 revolutions?" and the answer was, "It just turned out that way." Anyway, they would lift me up to watch the old Columbia Blue Seal records go round and round, then they would change the needle and wind it up again. Some fellow sang "It's a Long Way to Tipperary" and the band played "The Stars and Stripes Forever."

What really started us listening in earnest was when they brought in Vernon Dalhart's "The Prisoner's Song" . . .

"If I had the wings of an Angel . . . "—how fascinating—how realistic!

Some fellow by the name of Floyd Collins got lost in a cave and the whole family discussed it. We couldn't wait for the next day's newspaper to come so we could find out if he made it out. No, he was lost in the cave, which became his tomb. We were sad about that and even sadder after we heard Vernon Dalhart sing about "The Death of Floyd Collins." What a beautiful song and what a unique way to transmit the news. First we saw it in the papers and then we heard it on the phonograph!

In 1927, our ears really perked up at a new sound coming from our neighbor's windows. They were playing their phonograph and some fellow was yodeling and singing the blues. At first we didn't know who this new voice was, but we knew one thing. He was in trouble. He had some kind of a problem and was singing his heart out about it. Soon all of us had Victor Records by the Blue Yodeler, Jimmie Rodgers. What's more, we believed everything he sang about.

"Perhaps he was singing the news too!"

If he said that he was going to buy a pistol and shoot 'pore Thelma,' we believed it. If he sang his "Lullaby Yodel," we knew that his wife had left him and taken the baby with her. If he sang about being stranded ' . . . around the Water Tank', we knew what he was talking about because we had one of the biggest water tank stops on the Santa Fe Railroad. This fellow and his songs were authentic and realistic. You'd better believe it! We were hooked on Jimmie Rodgers and I was hooked on the idea of playing, singing and picking the guitar; and, making phonograph records.

None of the family could understand why I didn't want to go out into the fields and get the chaff down the back of my shirt collar. Not me! I was out rounding up more Jimmie Rodgers records. It was as though I had to learn how his story came out. Weldon Peden's Music Store closed and they sold out their entire stock at auction. I picked up four brand new Victor Records by Jimmie Rodgers for only a quarter. It was probably the best bargain that I ever ran across. I even remember that one of them was "Roll Along Kentucky Moon" backed with "For the Sake of Days Gone By."

When the depression hit in 1930 it didn't bother us too much for, by that time we didn't have much left to speak of anyway. We'd since lost the farm/ranch, the house and even the Victrola. I was in High School (1930–1934) and Leonard Little, the Bandmaster, approached, asking if I would like to play in the brass band. It was April First and I accused him of playing an April fool's joke- on me. "Okay," he said. "I'll ask you again tomorrow." The Principal, Ike Armstrong, loaned me his E flat alto brass horn and I I learned some music. By that time my sister, Mary, and her husband, had bought a brand new radio and they let me listen to it a lot. I discovered that Milton Brown and his Musical Brownies came in over KTAT, Fort Worth, at twelve noon. Then at 12:30, by switching over to WBAP, I could get W. Lee O'Daniels and the Lightcrust Doughboys.

Now, that was music!

Instead of going home for lunch like we were supposed to, I'd stop off and listen to those broadcasts coming through 'live'. Then on certain evenings we could get Carson Robison and his Buckaroos over KRLD and the CBS Network. (This meant that they even had our type of music up in New York City). Oh, for a tape recorder. What treasures could have been captured!

The subject of Jimmie Rodgers music came up in school. Our teacher went to great lengths to explain to us just how awful that type of music was.

"I can't stand Jimmie Rodgers," he said.

Then all of my classmates looked at me and laughed. They knew where my treasures untold were hidden away. When they tell you that 'no man is an island'—forget it. I was alone. Later on, during vacation time, that same teacher went to New York and wrote back a post card, saying, "Guess what? I saw Jimmie Rodgers on stage—in person!" At first he had panned the man, now he was bragging, rubbing it in, after seeing the great Blue Yodeler in person, something that a lot of us would like to have done. To me that was just about the greatest example of hypocrisy that I'd ever encountered. At any rate, I'm glad that I was able to stand up and be counted even if I was only a majority of one.

When Jimmie Rodgers died a short time later, W. Lee O'Daniels announced that he had written a song of tribute and that they would perform it on a certain days broadcast. I was right there, listening to my sister's radio when they played it. It was super inspirational. Then they announced that they would play it again on the evening's broadcast. Well, I didn't like to bother my relatives at that time of night so I had to seek out another radio. There was one in the pool hall! I went down there and waited for the broad- cast and turned the set to WBAP.

When the Lightcrust Doughboy's theme came on,

> *"Now listen everybody from near and far*
> *If you wan'na know who we are*
> *We're the Lightcrust Doughboys, from the Burrus Mill"*

. . . everybody else in the pool hall yelled out, "Git rid of that hillbilly crap!"

Then they turned it to another station.

The Doughboys later recorded the song, but it was wasn't the same. O'Daniels had woven into the number many of Rodger's hits and they couldn't use them because of copyright restrictions. Oh, well. I can still remember the one performance that I caught. The melody lingers on!

Whenever my classmates learned that I was listening to that 'hill-billy' music, I thought they were going to kick me out of school. The very idea! My chums dug Benny Goodman, Duke Ellington and Bing Crosby. I liked them too and I listened, but by that time my mind was made up.

The County (Love County, Oklahoma) paid me $8.oo for drawing some maps. Before I got the money, I laid out my budget. There were necessities—clothes, shoes, pencils, books—still I managed to hold out a dollar because I'd been scanning the pages of the Montgomery Ward catalog and they had the grandest Ukulele I'd ever seen; total price 98¢, which included a book of self-instructions.

With the little bit of musical knowledge that I'd picked up in the Brass Band, I taught myself to play the uke. After that came the guitar, and then the banjo, both of which I borrowed. Bill Lofton had a local string band and they let me sit in with them.

John Steele Batson ran for Congress-at-large and asked Glennis Stice and me to go along on his campaign. He bought me my first guitar, another mail order job; only this one cost all of $8.00. Then we'd go out to some Pie Supper or local private dance with Bill Lofton's band and pick up a quarter, or less.

Over the objections of my parents and the ridicule of my brothers, sisters and classmates, I became a professional "hillbilly" musician and singer long before my graduation in 1934. Perhaps it should be noted that they didn't refer to it as "country" music then. If they called you a 'hillbilly', that was a put-down of the worst kind. As a matter of fact, if we called each other "country," that was a put-down also. You can't win!

There wasn't too much for us to do in Marietta, so we attended all of the Church activities. They told me that God would give us anything that we asked for, so I decided to find out; I prayed that He would let me make phonograph records. My only regret is that I now wish that I'd also asked Him to help me pick my material, for I now see all too clearly that I've recorded a lot of songs that I wish I hadn't.

My brother, Howard, upon learning of my chosen career, came down from Oklahoma City and took me home with him. It was only five years away from Gene Autry, national broadcasting and phonograph records, but, my, oh, my, what long years those were!

When I arrived in Oklahoma City in 1934, standing on the brink of a long but interesting career in Country and Western Music, here is how things stood in the over-all field at that time—as I saw it then and still see it now.

Our great Blue Yodeler, whose songs, records and haunting style had planted the seeds of inspiration in so many fond hearts, this one included, was gone. Only the echo remained. Gene Autry had already picked up the reins and was sailing smoothly with "That Silver Haired

Daddy of Mine," while being featured daily on WLS, Chicago, and each Saturday night on *The National Barn Dance*, along with Lulu Belle and Scotty, The Hoosier Hot Shots, Uncle Ezra, Louise Massey and the Westerners, Red Foley, The Prairie Ramblers, and countless other fine acts. It is my opinion, inasmuch as an hour of this fine show was fed to the NBC Radio Network, that it had to be number one at the time.

WSM's *The Grand Ole Opry* was thriving and growing, but was still considered to be regional (Southeast). As far as we, the listeners, were concerned the Delmore Brothers, Uncle Dave Macon and DeFord Bailey were about the best acts that they had. Roy Acuff had yet to come upon the scene. Tex Ritter was making a name for himself in New York City on radio, records (Rye Whiskey) and in an area that few others of us have ever touched upon-Broadway!

In the southwest, Bob Wills and Tommy Duncan had pulled away from Lee O'Daniels and the Lightcrust Doughboys, taking several of the gang with them, forming The Texas Playboys. They had stopped, first in Waco, Texas, then WKY, Oklahoma City, before moving on to KVOO in Tulsa, where they stayed until the early forties. Milton Brown would meet an untimely death in a highway accident, silencing forever a great career that could have been.

There were no big name acts in Oklahoma City then, even though there were many of us with stars in our eyes. I auditioned at all of the radio stations and landed a 15-minute spot daily on KFXR (now KOCY) with no difficulty whatsoever, using "Tumbling Tumbleweeds" as my audition number. This radio bit was a cinch! So I thought. Later, I realized why when I learned that there was no salary connected with the job and that they were taking on any and all comers who sang and played the guitar.

After months of trying, knocking on doors, I finally connected with a western dance band known as Billy McGinty's Oklahoma Cowboys only to learn that there was no such person as Billy McGinty. Later the name was changed to Pop Moore and his Oklahomans. We broadcast daily on KOMA and played a few dances at night if we were lucky enough to get them. One Dollar per dance date for each of us was considered to be about an average take. Heliotrope Flour picked up our noontime broadcast and we were in the chips with an extra $5 a week for the radio show. I had been experimenting with song writing, but the band refused to play them.

I couldn't understand why then, but I know now. After the sponsor moved in, Pop moved me out. He said I was too "country" and too "hillbilly" and that they wanted to play more popular music. He did ask me to come back later, but I was with The Bell Boys then and had the pleasure of turning him down.

Johnny Marvin, 'The Lonesome Singer Of The Air', a one-time big name record seller, left New York and came to town. I just happened to be standing in front of Pop Moore's barbershop one day when Marvin drove by with his signs allover his car. Jimmy Wakely participated in one of Marvin's amateur shows and joined him on WKY. Wakely and I met and began performing together. Meanwhile, Johnny Marvin moved on to Hollywood where he joined his brother, Frankie, in Gene Autry's musical unit.

Both Johnny and Frankie had been instrumental in getting Gene his big break in New York City by taking him to various record companies for auditions. Later, they allowed him to participate in some of their vaudeville shows. Now the Marvin's could work for Autry anytime that they chose. Gene began making singing Western movies, so our type of music was given a giant boost forward. I believe that it can be safely said that it was during this time (1935-1939) that the term 'hillbilly' began to wane and the name of "Cowboy" or "Western" music began to come to the forefront. At any rate, it became fashionable to don western garb, Stetson hats and cowboy boots; as long as we were playing guitars we could sing any type of song. Prior to that time we had only seen publicity photographs of Jimmie Rodgers and Carson J. Robison wearing cowboy costumes. Now, with the Western movies so popular, everybody was following suit.

In Los Angeles, the Sons Of The Pioneers had made a series of electrical transcriptions (records for radio broadcast only), which began getting nationwide airplay to popular reception. When Jimmy Wakely, Scotty Harrel and I formed our singing cowboy trio, broadcasting on WKY (and sometimes KVOO), it was a combination of Pioneers and Autry music that we leaned toward. We drove to Tulsa once a week and recorded six fifteen minute shows in the KVOO studios as The Bell Boys,

The Marvin Brothers,
Frankie and Johnny.

named for the Bell Clothing Company, our sponsor. Although Bob Wills and his Texas Playboys were then on KVOO, we never made connec-tions' in person. They had finished their week's broadcasts before we came in and were out and gone into the hinterlands where their western dances drew large crowds.

Even though The Bell Boys were meeting with some success, I had entered the University of Oklahoma at nearby Norman because the future didn't look that bright at the time (1937). One of my subjects at OU was English. They had us write various types of themes and I will re-port only that my grades were about average. If I had it to do all over again, what with my trying to write a biography of Tex Ritter and about my years with Gene Autry and this work, I believe that I would have taken that subject to it's fullest degree as I now admit that more enlightenment and knowledge is needed. After only one year of studies, I felt that I was getting nowhere on that front and our Trio was then talk-ing of making a stab at the Big Time.

Gene Autry came through our area, playing premiers of his *Rancho Grande* at Okemah, Oklahoma and Lawrence, Kansas. Having been

The Bell Boys, Jimmy, Scotty and Johnny, circa 1938.

schooled on the 'build a better mousetrap' theory, it was then my belief that, if we were good enough, Autry would come to us. When I said this to Jimmy Wakely, his reply was, "If we wait—we may starve to death. We have to go to him—we must force the issue." We did that very thing, driving to both premiers and talking our way in. Gene received us cordially and asked us to sing for him, which we were glad to do. He then invited us to accompany him on the stage at Lawrence, Kansas, and he appeared on our WKY broadcast.

Before taking our leave of Oklahoma and WKY, and since numerous interested listeners to the song "Cimarron (Roll On)" have made inquiries as to how this composition came about, I trust a brief word on that subject will be appropriate here. It was the policy of The Bell Boys to open our show with a fast, rollicking Cowboy/Western song. Still trying to compose songs, I informed both Jimmy and Scotty that I was going to make the attempt at writing a new 'opener' for us.

I had gone to see the movie, *Cimarron*, starring Richard Dix and Irene Dunne, and was surprised to learn that no song or musical background by that title was included therein. We had, in our travels, crossed the Cimarron River many times, always commenting on the fact that no song about the river existed. I then composed the number in my bachelor room at the YMCA, after which the other two agreed that we could include it in our programs, both on radio and on our personal appearances.

It was, the first song that we used on CBS when we later joined Gene Autry. Wakely recorded it on Decca as our Trio performed with him. Les Paul and Mary Ford had a nice rendition on Capitol, but it was Billy Vaughn's version on Dot Records that topped the million sales mark. We also sung it in two Western movies, *Heart of the Rio Grande*, with Autry, and *Twilight on the Trail* with Hopalong Cassidy. They call it a 'standard' now and I'm happy to report that the continuing royalties are most welcome into the Bond household. "Cimarron" was written in 1938.

The Oklahoma City years (1934-1940) had been long, lean and both encouraging and discouraging. We didn't know it then, but we were gaining valuable experience—the cornerstone of this or any other career and we now realize it's worth.

On May 31, 1940, seven people piled into Jimmy's new Dodge pulling an overloaded one-wheel trailer and took off on Route 66, heading into an uncertain future in California. Not only were our funds very low, we had no firm offer of a job from Gene Autry. True, he had said, "If you ever come to California, look me up." But that was it.

Still, it was good enough for us.

PART TWO
Thirty Years on the Road

The Wakely Trio (JW, JB, DR) with the Bossman.

CHAPTER ONE

Oklahoma City, 1935

What's a 'Singing Western'?
Or, Who's Gene Autry? Or, Don't You Mean, Gene Austin?
Or, Why'm I standing Here In The Cold?

Gene Autry stood alone behind a microphone on a platform that had been assembled hastily for this brief occasion. He wore dungarees, blue shirt, black cowboy hat, western boots, and a gun belt with its holster and gun swinging low against his right hip. He strummed nervously on his guitar as he glanced uneasily both to the right and left leading me to wonder if he knew the right chords or not. There was only a small crowd of about twenty people waiting in the severe cold wind for him to begin his free concert, which had been advertised in the back pages of *The Daily Oklahoman.*

There were several reasons why I had not planned to attend this show. In addition to the cold, the Autry singing voice was not as appealing to me as some others I could think of. The only record of his that had been in our farm home collection was given to us by neighbors and it certainly couldn't measure up to those of Jimmie Rodgers or Tommy Duncan, who sang with the Lightcrust Doughboys, to mention only two of the many artists who planted the seeds of inspiration, leading me to make an attempt to get in on this business. What kind of a thrill can you get by listening to "The Yodel-ing Hobo" or "He's in the Jailhouse Now #2"? Both of those songs were on that one Autry record. Even the name, we thought, had a bit of a phony ring to it for it was Gene Austin who was making all the ladies hearts, including my older sister's, beat faster. Autry? Gene Autry?

"Wonder if he's any kin to old Doc Autry, or Bud Autry?" Papa had asked, not really caring to hear an answer. "We got Autry's all over this part of the country."

Papa was no fan of recording stars. Doc and Bud were local citizens of Marietta, my hometown. Papa's question would remain unanswered for another 20 years or so (When I asked and found out that they were cousins).

Another reason that almost kept me away was that Gene was plugging his first starring Western movie, *Tumbling Tumbleweeds*. It was showing down the street at the Majestic Theater, but I certainly wasn't going to see that. Not when I could see *Mutiny on the Bounty* with some real, he-man stars. Or even a re-issue of *Cimarron* with Richard Dix and Irene Dunne. The only reason I'd stopped by here just now was because it was on the way downtown to the theaters. It wasn't much out of the way.

"Tumbling Tumbleweeds" was my song and here he's singing it and using it as the title of his picture. Probably the only one he'll ever make. When I say it was 'my song', I don't mean to imply that I wrote it or owned it. But didn't I use it as my audition song at KFXR last year, and hadn't it got me the job on the fifteen-minute daily radio show? Of course, that hadn't paid anything yet, but it did get me acquainted with some of the musicians around town and now a few dance jobs were coming my way. Nobody could sing "Tumbleweeds" like me. So I thought.

"I wish he'd hurry up and do something," I mumbled through chattering teeth, standing there shivering with the others. Not many of them had overcoats either.

At last Gene spoke. "Well, let's see now. What'da you say we try just a little bit of "Old Faithful". He strummed some more chords then sang the song. There was something repulsive about that voice, at least to me. The others applauded politely when he finished. But me? I turned around and left. I might have stayed, but the cold was penetrating . . . it would be warm in the Midwest Theater.

I've often wondered what would have happened if I'd decided to stick around. What if I'd gone backstage and introduced myself? I could have said, "Hey, Gene! My name is Johnny Bond. I have a crystal ball here that tells me in five years from now, you'll put me to work in your show. That job will last for about thirty years and you and I will eventually become real good friends and co-workers, so why don't we just start now instead of waiting?" Perhaps if I'd done that my association with him may have started before 1940. But then, I didn't do or say that . . . instead, I walked away while he was introducing another song. By now I was too far away to hear the name of it.

Standing in front of the Midwest Theater, two things kept me from going inside; the feature had been on for at least an hour and the price had changed, going up to 25 cents, much more than last night's dance job had paid me. Besides that, it didn't look too enticing. Down on Grand there were three theaters in one block. I'd seen the one showing at the Warners, as well as the one at the Rialto . . . that left the Majestic and Gene Autry.

Being just 20 years old at the time, I was having difficulty making decisions on various subjects. If my fellow schoolmates from last year's graduating class had been looking on, I most certainly would not have even ventured near the Majestic since they'd gone all out in denouncing my chosen type of music.

"Get rid of that hillbilly stuff," they all advised. "Better start playing something out of the *Goldiggers* movies, like "Lullaby of Broadway," or a Bing Crosby song. That corn stuff has got to go."

And Papa hadn't been too encouraging either. "I wish you'd put away that old loud Banjo and go down to the feed store and start working for a change," he and my older brother Cecil had said to me more than once.

Lucky for me, Howard, another older brother, had been the one in the family to give encouragement. He had brought me up to the Big City to stay with him and his wife until I could determine whether or not I could make the grade.

"TUMBLING TUMBLEWEEDS"
Starring America's New Singing Cowboy
GENE AUTRY

That's what the posters said.

I looked all around. Nobody much in the streets, let alone anyone that I knew. The price was only 10 cents. It was still cold outside. It would be warm in there. I looked at the poster again.

"with Smiley Burnette
and Frankie Marvin"

Hey! That's more like it. I like them, I think. I looked around again, plunked down my dime and went in.

The feature was already in progress. Gene Autry was on the screen with a full facial close-up. That round face! Those pearly white teeth! That big smile! Seemed to me like he was much too happy. He was singing something other than the title song. And that voice! Much too high. Much too smooth. The way he swayed his head, rolled his eyes, opened his mouth too wide. Plus the extra volume which he employed in his voice; all of this found my ears still unreceptive. Something inside me was trying to build a wall between Gene Autry and me and I refused to try to suppress it. I began to wonder if I hadn't wasted my dime. This wasn't my idea of a Western movie. My heroes had been the big silent stars like Tom Mix, Buck Jones, Hoot Gibson, Jack Hoxie and all of the others.

When sound finally came to Lamont King's one and only movie house in Marietta, those same stars did sound a little on the silly side, not at all like we'd imagined they would sound. We didn't know then that the movies were using primitive equipment while trying to adjust to the new trend. Even though a lot of the town's folk had laughed at this new 'sound' thing, a lot of us kids had still continued to patronize the Westerns during these experimental years.

"Did you hear that horse fart?" Snooks Monroe had asked during one of the chases.

"No, but I smelt it," said his cousin Heck. We all laughed loud and long after that one. Soon we were drowned out by the ensuing gunfire. I was glad that those two friends were not here with me now. Boy, would I have caught it!

The Autry movie proceeded. I had long since made up my mind that I wasn't going to enjoy this picture, whether I liked it or not. For some unconscious reason, I'd already begun to resent it a little.

When Gene, Smiley and Frankie sang the title song in three-part harmony, you could hear each voice separately. No close blend! Unforgivable! But then, because all three were riding their horses, following the medicine show wagon, perhaps they couldn't get in close to the microphone. That could account for that.

Later on Gene sang "Ridin' Down the Canyon" in duet with himself. That was neat, almost. I'd never seen that trick before. Then Gene put a dummy in a rocking chair and the villain shot the dummy thinking it was Gene. Not Too Bad!

Still, too many things had been left out, such as the many fistfights, the long chases, the tougher bad guys, the Indian raids. Seems like it had been slightly on the sissy side. Couldn't possibly last, this Autry fellow. A one-time deal . . . that had to be it. There had been other such Westerns in the past. You saw them once, wham-o! Instant oblivion. That's all this one was.

As *Tumbling Tumbleweeds* came to an end, my mind was made up that there had been way too much time taken up with the medicine show stuff plus all that music. The picture was so bad I decided to sit through it again. After all, I'd come in on the middle of it and had to get my dime's worth. Besides, I didn't have anyplace else to go. Cold outside!

♫   ♫   ♫

Over the next few weeks, other Gene Autry movies came to the Majestic Theater. Because of the fact that the admission price was to my liking, and for no other reason, I saw them all. There was *Melody Trail, The Sagebrush Troubadour, The Singing Vagabond,* and a whole bunch of others. I couldn't believe that they were still making movies with this lightweight. I still kept telling myself that I didn't like this Autry fellow. There were others up on that screen that I came to see . . . Smiley "Frog" Burnette, Frankie Marvin, Carl Cotner, just to mention a few. It's a real good thing that Gene had those guys to carry him.

♫   ♫   ♫

In 1937 I had the opportunity to team up with Jimmy Wakely, a young lad fresh off the farm. Jim was an avid Autry fan and proudly admitted it. He was well ahead of me on that score since he'd worked with Johnny Marvin in Oklahoma City and had even met Gene when the movie star had slipped into town without my knowing it. After being around Wakely for a while, I finally worked through whatever had been bugging me and admitted that I really liked Autry, his movies and his music. Hometown opinions were out the window and at long last, I realized I'd found myself.

Jimmy Wakely and I started buying Gene Autry records and attending all of his films, which by now had moved out of the Majestic and up-town to the State Theater, where the admission price might go up to 35 cents and higher. Here, crowds began to form a line while other theaters downtown played to smaller crowds. Even the big-time stars were not drawing in the city like Gene was.

Publicity began coming out on the new "Singing Cowboy" star. We heard him on network radio shows while jukeboxes began offering more and more of his records. Newspaper publicity increased until the obvious soon came to light; Gene Autry was rapidly becoming one of the biggest stars in Hollywood and the entire country.

♫   ♫   ♫

Beginning in 1937, the singing trio that Jimmy Wakely and I had formed with Scotty Harrel began to make it's own showing, but only on a local level. If we were ever going to make the big-time we'd have to strike while the trio was hot. One thing was certain; if Gene Autry could only hear us sing, we might stand a chance. After all, our type of music was the same as his and if we could convince him that we would fit into his act, it would be good for him and super for us.

We saved up for a vacation. We hit the road to California where, with the assistance of Wakely's friend Johnny Marvin, we visited the Autry home, which was then close to Republic Studios in Studio City. Both Mr. and Mrs. Autry welcomed us cordially, listened to us sing and gave us the run of the place, including the use of their swimming pool.

No offers, or even a faint hint of an offer, came from this first visit with Autry. Back home in Oklahoma City, Mr. Lowenstein, owner of the Majestic Theater, used his influence in our behalf, getting us a small part in a Roy Rogers picture titled *Saga of Death Valley*.

Before and after the filming of this, our first cinema effort, we knocked on Autry's door, renewing acquaintances.

"Hi, Gene," we said. "Remember us?"

"Sure do," said Gene Autry, politely. "What's up?"

"We come back out here to make a movie with Roy Rogers," we said, chins up, chests out, eyes opened widely.

"That so?" said Gene, paring his fingernails. "How's my old friend, Maurice Lowenstein?" He also inquired about several other prominent Oklahoma citizens, mentioning them all by name. It later dawned on us that the mentioning of the Roy Rogers name carried no special weight with Gene. We had heard various rumors about how the studio had brought Roy in when Gene had gone on strike some time back, but we did not then know how deep the feelings between the two had gone.

Rufe Davis was a guest on the *Bell Boy's Show*, 1939.

Still, the Autry's again welcomed us into their home with open arms and we had the occasion to sing a lot of songs for them and their guests.

"Do you guys know "Tumbling Tumbleweeds?" Gene asked. We'd sung it for him before.

"Do we?" we said, eagerly. We sang it for them again and again. Each time he nodded his approval.

Still no offers.

After the Rogers picture was completed, we hit the road back to Oklahoma. disappointed that Gene Autry hadn't grabbed us up while the grabbing was good.

As the months went by, we learned that Gene would be making personal appearances in such nearby places as Lawrence, Kansas, and Okemah, Oklahoma, where he was promoting his latest film, *Rancho Grande*. In each city, we showed up, renewing acquaintances with a determination that knew no bounds. In Lawrence he invited us to appear on the stage with him.

We played for Gene Autry while he sang!

At Okemah he sang on our radio show, broadcast over WKY.

Gene Autry sang on our show!

That was April 22, 1940. In a few more months, Gene would hire us. But, boy! Those were long months.

At the end of the shows in Lawrence and Okemah, Gene invited us to his hotel where other activities were going on. Included among the guests were many other Hollywood personalities as well as high ranking political dignitaries from both Oklahoma and Kansas. Governor Red Phillips, a staunch Autry fan and friend, was one of those in attendance.

Gene introduced us and had us sing for his guests while he left the room for periods of ten to fifteen minutes, making the rounds to other important guests in various rooms in the hotel. When he returned he asked us to accompany him while he sang a few songs. After several numbers, he would always come back to "Tumbling Tumbleweeds." It was a must.

As we left him at the conclusion of this, our fourth meeting, I can well remember his parting words:

"Well, fellows. Good to see you again. Where do you go from here?"

"Back home to Oklahoma City," we answered as one. "Back to W K Y."

Good station," said Gene Autry. "Be sure and give my best to Perry Ward and Alan Clark and all the rest."

"We'll do that," we said, still waiting for those magic words.

"Why don't you hire us?" the tree of us thought as one. Out loud we said, "Bye, Gene."

"You boys ever think about moving to Hollywood?" Gene asked, casually.

"We thought about it."

"Well," Gene said softly without looking at us. "If you ever do, be sure to look me up.."

That was it. As we drove home we discussed this farewell conversation.

"I think he just let us sing because we didn't charge him anything," Scotty said.

"I don't think he liked us well enough to offer us a job," I said, disappointedly.

Jimmy Wakely was the optimist of our group. I had been brought up on the build-a-better-mousetrap theory. For years now I'd been waiting for the world to beat its path to my door. Had it been left in my hands, perhaps I'd still be there, waiting, and waiting, and waiting.

"You guys are both wrong," Jimmy said, smiling from ear to ear. "That was Gene's way of saying to us, 'come on out to Hollywood and I'll put you to work.'"

That was good enough for me. I bought it.

April 22, 1940. Lawrence, Kansas, where Gene is promoting the movie, Rancho Grande.
l to r: Scotty, Johnny, June Storey, Gene Autry, Jimmy Wakely, Noel Boggs.

In April of 1940, we gave our notice to WKY. Two months later, with Dick Reinhart replacing Scotty Harrel, we piled everyone into Wakely's new Dodge and took off for California. After three long months of waiting, fingers crossed, teeth clentched, Gene Autry hired us to work on his CBS Radio show, *"The Melody Ranch Show"* sponsored by Wrigley's Doublemint Chewing Gum.

In November of that same year, he took us to New York's Madison Square Garden Rodeo.

At long last . . . we had arrived.

CHAPTER TWO

1940

Mister Clean
The Man of the Hour
Or, Double Your Pleasure

Who was this man, Gene Autry, who, in his own nonchalant manner, and just lifted three unknown Okie musicians and singers from virtual obscurity into a worldwide spotlight of fame glory?

When we joined him in September of 1940, Gene Autry was already the biggest star that Western movies had ever produced. Forerunners, such as William S. Hart, Tom Mix and others, had been big stars, true, but they had been handicapped for the most part by a silent screen. When sound came along near the end of the twenties it did not flatter the rough and tumble 'he-men' of the westerns and by 1934 cowboy movies were definitely on their way out. Autry's singing westerns not only reversed the trend, they made it still bigger. In 1937, Gene was the first Western star voted into the Top 10 moneymakers in Hollywood box office reports. He would remain in those ranks until 1942, when fate, and a uniform, would intervene.

The public knew most of their silent heroes only from screen or within the pages of the movie magazines. Tom Mix, Ken Maynard, Tim McCoy, Hoot Gibson and Jack Hoxie all toured extensively with rodeos. Few of the others made public appearances at all. With Autry it was different. Personal appearances took him to the people who were also listening to him on the radio as well as buying his phonograph records. He was in millions of homes already.

These are only some of the advantages that Gene had over his predecessors. Other 'firsts,' such as merchandising and television, would follow.

In 1940, at the age of 33, he had been a recording star for ten years and a movie star for six. For the next 15 years his career as an entertainer would continue on it's upward climb.

In 1939, the year before we joined his show, several important things happened to Gene Autry. He made a very successful tour of England and Ireland, where thousands upon thousands of local citizens gathered in the street underneath his hotel window and sang to him . . . "Come Back to Erin."

"It was pretty touching at that," said Gene to us many times later.

Another great thing that happened to Gene in 1939 was the advent of his *Melody Ranch Show* sponsored by Wrigley's Doublemint Chewing Gum over the CBS Radio Network. This popular show would remain on the air, with the same sponsorship for the next 16 years, and might have lasted longer . . . if only . . . but then, we'll discuss that later.

The third (and most wonderfullest) thing that happened in 1939, involved me. I shook hands with the great star for the first time. As stated previously, Jimmy Wakely, Scotty Harrel and I drove out to Hollywood just to 'look around' that year. Johnny Marvin had introduced us at the Autry home. Gene was standing outside his poolside office. As Marvin called our names, the star shook hands with of each of us. I was shocked. The hand was cold and limp. He never looked at me. Turned his head to the skies and said, "I'll be damned glad when this blamed weather clears up. We've got pictures to shoot."

Of course, the shock wore off quickly and shortly thereafter we were given the run of the place. We swam and sang and were treated royally by both Mr. and Mrs. Autry during our brief stay.

"I was hoping he'd offer us a job," the three of us said on the way back to Oklahoma. That, of course, would come next year.

♪　　♪　　♪

Over the years, the most common question I was asked was. "What was he like?"

Every single time that I ever saw Gene Autry I got the impression that he had just stepped out of a steam bath. Both his person and his clothes were spotless.

His ten-gallon Stetson was always solid white, with the traditional 3½ inch brim. Had it been wider, or even more narrow, it would have been quite conspicuous and out of place. The world would have noticed.

He had many of these white hats at his fingertips. In the event the one that he was wearing became even slightly smudged or soiled, it was immediately replaced without anyone noticing. He wore the hat always, seldom taking it off in public except where it would be indiscreet to wear it. Whenever he was introduced to a lady, you could bet your boots that he would remove it promptly, only to replace it shortly thereafter.

Gene was proud of that white hat. Even though he had many, he never gave one up recklessly or carelessly.

I remember a man coming to me one time at a social function.

"That hat Gene's wearing," the man said to me over his martini. "I've got to have it. I want my boy to have it. Can you get me that hat?"

"Why don't you ask Gene for it?" I said, not really knowing what the man would run into.

"I'll do that," said the man, turning away. Later on he returned.

"Get me that hat," said the man. "I'll give you anything if you'll only get me that hat for my boy."

"Why don't you buy one for your boy," I said. "They don't cost that much."

"BUY ONE!" he roared at me, indignantly. "Buy one, indeed. I've got to have THAT one!"

"Ask Gene for it. What have you got to lose?"

At the end of the festivities I approached Gene, now hatless.

"Lost your white hat, I see."

"Yeah," Gene replied, disgustedly. "I knew the s. o. b. was after it. Stole it, he did. I'd have given it to him if he'd asked me for it, but no. He stole it."

Thousands of people came to me over the years trying to get to Gene or to get something from him. I began to feel like a gate, or a bridge, or both.

Almost everything that Gene Autry wore was tailor made for him. He didn't go for the 'loud' cowboy clothes except during those occasions when the script called for it. For street-wear, he had conservative suits with only enough trimming to show that it was Western upon close inspection. The suits were always immaculately cleaned and pressed. His boots were hand-made, very expensive and quite colorful, mostly on the tops.

We had been told all along that Mrs. Autry had much influence upon Gene's dress and mannerisms. Rest assured that anything that she might have done or said was always in private, for we never saw her direct any words on this subject to him in public.

I can believe this story that goes on to say that this 'coaching' of his etiquette had to have much to do with his eventual success in the industry.

To be a big Hollywood star is one thing, but to be able to mingle socially with big businessmen, their wives, children and sometimes, high-toned friends, is another., I should know, for it is one of the first things that I ran into after landing the job with him. It can be rough. I only hope that I made it. I know Gene Autry did.

Let me give here one brief, first hand example of the care, the thought and tactfulness that Ina Mae used on her husband to insure him of his eventual acceptance in a forthcoming, seemingly important business meeting.

We closed a tour of State Fairs in Trenton, New Jersey, on Saturday, September 24, 1960. Gene and Ina invited me to fly home with them in their private plane as I'd flown with them often before. Herb Green was the pilot., While the Autrys did not go into detail, they did alert me to the fact that we would be stopping over in Detroit while Gene meet with Mr. Bob Reynolds. It seems that there was a radio station in that vicinity they were interested in buying and they would be meeting with various executives.

Our plane landed at the Detroit airport after dark. Being a private plane, we landed and taxied to a spot not near the regular airlines traffic. Herb had called ahead for a taxicab that drove all the way up to the plane. Here several minutes elapsed while Mr. and Mrs. Autry debated about what wardrobe should be taken along and what could be left in the plane. Once this was decided, Gene, Ina and I got in the taxi and left with Herb staying behind to care for the plane. He would join us at the hotel later.

Almost all airports are a considerable distance from the downtown areas, Detroit being no exception. Along the way Gene talked to the driver about this and that, mostly local conditions and politics. Casually, Ina Mae said to her husband, "What suit did you bring along for your meeting tomorrow?"

"Did you bring the boots to go with it?" she asked.

"No," returned Gene, holding up one foot, displaying the boots he was wearing. "I'll just wear these."

"You can't wear those boots," Ina said. "They don't go with the other suit."

"Oh, hell, Ina Mae. Boots is boots. One pair goes with any suit. I just brought this one pair. We're not going to be here long."

"You have to have another pair," said Ina, leaning forward toward the driver of the cab. "Driver, turn around and go back to the airport."

"Oh, for cryin' . . . " said Gene. "It's too far and too late. Straight ahead, driver."

"Never mind! Driver, I said turn around!"

"And I said, go on to the hotel. To hell with the measly pair of boots. Who's going to notice. What difference does it make?"

"Driver," said Mrs. Autry. "Turn around."

The cab driver turned the taxicab around, returned to the airport where another pair of cowboy boots was procured for the meeting of the following day.

There you have just one brief insight into the manner in which Mrs. Autry showed care and concern over the star's personal appearance. The boots must fit the occasion. Keep in mind that by 1960 Gene Autry had been in the limelight for 30 years. One can imagine the concern that she might have shown during earlier times.

CHAPTER THREE

Sell That Gum Chum

Melody Ranch
Double Your Fun

Our primary assignment in our new job with Autry was to play and sing on his thirty minute 'live' CBS broadcast, *The Melody Ranch Show*. The show had been on the air for seven or eight months and, naturally, we had heard just about every broadcast over K O M A while we were still in Oklahoma City. Even though we had done a few network shows while at W K Y, the thought of standing before a microphone hooked up to a nationwide audience was still frightening to us.

In those days, there was a Friday night script rehearsal (the live broadcast itself being on Sunday night). We would gather in one of CBS' small studios at Columbia Square, Sunset at Gower Streets in Hollywood, in order to read the script and to make possible changes.

We usually sat around in an informal circle, most of us in casual attire. Gene would always arrive on time, stop in the doorway of the studio and speak to the entire cast, the director, and any others called in to be there. Usually it was just, "Gentlemen," or "Ladies and Gentlemen." Then he would take his seat within the circle, pick up his script and say, "Well, where are we?"

Gene's first reading was usually a bit on the rough side leading us to wonder if he was going to be able to handle it or not. However, after a couple of times through, he fell into it pretty good, although he was never completely relaxed in all of the years that the show was on the air. He took direction well, hardly ever making changes or suggestions of his own. When he did, he usually tried to drive home his point with gentle emphasis.

While Autry was the quiet, easy-going sort, director Tony Stanford was just the opposite. He drove everyone pretty hard, so much that we newcomers were often shaking in our boots for fear we were not yet ready for the big time.

After rehearsal was over, Gene usually stayed around for a short while, having a few words with this person and that. If he talked to us he might say, "Found a place to live yet?" Or, "Writing any good songs?"

He would have corner conferences with the director or Johnny Marvin, who was then acting as musician's contractor for the show. Mitch Hamilburg, his agent, was often around, so they, too, would steal off into a corner going over things which we could not hear. At last he would wave a hand to the entire cast and say, "Goodnight, everybody. See you Sunday Morning."

The music rehearsals came about 10:00 A. M. on the day of the broadcast. Most times the show was on Sundays, but there were times when it was moved to Saturday evening. His routine was about the same as it had been on the night of the script rehearsal. After speaking to everyone, he would wander over to the orchestra leader's podium to go over each song alone before taking it on mike with the rest of us.

Once all of the music was rehearsed, another script reading took place, after which a full dress rehearsal was run. This was clocked with a stopwatch to make certain that the show came out on the very split second. We couldn't afford to run over or under time. If cuts became necessary, it usually came out of the script, but musical cuts were not out of the question.

We had approximately an hour between the end of the dress rehearsal and show time. This enabled the director to give us final instructions after which we all got into our uniforms. The radio show was broadcast before a live audience who got into the studio with complimentary passes.

CBS, Hollywood, was made up of Studio A, the largest, designed exactly like a typical auditorium. This one held about a thousand people with a small balcony upstairs. Studios B and C were slightly smaller, containing no balcony. Over a period of ten years or more, we broadcast from each of the three studios.

When the signal came from the director that we were on the air, that was it. The broadcasts were live. If a mistake was made, there was no turning back or dubbing out. It had to be as perfect as we were capable of making it. The transcribed, or taped, show didn't come about until after 1950, when they could be recorded in advance and broadcast at a later time. In this format, mistakes could be covered up and re-taped. Mr. Wrigley complained

Awaiting signal from the director that the live broadcast is on the air. JB is standing at back ready to cord the opening theme.

about the taped shows, saying that they were too perfect. "Let's hear a little flub now and then," we were told he had said.

Here, then, is the way the broadcast of *The Melody Ranch Show* shaped up in September 1940:

Gene Autry began with his instantly recognizable theme song, "Back in the Saddle Again." On cue from announcer Tom Hanlon, the studio audience would applaud and we were under way.

After a few opening remarks, Gene would sing a lively song on the order of "When the Bloom is on the Sage," backed up by the full orchestra, with harmony provided by us newcomers.

Following this song came a commercial extolling the many virtues of Wrigley's Doublemint Chewing Gum. At the time, the announcer read this. Later on the chore was handed to Gene, himself, who is reported to have sold many, many tons of the product.

According to the description from the advertising agency who represented Wrigley, the gum was not only economical to the purchaser, then 5 cents per pack of five sticks, it was refreshing to the taste, did not spoil youngsters appetites, and left both hands free for other assignments as opposed to the holding on to a candy bar. The latter part was merely implied, never spelled out.

Once Gene began reading the commercial, it became part of my job to strum soft guitar chords behind the pitch so that the listener would get the impression that Gene was seated on a log or a stump, strumming his own guitar and simply talking about his favorite brand of gum. The Wrigley people were always happy with the results of the broadcast. They never worried about ratings, saying only, that as long as it sold chewing gum they intended to keep the show on the air, which they did until 1956.

Doublemint was the only sponsor that *The Melody Ranch Show* ever had. During wartime shortages of product, when Wrigley was unable to turn out a package that he considered up to his top standard, they continued to advertise Doublemint even though the public may not have been able to find it over the counters. About 1944, Wrigley produced a gum which they called 'Orbit'. Even though it had the Wrigley name on it, it was never mentioned on the broadcast. Shortly after World War II, they did mention another of their products, Spearmint, but this was for a very brief time. From then on . . . Doublemint.

Following the first commercial came another song by Gene. This one was usually a ballad as opposed to the rousing opener. Typical examples here would be, "The One Rose," "Mexicali Rose," or "It Makes No Difference Now."

Now for the comedy! In 1940 there were two comedy characters. Horace Murphy played the part of Shorty, and Frank Nelson was Reno. "Little" Mary Lee, who had become an overnight sensation when she sang "Goodbye Little Darling" with Gene in one of his movies, was also a regular on the show. Her featured solo usually followed the comedy spot.

Now came the Trio's big moment. We were given one song on each show. The very first one we sang was "Cimarron," a number that I had composed a couple of years earlier. It was fast and short. Everybody liked it and the applause was loud. It had to be, Tom Hanlon was milking them on like mad.

Immediately after "Cimarron," I can still recall some of Shorty's dialogue; "Cinnamon roll, Cinnamon roll!" More laughs. Although our knees

Doublemint's Melody Ranch cast, 1941. front l to r: Frank Nelson, Horace Murphy, Mary Lee, Gene Autry, Jimmy Wakely Trio (JW,JB & DR, standing). Frankie Marvin is standing at left with Lou Bing and the orchestra behind cast.

were shaking from stage fright, we had crossed the great divide. Gene Autry's massive audience was placed at our disposal.

Lou Bing was the leader of the orchestra in the early days. Carl Cotner, then playing one of the four fiddles in the band, later took over. Frankie Marvin played the steel guitar.

Perhaps it should be noted here that, while Smiley 'Frog' Burnette was then still a member of the movie cast, he was not on the radio broadcast. We wondered about this, even making inquiries, but the absence of logical answers prompted us to drop the subject quickly. Smiley did join the cast in the late forties but his stay was quite brief.

As time went by, the characters of Shorty and Reno were dropped. Since I was there, they began giving me some 'Okie' type lines. Tom Hanlon was also replaced by Lou Crosby, best known then for his being regular announcer for the popular *Lum and Abner Show*.

Finally, an old friend of Gene's from the Chicago days, Pat Buttram, joined the show in late 1947.

At this point in the show, about half-way into the broadcast, Gene would begin his Western Tale of the day; a 10 minute fictional story written especially for the show which, with added musical cues and sound effects, made quite an impression on Autry fans wherever the broadcast was received. Veteran Hollywood actors were called in to participate in these stories and I was later included to ride along with him as sidekick. The story endings were almost always the same, the triumph of good over evil, with Gene just a bit bigger hero than he ever was before.

Next came another commercial selling gobs and gobs of gum, followed by the traditional cowboy classic sung by Gene and the entire gang. A typical song here would be on the order of "Empty Saddles", "Cool Water," "Tumbling Tumbleweeds," or any other great cowboy ballad.

Much applause was requested as the program came to a conclusion with Gene's usual goodnights, followed by "Back In the Saddle Again." In years to come the show would undergo many changes, but this is the way the show was done in 1940.

It goes without saying that listening to these weekly broadcasts of *The Melody Ranch Show* became a very popular pastime with the public. Even today someone will mention that they remember them with a fond longing for the good old days.

Autry had each broadcast recorded on disk for his own personal use and reference. With the advent of tape and home recordings, we would all record these broadcasts for our own use. Since our live broadcast was scheduled early evening in the East, our local West Coast listeners had to tune in quite early. Later on, KNX in Los Angeles, would delay the broadcast, giving us a chance to listen and record the show in one form or another.

Today people ask the question, "Where did *The Melody Ranch Show* broadcast originate?" The answer is, at one time or another, it came from just about every large city in the US and Canada. Since the radio show was broadcast live, it was necessary that we "take it with us" as we hit the road for personal appearance tours and rodeos. Most of the shows originated in Hollywood. Many were from Chicago, home of the Wrigley people, while many others came from New York City, as we were there for long periods with the rodeo. On the later one-nighter tours, the broadcast emanated from the particular city in which we happened to be playing on the day that it was due to hit the air. Sometimes it was broadcast from auditoriums, sometimes from high schools, and sometimes it was from the local CBS affiliate in that city. After Gene entered the Armed Services, many broadcasts originated from Luke Field in Phoenix, Arizona. One show in particular was performed on a railroad flatcar in Berwyn, Oklahoma late in 1941, when they changed the name of the small town from Berwyn to Gene Autry. There is really no reason to add that Gene felt quite at home on that railroad line since he had worked in and around there many times before.

♪   ♪   ♪

From the outset, following our first radio broadcast, the Trio found that we were in serious trouble with both Autry and the advertising agency that represented the sponsor.

When we had performed our four auditions for the star, two in California in 1939 and two more in 1940 at Okemah, Oklahoma and Lawrence, Kansas,

The Jimmy Wakely Trio, Jimmy Wakely, Johnny Bond and Dick Reinhart.

our trio consisted of Jimmy Wakely, Scotty Harrel and myself. We had been working together for about four years, concentrating on as near perfect blend of vocal harmony as might possibly be attained. Many critics assured us that we sang together as one. This was the trio that Autry heard and it had to be the one that he had made up his mind to hire.

He never hired us in so many words: as, "You boys are hired — you go on the payroll tomorrow." The closest he came to saying it was, "be sure and look me up." We had taken that statement as his way of taking us on.

For reasons of his own, Scotty Harrel decided to remain in Oklahoma City when Jimmy and I pulled up stakes. Dick Reinhart, who just happened to be standing by, ready, willing, available, agreed to come with us on a moment's notice. The only rehearsals that we had were in the automobile as we drove from Oklahoma to California. Even though Dick was an accomplished musician and fine tenor singer, practice, time, and practice time alone, builds a singing trio. When we approached Gene with our new addition, he made no comment to us other than to listen to us sing in his office, and nod his head politely as we concluded.

He did not say, "Well, you boys sound alright, but I believe that I liked you better the way I first heard you." As it turned out, he didn't have to say it.

Shortly after our arrival in California, the Autry troupe went to Duluth, Minnesota, leaving us with no assurance that he was going to use us in any capacity.

We learned later that Autry had gone to Oklahoma City, went to Scotty Harrel, and made the following commitment to him: "If you will go out and re-join the trio, I'll put you all on my radio show." It was then that Scotty showed up in Hollywood with the message.

After the passage of several weeks, we were, in fact, called in to do the show. Therefore, the first few programs that we did were with Harrel. Since we were also working other jobs such as recordings, a few night clubs, and an occasional motion picture, Dick Reinhart was able to stay on and we were able to practice and concentrate on our blend.

Johnny Marvin came to us right away with the news that our trio wasn't quite 'cutting the mustard' on the radio show. He pointed out several weaknesses, one being the fact that certain tenor requirements written for us were a bit out of Scotty's vocal range. After a few more weeks (and shows) went by, we were informed that some kind of correction would have to be made.

Our big time careers hung in the balance.

In order to try to prove that our trio had now improved with Reinhart as the high tenor we hired a studio and made a recording of "Sierra Sue," one of Gene's favorites at the time. We sang and recorded it over and over until we turned out a 'perfect' blend. We then had Johnny Marvin take it to Autry, who, after learning that Dick had a much higher range, enough so that he would be able to reach the high notes in question, the change was made, after which things progressed smoothly.

We learned much about Autry's methods from this incident, which taught us that we were not dealing with just another ordinary businessman. A similar situation would arise between Gene and myself in years to come, that I can truthfully say would become my most frustrating experience, demanding from me the most difficult decision of my life.

CHAPTER FOUR

Getting Acquainted

Or, It's Your Turn To Throw The Party

Working with Gene Autry and all of those who had been part of the musical portions of his show before our arrival in California afforded our trio an opportunity to get more fully acquainted with him and all the others. We soon fell in step with the rest of his immediate gang, Carl, Frankie, and the rest, but it would take a few more weeks to bring the wives into the circle. I had brought a young bride of six months with us in the one automobile that transported Jimmy Wakely, his wife of some years, their two young daughters and the newest member, Dick Reinhart, who would bring his wife and young son out a bit later.

When Gene was not on tour, whether he was working on a movie or not, there was a steady stream of parties thrown strictly for this one circle of individuals. It was Mary Lee Wooters, living in the heart of Hollywood, who invited us first. Mom and Dad Wooters were average, down-to-earth, neighborly, friendly people and their gatherings were the same that we had experienced back home. Every two or three weeks, someone else would throw a party and before you knew it we were all feeling as though we had been friends and neighbors all along.

These get-togethers afforded us the opportunity, not only to meet and visit with Mrs. Autry, his wife of about eight years, but also to get to know a side of Gene that was not strictly business. Gene and Ina seldom arrived late. They would shake hands all around; comment about the last radio show or record session, or, perhaps he would come forward with a story or two about that day's shooting at Republic. It was not unusual for him to arrive in costume and make-up directly from the studio.

The early parties (1940) usually involved a whole lot of plain old visiting like ordinary folks. Refreshments would usually consist of coffee, tea, soda pop, cakes, cookies, sandwiches, ice cream and the like. There were no alcoholic beverages served at this time. That came a few years later. Whether or not the others used it at home was something that didn't enter our minds. Being from the dry state of Oklahoma, we had not yet been exposed to it except for those rare occasions when famous personalities came to town and we would be called in to play for their socials.

After about an hour or so of visiting and chatting, Gene usually wound up seated in a corner with several of us gathered about him and the musical instruments would start coming out. The playing and singing would then begin and last until about midnight. We learned that Gene loved to sing whether on stage or off. We would begin with some of the older, more familiar favorites, followed by some new songs that he and others in the group were working on. In this manner we all learned the new songs, sometimes even helping revise certain parts of them.

Present at most of these early parties were friends and co-workers and their wives. The Autry's were usually the unofficial hosts to co-workers Frank and Johnny Marvin, Carl Cotner, Jimmy Wakely, Dick Reinhart, Scotty Harrel and such friends as Fred Rose and Ray Whitley. Also included were the entire Wooter family, Mary Lee and Mom and Pop Wooter, and, of course, my wife Dorothy and me. This list of guests was by no means static, depending upon the occasion and the size of the household.

Fred Rose and Ray Whitley were close friends of the Autry's and were constantly writing songs and singing their latest creations, which then might have been "Be Honest With Me," "Tweedle-O-Twill," "Hang My Head and Cry" and others. These two had turned out Autry's theme song, "Back in the Saddle Again" a few years earlier. Always, Gene would ask each of us to perform any new compositions; so naturally, we started writing like mad.

Smiley Burnette was conspicuously absent from both the parties and other Autry gatherings where we were present the first few years. We wondered about this only to learn that Smiley was now a star independent of Gene and might be out on the road with his own show. Later on there would be huge parties at the Burnette home in Studio City, not too far from the Autry's, where the guest list was always larger and Gene and Ina were usually present.

It was at one of the informal parties that Gene first broke the news to us that the time was approaching for him to take off on another tour. This one would be his annual trek to New York and Boston for the greatest of all rodeos at Madison Square Garden and The Boston Garden. We had been aware of the impending trip but had not yet been officially notified that the Trio would be expected to go along. This was double-good news for us as he would take the radio troupe with him and we would not miss out on any of the shows.

CHAPTER FIVE

New York and Boston—Rodeo

Or, Would You Get A Load Of Those Skyscrapers

It is difficult to describe the thrill that came to us as we made our first tour with the popular cowboy entertainer. Merely thinking about our first visit to New York and Boston left us practically speechless.

The last instructions that Gene gave us came at the conclusion of one of the Melody Ranch Broadcasts.

"OK, fellows," Gene said to us. "I'll be flying out in a day or so. You've got a whole week ahead of you. When you get to New York, you're to call Mr. Tony Stanford at the J. Walter Thompson Agency. Let him know where you're staying and he'll be in contact with me. See you in the Big City."

He didn't give us a chance to remind him that we'd never been in New York but it didn't matter. We figured that we were grown men now and could get around by ourselves.

Our first entrance into New York was enough to give a person heart failure. We tried to make a U turn in the Holland Tunnel. We picked up a man we thought was an officer but who turned out to be a representative for a run-down hotel who'd spotted our Oklahoma license plates. We stayed at this flop-house for one night before moving over to the Belvedere, next door to Madison Square Garden.

"Why are you taking up all of the carpets from the hallways?" we asked of our Bell Boy.

"We do it every fall when the rodeo hits town and the cowboys check in," the lad informed us.

Gene Autry's name and picture were all over the Big City . . . even overlooking Broadway. They not only knew who he was, but they also knew that he was in town.

There were meetings to talk over the rodeo performance as well as be sure we knew directions to the CBS Studios where we would do the broadcast.

The old Madison Square Garden Arena held a lot of people. Some say 25,000 per show when filled. I can verify that each show was full at every performance, seven nights a week with four matinees for six weeks running. Boston, for the next two weeks, was sold out as well. Times were good and the fans were filled with excitement at the prospect of being able to see their Cowboy Hero in person.

The rodeo itself was nothing new to me or to the New Yorkers. It had been appearing there for a number of years, but not necessarily with Gene the headliner. I'd seen my share of them while growing up in the Oklahoma ranch lands, but this was different. This was Big Time!

The typical rodeo and show would follow a fairly standard format.

After the playing of the "Star Spangled Banner" by the big brass band, Abe Lefton, the famous rodeo announcer and close friend to Gene, would introduce us as Gene Autry's Melody Ranch Gang. From a side entrance, Jimmy, Dick, Carl, Frankie and I would run out into the center of the arena directly underneath the enormous circle of loud speakers which re-layed the sound clearly into every corner of the huge building. Four or five short, snappy numbers were all that we did, after which the big brass band struck up a march for the grand entry which consisted of every cow-boy and cowgirl and official connected with the event, except Gene Autry and ourselves.

This entrance, single file, with flags and colorful costumes began with the horses at a walk. They proceeded along the outer edge of the arena, the band playing while the announcer gave a running commentary until the several hundred mounted riders completed a full circle. When the leader reached the spot from where he had first entered, he then changed his course to a right angle, marching directly over to the other side with the others following closely behind. As they reached the other side, they made a sharp U turn, returning to the opposite side. All the time this was happening, fresh riders were coming in through the entrance. By the time the leading rider reached the center of the arena, the pace of all the animals had reached a trot and shortly thereafter, a full gallop., The band was playing louder and faster as the gait of the horses increased. Now there was a small amount of gunfire with chosen cowboys shooting blanks.

By the time that all of the members of the Grand Entry were out in the ring, the pace and the excitement was at it's highest and the crowd was going wild with shouts and applause. It was truly one of the grandest beginnings to any show that I ever saw anywhere.

The rodeo contests were next. The cowboy contestant did not receive a fee or salary for his appearance. On the contrary, unlike any other form of show business, he paid an entry fee for the right to participate. If he won, he came out pretty good on the money end. If he lost, he was out not only his entry fee, but his expenses and time lost as well.

First came the bareback bronco riding, followed by calf roping and sometimes women's saddle bronco riding. The running commentary supplied by Abe Lefton was the added spice to the show since his deep voice and special sense of humor often made the difference between a great show and an otherwise dull routine.

After about 45 minutes had elapsed, they would introduce Gene Autry for the first time. A large hoop, covered with paper with his name painted on it, was held near the entrance, right under the balcony where the band and the announcer were seated. A drum roll began, ending in a loud fanfare as Champion jumped through the hoop breaking the paper. The spotlight followed Gene and Champ as they raced at a very fast gallop around the arena, coming to a stop in the very center. Then, on cue from music written especially for this act, Champion went through a series of steps, tricks and dances, taught him by his trainer, John Agee. There was a march, a waltz, a rumba, etc., all topped by bows and ending with the duplication of the famous painting, "The End of the Trail." The reception was tremendous. One would think that Gene Autry was the greatest personality to ever hit the Big City.

Following Gene's initial appearance, there were more rodeo contests such as bulldogging and trick riding, intermingled with other specialty acts which varied from year to year. Then, on cue, the lights would dim and we would enter the arena again with instruments in hand. This time Gene would ride Champ straight to the center where we all came together as he dismounted and spoke to the audience for the first time. This was usually a simple greeting leading into "Back In the Saddle Again."

This musical act lasted approximately 15 minutes and included many of his popular recorded hits. During World War II, he usually included an old song with the soft protest, "Don't Bite the Hand That's Feeding You."

Both of his appearances during each show were greeted with tremendous applause. There was no question about it . . . Easterners loved the Great West that Gene represented.

Following the songs he would mount Champion and ride slowly around the entire arena giving everyone present the best close-up view possible. Standing ovations were often given him as he reached the immediate vicinity of the overflowing boxes.

The rodeo, of course, was not over. More contests followed ending with the Brahma Bull riding contest that usually produced more exciting thrills than all the rest of the events put together. Gene and the rest of us always stayed around for this one.

As this event was introduced, two rodeo clowns ran out onto the area floor dressed in shabby overalls and wearing circus type makeup. They were Hank Mills, veteran of many seasons, who also entered other events as a contestant, and Jasbo Fulkerson. Hank's specialty was to run straight toward a big Brahma just missing his horns by a very few inches. Had they made contact at this speed Hank would surely have been finished.

Jasbo Fulkerson, short and chubby, entered the arena rolling a barrel, which he had built especially for his act. It was open at both ends with a handle inside that he could cling to in safety as some big bull tossed it about.

Backstage Gene would often say to Jasbo, "One of these days that old bull's gona' climb inside of that barrel with you," to which the little man would only laugh and say in his gravel voice, "And if he does don't you know I'll be climbing out. I'll just give it up and take the coward's way out, singing and pickin' the gee'tar." Then, turning to me, Jasbo continued,, "Play me a little bit of that "Roundup Time In Texas" on that stick-o-wood, Slim."

The bulls never got Jasbo. One longhorn took one of the clown's eyes, but he continued his act for years. The end came, ironically, to the little man on an icy highway somewhere between Fort Worth and Dallas where his overturned truck pinned him underneath.

Other rodeo clowns have adopted the 'barrel act,' but, as Gene always put it, "There was only one Jasbo."

With this event the rodeo and the Gene Autry Show came to a close. Outside the arena, Gene was mobbed by thousands of screaming youngsters clamoring for his autograph or some other souvenir. Hero worship such as he experienced was equaled only by that bestowed on Frank Sinatra a few years earlier or Elvis Presley a few years later.

We had known all along that Gene Autry was a big Star. Just how big, we never dreamed. And now, we were sharing his spotlight with him. Not only was the man a Star, he was a tremendous drawing card. There is a difference.

So ended our dream year, 1940. We had been in the big time for a little more than four months.

Bigger things were yet to come.

CHAPTER SIX

1941

Or, Where Were You When The Bombs Hit Pearl Harbor?

It was a very good year, so the ad goes. A common question connected with the year 1941 is, "Where were you when they bombed Pearl Harbor?" My answer has always been, "I spent the entire day with Gene Autry."

This year began just as busy and as exciting as the previous one had left off . . . nationwide radio broadcasts, extensive tours, getting our feet wet in the movies and phonograph records.

Gene made his usual quota of western films, eight per year, but none included our Trio. While we did appear in other films, it was always a mystery, as well as a disappointment, that we were not included. We made the broadcasts, the tours and the records; then, why not the movies?

We didn't have the nerve to ask Gene about this, but we did approach our agent, Mitch Hamilburg, who referred us to our contact man, Johnny Marvin. None of the answers were satisfactory so we endured the entire year of 1941 waiting and wondering. In the meantime, however, we did manage to land some pictures with other stars, such as Hopalong Cassidy, Tex Ritter, Johnny Mack Brown, Don Barry, and others, which helped to soothe our disappointments somewhat.

Now that we've all grown older and we hope, wiser, an answer has come to us, which in all probability, is at least partly correct.

By the time we joined forces with Gene Autry, he had been making successful movies for six years without us. His writers and producers at Republic probably did not know that we existed; therefore, when the scripts were written, they were done as they had been all along, with Gene, Smiley, and the regular Hollywood actors in mind. It is now clear that there simply was no part for us.

The successes of the New York and Boston rodeos prompted other bookings. This time it was Washington, DC, Pittsburg, Hershey, New Haven, Cleveland, Houston, and other points North, East, and South. While most of these stops enjoyed the turn-away crowds, the impact was not that of Madison Square Garden, so everyone looked forward to our return the next fall.

♫ ♫ ♫

Of all the cities played, two stand out in memory. One was the Nation's Capitol, because it was my first visit there. Since the European War was raging and we were beginning to feel the pinch, I had the unique opportunity of seeing all of the famous landmarks almost entirely alone. No tourists, no travelers, just one lone Okie viewing all of the sights. The rest of the gang was playing poker at the hotel.

A day or so later Gene surprised me with an invitation to go with him to the Capitol to attend a luncheon given him by the Oklahoma Senators and Congressmen. Here we met and chatted with such dignitaries as Senator Josh Lee, Congressman Wilbur Cartwright, Jack Nichols, and Will Rogers. The latter was not the famous humorist but a gentleman by the same name against whom I had helped campaign in Oklahoma in 1934. His opponent, John Steel Batson, from my hometown of Marietta, had tried to gain the newly created seat of Congressman-at-large. It was during these times that we all came to realize that Gene was very much interested in politics. On each subsequent visit he always placed the Capitol or White House on his itinerary. Years later he would say to us, "

I guess I should have run for Governor or Senator."

The second city that I remember well was Cleveland. It was early in the morning, April 20, 1941, that I received a telegram informing me that our first daughter, Sherry, was born. It had been a difficult decision for me to leave home knowing that this event was due. However, since my staying behind would have had a direct bearing on the jobs of Wakely and Reinhart, and Dorothy and I had the added comfort of her parents being present in my place at home, the two of us had decided that it would be to our advantage if I stayed on this new and exciting job.

I purchased a pocketful of cigars and hastened to the Cleveland Arena and Autry's dressing room where I beamed radiantly and said, "Hey, Gene! Guess what? Have a cigar."

Johnny and Dorothy Bond and daughter Sherry, 1941.

"Don't tell me," said Gene. He was aware of the impending event. Hadn't I spread the news around loudly enough? "Boy or girl?"

"Girl," I said, trying to force more cigars on him.

"Well, congratulations, son. That's something I've never experienced. I'll just take the one cigar. You know I don't smoke."

"Neither do I. Especially cigars."

"Is that all the cigars you have on you?" asked Autry, gazing at my small pocketful, cleverly concealing his inner motives. "Sure. I got enough for our gang."

"That so," said Gene as I made my move to leave.

Not long afterward I was confronted by some of the rodeo cowboys with whom I had previously had little or no contact.

"Hey, congratulations, Bond!" they shouted, hands out. "Where's our cigar?"

"Oh, sure," I said, nervously, surprised. "Have a cigar."

One by one, little by little, my supply of cigars soon evaporated into an ever-increasing flow of oncoming cowpokes, all of which had just been informed by Gene Autry.

"That's my last one," I said to a group of newcomers, some of whom had arrived too late for a stogie.

"That's just too damned bad," said a tall one, grabbing me by the arm.

"Where you taking me?" I exclaimed.

"No cigars? A beer will do just fine," said the cowpoke, beckoning for the others to follow us to the nearby bar.

After getting rid of this group of riders, I ducked out in a hurry, and re-armed myself with a full new box of Havana's. The beer bit was too steep for my pocketbook. I was learning things about my new boss . . . fast!

Cleveland happened to be our closing date after which I grabbed my very first airplane flight, hurrying home to see my three-week-old youngster. Still more surprises awaited my arrival, for there at the Burbank Airport, waiting to greet me, was my bride, Johnny Marvin, and Ina Mae Autry, all three smiling broadly.

♪   ♪   ♪

So passed the spring rodeo tours. Summertime is a good time for movie making, so while Gene made his, the Trio spent those days making movies with other Western stars. Gene placed no restrictions whatsoever on our activities so long as we showed up on time for our chores with him. Every Friday and Sunday, it was back to the CBS Studios and Gene Autry's *The Melody Ranch Show*, into which we had now begun to fit quite nicely.

That fall brought a return to New York and Boston, each even more successful than the previous year if such a thing is possible. At the close of this particular season we were instructed to stop off at Berwyn, Oklahoma, where we were to do the next broadcast.

When both of us were much younger, Gene Autry and I had crossed many a trail and junction over the same areas of South Central Oklahoma, though not at the same time. Tioga, Texas, and Ravia, Oklahoma, is a very short distance from my hometown of Marietta. At different times both of us had visited Ardmore and Berwyn laying directly on the Santa Fe Railroad.

When Gene realized that he was going to become heavily involved in the shipment of rodeo stock (one of his earliest investments was in a ranch which bred stock for rodeos) from Texas to the Northeastern States, he acquired a rest stop for the cattle and horses along the way. Being a railroad man, he was well aware of the law that stated that livestock being transported by rail had to be given this privilege. It was a mere coincidence that a convenient spot just happened to be near Berwyn.

At one time or another he had gone to Carter County and selected the acreage that he purchased for the purpose. When the local citizens discovered that their new neighbor was the singing star, they promptly made the motion that Berwyn be renamed Gene Autry, Oklahoma. The motion passed.

We went there for the name changing ceremonies, which included an all-day affair with Governor Red Phillips coming down for the occasion. Huge crowds turned out in full. Being so close to my home, I soon discovered that I was almost as big a star as was my boss. Here they came, friends, relatives, and kinfolks I hadn't seen or talked to for ages. The only thing about it was, all of the dialogue was the same. "Hi, kid. Take me to Gene!" Half a dozen local Autry's were there, most of who had never mentioned their close relative before now. At long last, Gene was their buddy come home.

We went through the name changing ceremony, broadcast *Melody Ranch* from the flatcar, and headed home for California. November was coming to a close. The whole world was about to undergo drastic changes.

♬   ♬   ♬

"Where were you on December 7, 1941. How often has that one been asked? Here's where we were:

We came to the CBS Studios in Hollywood just as we had been doing for over a year. Rehearsals went without incident followed by the usual break to don our costumes and receive any necessary changes or cuts in the script. We then took our places on stage before the full audience in Studio C, preparing to feed the full CBS network with our live broadcast. The time was 3:30 PM Pacific time making it 6:30 PM in the East. The KNX West Coast replay did not come until later so whoever was to hear us this day would all hear the same broadcast.

As was customary with most musical-comedy-variety radio shows, a 'warm-up' preceded the actual broadcast in order to "break the ice" with the studio audience, getting acquainted and, hopefully, encourage them to give out with louder, longer applause and to laugh at our corny jokes. About ten minutes before airtime the curtain was drawn as the entire cast took their place on stage. Gene strolled to the microphone, introduced himself and then the cast. Several bits of humor were passed along and, in no time at all, the audience was with us, which helped give the folks at home the impression that everyone was having a grand time.

We didn't know it, but the director had received a message during the warm-up that our show was to be delayed for a special announcement from the CBS newsroom in New York. So, at the moment when our theme usually began, we, along with the hundreds of people seated in the audience heard the shocking news together.

This was the first announcement of the Pearl Harbor incident and was lacking in detail. Everyone was alerted to standby for further news reports.

It goes without saying that each of us, Gene included, was stunned. We looked out at our room full of people while they sat motionless looking back at us. Autry made no comment but, on cue, went into his theme at the conclusion of the news bulletin.

It was an awkward show, for the performers as well as the listeners. We sang, played and spoke in one mood, always a carefree, lighthearted one, while millions of terrifying thoughts raced through our minds. During the broadcast, there were no more interruptions except for the time cuts. I can only suppose that there were plenty of things that Gene would like to have said to his fans; but, like a true showman, he stuck to the script and let it go at that.

The beginning of the American participation in the war brought changes in everybody's life. Gene Autry and his crew were no exception. At rehearsals, the male members of the cast would compare draft registrations and classifications. While there was no immediate likelihood of any of us being taken into the Armed Forces, it was pointed out, even in his presence, that the Autry's were childless while the rest of us were all proud fathers. So, while most of the troupe might not be taking up arms, there was a definite possibility that our Boss would.

Gene was not in the habit of revealing everything about his personal plans and movements, but we did begin to hear rumors from sources close to him that he was preparing to enter the service in some manner. We knew that he was taking flying lessons, and, various strangers in uniform began to appear at rehearsals and other gatherings.

In the meantime, back at *Melody Ranch*, it was business as usual. The Trio received the good news that we had been waiting a year and a half for . . . we would appear in the next Autry movie.

One of the popular songs of the day was "Deep in the Heart of Texas," which Gene had recorded and began singing on the radio show. When we reported to Republic Studios for consultation and wardrobe, we noted that this was to be the title of the picture. Almost all of his past films carried the title of some outstanding song so this came as no special surprise to us. Once we began filming the picture, however, we were told that the publishers had sold the title rights to Universal Pictures instead, so our picture was re-titled, *Heart of the Rio Grande*.

Gene was somewhat put out by this loss but said little about it. It was by a strange co-incidence that we would also work in that Universal Picture, *Deep in the Hear t of Texas*, starring Tex Ritter and Johnny Mack Brown.

As we got into the Autry picture we soon noted that Gene worked before the cameras just about the same as he did on radio and on the tours . . . relaxed and unconcerned. He very seldom ever blew his stack. He took everything in stride, reading his lines in his semi-amateurish way, donning a boyish/bashful approach to the leading lady, Fay McKenzie, while working the horses and fighting scenes with much authority.

Whenever our paths crossed during the day's shooting, he would stare at the crude sombrero that the wardrobe department had forced upon me and say, "Bond . . . where in the hell did you get that hat?"

It was while making this film that we got acquainted with the famous comic, Smiley 'Frog' Burnette, who had been conspicuously absent from all of the other Autry endeavors in which we had been participating.

About the only outstanding thing about this picture was that we were in it. Our parts were small, just cowboys around the ranch watching Gene, Smiley and the others do what had to be done. We did sing our song, "Cimarron." Evidently, the powers-that-be at Republic didn't care too much for the song, or at least our version, for they faded it out before we finished singing it. We did sing it all the way through, however, in a Hopalong Cassidy film entitled, "Twilight on the Trail."

During the filming of the Autry picture, we did notice that he had several visitors talking with him between takes. Gene would do one of his scenes, then, while the crew was changing camera angles, he would rush over into a distant corner and they would get their heads together in conversation. The cast included several teenaged girls, including the popular Edith Fellows, who began to needle Gene with some kind of verbal heckling. After a while Gene rode Champion over to the group of gigglers, giving them a firm but polite dressing down.

"Listen, you kids," he said to the girls. "Don't bug me when I'm talking business with somebody."

This was about as close to losing his temper that he had come to since we joined him. Five years hence he would come on with another one, yet stronger, a lashing in which I would find myself dead in the middle.

The next day on the movie set, the strangers of yesterday were absent. On this day Gene was talking between takes with many of the actors, actresses and extras working on the picture. It turned out he was inquiring as to their availability during the next month to work the Houston Rodeo as part of his show. Nearly all of them accepted. Upon completion of the picture, we all hit the road for Texas.

The Houston Fat Stock Show is one of the outstanding attractions in that area. Among other things, it is a rodeo that was programmed just about like the ones already described in Madison Square Garden. There were minor exceptions. For instance, they turned the clowns loose to work the full program instead of just the Brahma Bull riding as in New York. This made for a more interesting and colorful show over all. But, there was more. This is where Autry's thinking came in.

Opening the show was the entire group of actors, actresses and extras performing an old fashioned square dance in the arena. The costumes were colorful enough in the bright lights, but when these were turned off and the newly installed strobe lights hit the specially treated shirts, dresses, boots, and other ornaments, the fluorescent glow sent oohs and ahhhs throughout the crowded building.

Later on in the show, these same actors changed costumes, donned special Hollywood make-up and were introduced as they re-entered the arena one at a time.

First, out came Buffalo Bill, racing his horse across the arena floor. The old time actor and sometimes extra, Tex Cooper, looked exactly like the great frontier scout as he might have appeared in this hey-day. One by one came the others; Teddy Roosevelt, the Rough Rider, Kit Carson, Davy Crockett, Sitting Bull, Annie Oakely, General Custer . . . on they came until, standing at one end of the house, big hats swaying in the special lights, it appeared as if just about every great Western hero that ever rode the West was gathered in a group in front of us. It brought the house down with excited applause and standing ovations during each performance. It was one of the most colorful additions to a rodeo that I had ever seen. Unfortunately, this was the one and only show in which the event was used. I do know that it was never again done during any of the rodeos that we did with Gene. Perhaps it was because the use of the Hollywood actors proved to be much too expensive. Or possibly, the boom in motion picture production due to the War made it more profitable for the actors to stay in Hollywood.

♫   ♫   ♫

1941 produced many drastic changes amid the Autry camp. In July, Gene entered the Armed Services, taking his oath on the air during one of the *Melody Ranch* Broadcasts. Another major change was made in our singing Trio. By this time, we had appeared in a sufficient number of movies that Jimmy Wakely was beginning to get offers to star in his own vehicles. Naturally since we were an act unto ourselves, he wanted Dick Reinhart and me to stay with him. This entire process became both complicated and somewhat personal, so I will forego the details and give here only the end result.

We resigned the Autry show as a unit. Gene hired Eddie Dean and his brother, Jimmie, to take our place. Dick Reinhart changed his mind at the last minute and stayed on with Autry. For a period of a few months I was off the Autry payroll. Then, as the War got closer and closer to him, Dick resigned, taking his family back to Texas, and I was asked to fill his place. After consulting with Wakely, I returned to the fold to sing with Eddie and Jimmie Dean. Shortly afterward, Eddie left and was replaced by Wesley Tuttle. This Trio stayed with Gene and the show until wartime pressures caused its cancellation for the duration.

Gene entered the service wearing the uniform of a Sergeant in the Air Force. Carl Cotner entered about the same time and both were eventually stationed at Luke Field in Phoenix, Arizona, from where we performed many broadcasts. Mr. Wrigley told CBS that he would like to keep the show on the air as long as possible, so the rest of us were still in business, making the trip from Hollywood to Phoenix once a week.

Due to wartime travel restrictions and for financial considerations, most of our transportation was by train. The Southern Pacific Railroad had a convenient schedule whereby our weekly jaunts soon became routine. It was on one of these Pullman rides that I was afforded my first opportunity to visit and converse with Gene Autry.

Just the two of us.

CHAPTER SEVEN

1942

Or, Take That Night Train From Phoenix
Or, Gene Autry Talks and Talks

The decision to write this tale didn't come suddenly. As far back as the mid-forties, while riding the Autry bus down the open highways, someone would turn and say, "Somebody ought to write a book about this."

True, somebody should. For years it had been my belief that somebody would. During the fifties we were told that a man was hanging around, contemplating *The Gene Autry Story*. How can an outsider write such a story? It was always my belief that the writer had to be on hand, at least most of the time.

Mitch Hamilburg could have written much about Gene's financial matters since it was he that helped set up a lot of it and would have a first hand account of some of the negotiations. If Hamilburg left anything in writing behind him I don't know about it.

The one person who could have told the most complete story would be Ina Mae Spivey Autry, his wife of many years. But, she chose not to.

Naturally, there are many, many others who could give us an interesting, detailed account of the life of the great personality.

As time went by, I came to the conclusion that perhaps I might have something worthwhile to contribute. After all, Gene and I did have a number of private conversations together. While I am not so naïve as to imply that the subject matter of those talks will move mountains, they were, at least, interesting to me and, hopefully, to someone else. Still, if I don't tell about them, who will? Surely not Gene himself, for he has had too many other conversations with too many, much more important people to even try to recall anything that he might have ever said to me?

What I said to him was nothing.

What he said to me was interesting enough to be recorded indelibly into my feeble brain just itching for an opportunity to be turned on.

It was during the rehearsal of one of the Luke Field broadcasts that Sgt. Autry informed us that he would be making the train ride to the coast with us that night. He and Mrs. Autry had been staying in Phoenix so it came as welcome news that he might be coming back to discuss either a movie or record deal in which we all might participate.

Following the show, it was usually a quick dinner at the Adams Hotel, then on to the railway station where we boarded our Pullman car to prepare for the eight-hour sleeper jump. Brad Browne, the show's director, usually made all travel arrangements handing out tickets and berth numbers as he saw fit. There had been some mild grumbling that some of us had to take the upper or lower combinations while others received the privacy of the bedroom compartments, so I was pleased when Browne informed me that one of the latter would be mine for this particular run.

"I don't know who will be in with you just yet," Brad said.

"Doesn't matter," I said, hastening to ease his mind on that subject since I figured that his job was complicated enough.

Just as Autry came aboard the train, Brad Browne handed him a ticket and asked, "Do you two mind sharing a compartment together? Had I known in advance that you were going to be with us, Gene . . . "

"Oh, hell, that's okay," Gene said, indicating with both his hands and facial features that he was satisfied with less than something special in the way of accommodations. "Put me in there with Jonathan Q. We'll keep each other awake."

For the next hour or so after the train was under way, visits were made up and down the hallways where poker games and other gatherings were in progress. There had been a big fund raising affair in Phoenix that day and several Hollywood personalities were aboard. Jack Benny and Ann Southern stopped by and chatted with Gene for a little while before moving on to the next car. I said my goodnights to all and started for the compartment while Gene allowed he would play a couple of hands with the guys and would be along shortly.

I wasn't particularly nervous about this unexpected situation, as I knew Gene pretty well by now. While in his presence, it was hard to realize that he was one of the top moneymakers in Hollywood and a world famous personality. He had a way of putting a person at ease so that we soon looked upon him as just one of the gang. He was that down-to-earth.

Preparing myself for the night, I elected to take the top bunk as I felt that he not only deserved the lower but would need all the space he could get in this small, crowded room.

With that, I climbed into the upper berth and listened to the wheels making contact with the rail connections.

In a short while Sergeant Autry came in and our very first private conversation began:

"Well, Jonathan Q, it looks as though you've already hit the sack." I still don't know where the Jonathan Q came from, but like Tex Atchison said, Gene had a name for everybody.,

"Yeah," I said, delighted now that he'd come in with an 'ice-breaking' first line of conversation. "I thought I'd get out'a your way and let you have the lower."

"Oh, hell, you didn't have to do that. I could have jumped up there just as easy."

"How long are you going to be in LA," I asked, really not knowing if I should try and lead the conversation.

"Oh, I don't know. Only have a few days leave."

"I guess the service doesn't give you too much leeway, does it?"

"You better believe it. They let me live off base . . . outside of that I'm just another soldier."

"Think this mess will last very long?" I asked, still reaching for subject matter. I would be glad to have him take the ball and run with it.

"Who knows," Gene said, going through his preparations to hit the sack. "It'll last as long as that damned Hitler is alive. He's not going to give up until he buries every one of us."

"Sure has messed up the lives of a lot of people."

"Yeah. You spend half your life getting things gong like you want them, and wham, something like this comes along and puts the skids on it overnight. One day you're making good money and the next day you're on Army pay."

"That must make quite a hardship on you and Ina Mae."

"We've built up quite an overhead; and now, with the Republic money cut off, there's nothing coming in but some royalties and you damn sure can't depend on them alone!"

"You still get paid for the radio show, don't you?"

"Yeah, well, I'm not supposed to, but just between you and me, the Wrigley people slip ole Cotner and me a little something on the QT. We don't get it in cash. They make out a War Bond in our name."

"That helps."

"I'll tell you one thing, though," said the Sergeant, pulling off his shoes and socks. "I'll never again let myself get into a position where I'm depending on a salary which might be cut off by something like this. I'm going to get me some investments which will pay me whether I work or not."

"What kind of investments?" I asked, not yet being hip on big business matters.

"Lots of things, " Gene informed me. "Real estate, hotels, radio stations; I've got my eye on a couple of stations. One is here (Phoenix) and one down in Tucson. They tell me they're little gold mines."

"I see what you mean." This high finance was over my head. I tossed and turned a little as the train rounded some curves. Every so often it would stop at a railroad station, then, move on. The Sergeant walked back and forth within the diminutive confines of our small compartment. He was taking his time preparing for bed.

"By the way" Gene said, after a short pause. "How's our friend Wakely making out with his picture deals?" I gathered from this change of subject matter that he thought perhaps we were getting a bit too deep into his private financial dealings and would prefer to talk about something else.

"Okay I guess. He's had some meetings but I don't know too much about it. In the meantime we've been signed up to do a series with Tex Ritter and Johnny Mack Brown at Universal."

"Ritter is one hell of a fine guy. Finished any of them yet?"

"Yeah, one of them."

Deep in the Heart of Texas? he asked without looking at me.

"Yeah. How'd you know?"

"Oh," he hesitated. "I read the trades."

I should have known that information would be printed in the *Daily Variety* and *Hollywood Reporter*. Gene read those daily.,

"Did they have Ritter sing the title song?" he asked.

"No. Fuzzy Knight sang it."

"I see. What time setting did they use?"

"You mean the date of the picture? About 1870."

"That's about what I figured, " Gene said, nodding his head vigorously. I said nothing further as he wandered to and fro, taking care of certain pre-bedtime matters. Being in the upper berth, my position was about level with his head as he was standing. He walked over closer to me, looked me straight in the face and continued, "You see, that just goes to show you how short sighted and stupid some of these Hollywood executives can be. We offered the publisher a good deal for the title rights to that song. Universal heard about it and buys it out from under me for a few bucks more. I recorded the song. That'll make the publisher more money. Did anybody at Universal record the song for them? Hell no. Then, you take Universal. Here's a modern song and they take it all the way back to the middle ages. They have Tex Ritter, a recording artist with a big hit record (note: "I Got Spurs That Jingle Jangle Jingle") and do they give him the song? Hell, no, they give it to Fuzzy Knight. Oh, don't misunderstand me. Fuzzy is a fine guy and a great comedian. He did okay with that "Trail of the Lonesome Pine" stuff, but you should give your key songs to your stars. We had a modern, up-to-date story built around the song. As I see it, both the publisher and Universal missed the boat. See what I mean?"

"Yes," I said, meekly. "I see what you mean."

"Who's producing?"

"Oliver Drake," I told him.

"No wonder. He did some of mine years ago. I don't think he knows a damn thing about making singing westerns."

"I don't think so either."

"Every since I started making the musicals, every studio in town has tried to jump on the bandwagon. They think all you have to do is get some guy, any guy, who can carry a tune, stuff a few public domain songs down their throats, hire some two bit writer and turn out a money making western. We don't do it that way. We spend money on songs and stories and we turn out a good, modern picture. The rest of them want to stay back in the Stone Age. Do you ever see an automobile in one of their pictures? Hell, no. We even use motorcycles, radio. . .we go modern. So, they finally go out and buy a hit song, and look at what they do to it. Louse it up. What songs did they use other than "Deep in the Heart of Texas"?

I told him the names of some of the other songs. True, they were old traditional cowboy songs. Some of them were almost a hundred years old.

Johnny as he appeared in *Deep in the Heart Of Texas.*

"See what I mean. You just can't get through to them that it's important to use hit songs. Not just one hit, lots of them. They just won't put out the money for songs. They spend it all on everything else."

"They're dang sure not spending a lot for us," I confessed.

"You think I don't know that? Some guys I know would pay them just to get to be in the movies."

"Well, I learned one thing about these Hollywood executives. The only way you can get them to respect you is to make them pay. Remember that, make them pay!" The famous sergeant pounded his fist on the edge of my upper berth as the train rumbled through the night. By now we were probably crossing the Colorado River into California. Each time I go through that area, I think of myself as another Okie out of the "Grapes of Wrath."

"We don't feel we're in too good a position yet to make them pay us more, " I said, knowing not what else to say.

"Republic didn't pay me in the beginning . . . much, that is. I had to go on strike to get another dime out of them. That and a few other things."

"Yeah, I heard about your strike."

"How did you happen to hear about that?" Gene asked, somewhat surprised.

"Several places," I said, hurriedly, not wishing to let him know that I might have been prying into his personal business. "Wasn't it in the papers? Carl and Frankie were with you and Uncle Art Satherly might have mentioned it. I didn't mean that I knew all the details." I didn't know if I should have gone into this or not.

"Oh well," Gene said, putting me at ease, somewhat. "There wasn't that much to it. I was going along fine. I didn't pry into the studio's business. I knew the pictures were selling . . . that was good enough for me, but when I learned that they were using my pictures to move a lot of that other crap they've been turning out, it kind'a got my goat."

"The boys said you were really teed off."

"That's about it. Anyway, that's when I decided to make them pay. They did, and now they respect me more for it. But, you have to demand it in order to get it."

"Did Smiley go on strike with you?"

Sergeant Gene Autry stopped whatever he was doing at the time and looked at me coolly. "No, no," he said, after a slight pause. "He didn't strike. He wasn't even with me at the time. Frog was out on tours of his own."

Several things pertaining to the strike and Frog raced through my mind but I thought it best to remain silent about it and let Gene do the talking. I should be doing more listening at this point anyway.

"It doesn't matter," Gene went on, returning to his bedtime chores. "I'm not going to use him in my pictures anymore, anyway."

I sat up in the upper bunk, startled. "You're dropping Frog?"

"Not only him, but Republic as well," said Gene, looking around at our place of confinement as though he wanted to make certain that nobody else was listening.

"I can't believe it."

"They're too slow for me," the singing cowboy continued with his revelations. "I've given them every good idea they ever had. Then what do they do? Turn right around and fire up another series with this one and that one . . . some unknown who never made a picture, never made a record, and never rode a horse. Now they think they can make stars out of just anybody. I plan on making my own pictures. They'll be bigger and better Westerns. What's more, they'll be in color . . . every one of them."

At this point in history, very few, if any of the so-called B Westerns had been made in color. Even *Stagecoach,* about the biggest one up until that time, had been done in black and white.

"Getting back to Smiley" I said, fishing. "You gonna replace him?"

"I don't know yet," the Sergeant answered. "Neither Tom Mix or Buck Jones or Ken Maynard ever used a steady comic side-kick. I don't know if I need one or not. If I do, though, I have a guy in mind."

I was on edge, of the upper yet, because that was the kind of part I would have loved to have.

"Who's that?"

"Sterling Holloway."

"Sterling Holloway! He's not western."

"Doesn't have to be. We can dress him for that part. Besides, I like him. He has that 'Step'n' Fetchit look about him, and he enlisted in the service. I'm going to stay with the patriots because when this thing is over, I think the public is going to remember who served and who didn't."

That put me on the spot because I hadn't gone into the service myself. At any rate, that just about ended our conversation on any subject of consequence. Goodnights were said and we both called it a day.

Many, many things went through my mind as I lay there in my upper berth, listening to the clicking of the rails as the connections came in contact with the metal wheels. Every now and then the whistle would blow, or a swinging highway signal would be passed, causing the pitch of its bell to change and fade away as we raced past the intersection. I knew that Los Angeles and home lay in my immediate future. Beyond that, I couldn't comprehend.

♫   ♫   ♫

In going over this discussion between Gene Autry and myself, which took place over 30 years ago, several things come to my mind. Someone might ask, 'how can you remember one particular conversation after so long a time?' The answer is that I can't forget it. It was also repeated many times over in one form or another with other people on other occasions. I realize that time has somewhat diminished the full importance of some of the subject matter, but, look at it this way. Suppose that Louella Parsons, or the head of Republic Pictures had overheard the talk. What a nice juicy column with huge headlines that would have made in newspapers the next day. How much fur would have been flying in the front offices of Republic? How many lawyers would have dug out the Autry contract, going over and over it with a fine-tooth comb?

Another thing! Why would one of the biggest movie stars in the business make such confidential statements in the presence of an employee without pledging him to eternal silence? Why did I not repeat it with or without the pledge? The answer to the latter is obvious. He was my boss and idol. I wouldn't have repeated anything for personal reasons and pride. As for his reasons, I don't know why.

When I think over some of the subject matter of our discussion, I realize that much of it did, indeed, come to pass. Most of his plans worked out to his satisfaction. Other decisions would come back to haunt him.

Even as Gene Autry was talking, many of his projects were already under way. He had purchased the ranch near Berwyn, now known by his name. Just before that, he bought into *The World's Championship Rodeo* with the influential Texas rancher, Everett Coburn. The two radio stations mentioned, in Phoenix and Tucson, were acquired. Soon, other radio stations in other parts of the country were added to his holdings, as were hotels and oil properties. In the early fifties television would become dominate. The biggest and probably the most interesting and personally satisfying of his projects yet to come would have been the least on his mind during this railroad journey through the night . . . baseball.

Gene's viewpoints on the making of singing Westerns proved that it was mostly his own personal ideas that made his films great as well as highly commercial. Although most of the other studios in Hollywood did try to jump on the singing cowboy bandwagon, none had come near the success that he was enjoying. It was mostly the old, tired, traditional songs plus cheap, dull, out-dated scripts that finally drained the well dry. The B Westerns died out in the early fifties . . . even his. As for the songs, one has only to look at the great *High Noon* to see the intense value of the music. A good film, yes, but what would it have been without the song which may very well live on long after the film is forgotten. Too many highly paid executives in the movies are prone to under-rate the value and power of a good song.

Gene did file suit seeking the termination of his Republic contract after he was released from the service. He did leave Republic for Columbia, where he made his own films. He dropped Smiley Burnette, but only used Sterling Holloway in the last few Republic films. I learned over time that Gene did not necessarily push the use of Frog in the movies in the very beginning. Smiley had been a member of the Autry troupe and had a personal services contract with Gene. After a year or so of success with the singing Westerns featuring Frog as the eternal sidekick, Smiley's contract with Gene ended and he was signed to a separate contract with Republic. He also was able to form his own show for personal appearances. None of this is meant to imply that there was a personal difference or rift between the two. Anything there was always strictly professional. I can vouch for the fact that both Gene and Smiley always spoke well of each other. As time went by I am certain that they each learned to respect the other's talent and position more and more.

The only rift, if there actually was one, had to come at the time that Gene went on strike against the studio. With Gene on strike and a film all ready to start shooting, the studio decided to put Roy Rogers in the starring role and expected Smiley Burnette to proceed with the part that had been written for him. It was Autry who went on strike, not Smiley. For Frog to refuse to do the role might have jeopardized his entire career. Still, the incident had to leave its mark in Gene's mind, for it brought into being his nearest competitor, Roy Rogers.

Although Smiley Burnette was dropped from the Autry films after the war, Gene was most happy to bring him back before it was all over with the singing Westerns.

♫   ♫   ♫

My first private conversation with Gene Autry was informal, but most informative. Our get-together had been entirely accidental due to wartime restrictions on travel. He could have taken a plane home. He could have demanded and received a private bedroom on the train. They could have sent me to one of the uppers in the Pullmans, as they often did.

It was just one of those things. As the years went by, Gene and I had many such private conversations. His words may not have changed the world, but they certainly left their imprint upon my mind. Eighteen years after this 1942 date, he would cry on my shoulder for some of the mistakes he thought he made with some of those decisive moves.

CHAPTER EIGHT

Army Tours
1943
The Command Performance

Or, Sergeant Autry, I Order You To Sing My Baby Son To Sleep

Although I've heard about Command Performances all of my life, only one has come my way and I was compelled by irate instinct to throw a monkey wrench into the big middle of it.

As Red Skelton's "mean widdle kid" might say, "I'm glad I dood it.."

The Luke Field Broadcasts of *Melody Ranch* continued while Sergeant Gene Autry and Private Carl Cotner went through their basic training. With nothing keeping him in Los Angeles, Frankie Marvin moved his family to Phoenix, setting up a string of jukeboxes that he worked between broadcasts. Since I was still making a vain effort on my own to try to come up with a picture now and then, I found myself with the week in-between on my hands, so I went to the USO and volunteered my services to some of the Camp Shows on military bases in the Southern California area. Movie stars galore worked these same shows bringing in thousands of dollars worth of comedy material which I listened to backstage as the hoards of GI's roared with laughter. I always was a good listener, but my upbringing had cautioned me not to steal.

We have a saying in this business that goes like this: "I didn't steal his joke, I merely borrowed it. He can have it back any time that he wants it." There is another legal saying that implies that once a joke has been told in public, it is no longer copyrightable and therefore becomes public domain, belonging to anybody. After clearing my conscience on the matter, I set about lifting enough material to build myself a comedy act. It went over so well that before I knew it, some low down sneaky thieves were now stealing my material.

The dirty bums!

At any rate, the result of all this was that it soon came in handy. We were informed by the J. Walter Thompson Agency that arrangements had been made by the Defense Department and the Wrigley Company to send Sergeant. Autry and his troupe on a tour of Army and Air Force Bases throughout the US, where we would put on shows while continuing the radio broadcast once a week.

For the camp shows, Autry took Eddie and Jimmie Dean and myself as a playing/singing trio, with Private Carl Cotner on fiddle, now directing a larger orchestra for the broadcast. Brad Browne carried three Hollywood actors along for the radio show, while CBS arranged for staff musicians and radio engineers to come from Chicago to such places as Denver, Indianapolis, Louisville, Nashville, Birmingham, and any other place where our schedule might find us on a given Sunday.

While the radio broadcast might be about the same quality as all of the previous ones, the camp shows were rather light, having only a skeleton crew with which to work. A local Officer from the base would introduce Sergeant Autry who would, in turn, bring on Private Cotner for a few numbers on the fiddle while we backed him up. After that, our trio would do a few songs, and then Gene would sing several of his hits as a windup. The soldiers went for the show in a big way since many of them were from rural areas and grew up on Autry movies, records and radio. Seeing him in the same type of uniform that they were wearing gave them something in common.

It was pointed out that our show was good but short. Couldn't we do something about that? I was reluctant to push myself forward so Eddie went to Autry, informing him of my comedy act which was then added to the show to everyone's satisfaction. Especially mine.

One sample joke went like this:

"A group of nurses arrived today about the same time that we did. One nurse said to the Captain, "Where do we eat?" to which the Captain replied, "You'll mess with the Officers.""

"We figured that," said the nurse, "but where do we eat?"

Before long Gene and I were doing gags together. Gene Autry became my straight man!

Bond: I have a brother in the Army.

Gene: Did he go peacefully?

Bond: Yeah. After they come and got him he went peaceable.

Or:

Bond: I saw you trying to date that Wac.

Gene: Oh, you did, did you?

Bond: Yeah. She turned you down, didn't she?

Gene: Yes, she reminded me that I'm a Sergeant. She said she wouldn't go out with anything lower than a Second Lieutenant.

Bond: Hmmm. I didn't know there *was* anything lower than a Second Lieutenant.

♫　♫　♫

After we had a few shows under our belt we improved so much that soon thereafter we were all congratulating ourselves at the end of each day while relaxing in our quarters.

"That Bond is some funny-man, eh Gene?" said Eddie Dean to the Sergeant.

"You happen to be talking about the guy that's going to replace Smiley Burnette in my pictures," Gene said, slyly.

"How about that?" Dean said.

I said nothing. I'd already heard all the dialogue that I wanted to hear this day. Me, Gene's sidekick?

Thankfully, our show was a smash according to all of the Commanding Officers on every base, not to mention the draftees who let us know that they loved it by their thunderous applauses. It is a well-known fact that GI audiences during the early part of World War II were the most appreciative crowds to be found anywhere.

With the Autry troupe, there was something new and surprising with each passing day. One of our shows was staged at Casper, Wyoming, where we really found ourselves out in the wide-open spaces. The bases in and around Casper were populated enough but we learned that there was a very small group of enlistees stationed some distance from town out in the backlands. Gene was ordered to go there to entertain them so it was only natural that we went along.

♫　♫　♫

As we were being driven in army vehicles over long, unpaved roads, we soon found ourselves alone in an area where there was no other sign of civilization. There was nothing except a vast expanse of plains covered with scrub brush, with snow-capped mountains in the distance. It had snowed on us lightly and the weather was brisk. As our car topped a small hill, a lone horseman was spotted ahead of us. As we neared the rider we saw that it was a young cowpoke not more than 10 or 11 years of age. Our driver stopped the moment we pulled up even with the lad, who also pulled his mount up to a halt.

"Hey, there young fellow!" our driver called out to the young cowpuncher. "Ever heard of Gene Autry?"

The lad merely nodded his head, bashfully.

"Ever shake hands with Gene Autry?"

This question brought only the shaking of his head.

Gene climbed out of the car and greeted the young fellow by extending his hand.

"Hi, son," said Gene. "I'm Gene Autry."

The small cowpoke did not seem to comprehend that which was happening to him. Had Gene been attired in his western clothes with the big, white hat, the boy might have given out with some kind of response. As it was, he merely hung on to his silent composure.

"Johnny, is your guitar handy?" Gene asked.

"Sure is," I said, pulling my Martin out of the case. I struck a C chord while Gene Autry sang "Back In the Saddle Again" for his lone audience of one, his smallest ever. When it was over, Gene again offered his hand to the youngster who held on to his eternal silence. I believe that he did give out with one, diminutive grin.

Gene re-entered the car and we resumed our trip over the long, lonesome road. The lone horseman fell behind us, growing smaller and smaller with distance. Just before we cleared the next hill which would take us out of his sight, we saw him life his hand, waving it gently until the rise came between us.

♫   ♫   ♫

From Casper, Wyoming, we were shuttled in an army cargo plane to Rapid City, South Dakota, where the infamous Command Performance was

Carl Cotner, along with Frankie Marvin, Johnny Marvin and Johnny Bond participated in every area of Gens's entertainment. These were the only four to do so.

supposed to take place. Since I do not remember the Colonel's name, and since I wouldn't want to mention it even if I did, I'll resort to the old favorite standby of "Smith."

Colonel Smith, the Commanding Officer of the base, along with a dozen or so of his officers, met our plane. Gene de-planed first with the rest of us right behind him. Both Sergeant Autry and Private Carl Cotner snapped to attention, clicked their heels and saluted in formal Army fashion. We civilians merely stood there while the Colonel and his officers all smiled broadly while saluting in return. The welcome was warm enough and, after a period of rest and refreshment, they escorted us around the base. We had to have a cook's tour of every base. They couldn't read the minds of the Dean brothers and myself . . . when you've seen one Army base you've seen them all. But, we pretended to be impressed.

"These boys here are in the signal corps," the Colonel informed us. Autry shook hands with all of the young soldiers who then gave a brief sample of their ability to use the telegraph keys and the Morse code. They dotted and dashed off a few things, then stepped back, looked at each other as they grinned devilishly. Sergeant Autry said nothing, but I noticed that he, too, had a sly grin on his face as he stepped forward, touched the telegraph keys, tapping more dots and dashes, after which the entire signal corps burst into hysterical laughter. I doubt that the soldiers were aware that he used to be a telegrapher with the railroad. Neither Gene nor the boys volunteered the subject matter of their exchange of dot-dash dialogue.

"What did you and those boys discuss on the telegraph keys?" I finally got up the nerve to ask Gene years later.

"Oh," Autry hesitated. "I'll be damned if I know."

After the show, which was put on in one of their large hangers, the Colonel and his staff fell on our necks with praise and gratitude. It was then that Colonel Smith informed us that he would drive us back to our quarters where we were to spend the night on base. Nobody questioned his offer as we all piled into his car. On the way across the wide open spaces of the air base, the Colonel continued his appreciation for the show while pointing out various buildings here and there. Then he said, "By the way, Sergeant Autry, it just so happens that my home is nearby. How would all of you like to stop in for a moment?"

It would have been out of the question for Gene to refuse this offer of hospitality. He turned to those of us who were riding in the back seat and said, "I think that would be very enjoyable, don't you fellows?"

We all agreed.

"Now, don't get me wrong, men," the Colonel continued. "I'm not using this to show you off. Matter of fact, there's nobody home. Just thought you'd like to stop in for a minute."

We stopped in. He escorted us into the modest living room where he offered us a seat ... nothing else. When we had seated ourselves, the Colonel excused himself while he went off into another part of the house. As a matter of fact he left the room two or three times, always returning alone. Each time that he came back to our presence the smile on his face kept getting broader. He brought no one else out with him, not even a wife or a nurse. The next time he left our presence, he turned and said, "I have a surprise for you."

Here it came. He returned from another one of the rooms with an infant of about six months wrapped in a sleeping garment.

"Gentlemen, Sergeant Gene Autry," said the proud Colonel. "I'd like for you to meet my baby son."

All of us gathered around the infant expressing our great pleasure at this meeting.

"How are you, little Colonel?" Gene said to the baby. The proud father was beaming from ear to ear.

"I'm afraid I'm waking him," said the CO as he turned to go back into the child's bedroom. "If I wake him up, Sergeant Autry might have to sing him back to sleep. Isn't that right, Sergeant Autry?"

We let that one drop as Gene looked at us, showing a small amount of embarrassment. All he could do was to smile politely at the Colonel, who, with his young son, had now disappeared into the darkness of another part of his household.

"How about that, Sergeant Autry?" came the Colonel's voice from the nursery. "Don't you think this boy needs a bedtime song?"

All Gene could do was to look at us and shrug. "Well, I don't know, sir," he finally said loud enough for the Colonel to hear. At this point none of us, including Autry, could tell if the Colonel was putting us on, or just what. We soon got the message.

"I think he needs just one little song," continued the invisible voice of the CO. "After all, he did miss the show. Papa's baby didn't get to hear Sergeant Autry sing, not one song, did you, baby?"

In the living room there was complete silence as well as wonderment floating through the air among Gene, Carl, the two Dean brothers and myself. We were completely stumped.

"Sergeant Autry! My son is waiting for his song."

Now we knew that the Colonel meant it. He was not kidding. He was, in fact, ordering Sergeant Autry to sing a song for his own little son, now back in his crib. Gene was on the spot. Had he not been in uniform he would have told the Colonel, politely, that his throat was sore from just doing a heavy show and excuse himself thusly. If the Colonel then persisted, Gene could tell him where to get off. As it was, the Sergeant was definitely receiving orders from a superior officer. "Sing my baby to sleep!"

"Sergeant!" the Colonel's voice was now crisp and clear. That one came into our room riding icicles.

Being a civilian and not subject to the Colonel's whims, I was burned at this brazen call for action above and beyond the so-called Call-to-Duty. I got Gene's attention . . . pointed to myself and motioned for the other boys to join me ion a circle. Although the Colonel could not see us, we placed Gene in such a position that his back was to the doorway to the nursery in the event that the Colonel should re-appear.

Then, imitating Gene Autry to the very best of my ability, I sang, "Back in the Saddle Again," motioning to Gene that he could remain quiet whole the others joined me by humming the same song. We had not brought the musical instruments in from the Colonel's car. For several moments thereafter, the Command Performance of "Back in the Saddle Again" continued.

Once it was concluded, the Colonel, the proud happy father came back into the room smiling more broadly than ever.

"Thank you, Sergeant Autry, gentlemen," he said, radiantly. "My son thanks you for that fine song. You never sounded better. Now, I will be glad to drive you to your quarters."

In spite of this embarrassing incident, Gene Autry never complained about it. He always said of this Colonel, "He was one fine gentleman."

Perhaps I over-extended myself in this matter, but I couldn't stand to see Gene on the spot and I had to do what I had to do.

Somewhere out there in this land of the free there's a young man, a Colonel I suppose, who has proudly told many times about the night that Gene Autry serenaded him to sleep.

♫   ♫   ♫

As we prepared to leave Rapid City the next morning we were informed that we had no transportation. No one particular plane or crew had been put at our disposal. Instead, we had taken that which had been assigned to us at each base. As we waited with Colonel Smith and his staff, we noted a B26 Bomber sitting on the runway. After inquiries were made it was learned that this plane had been part of a flight that had left Fort Worth for Chicago. This one had to drop out of formation and land here for reasons not relayed to jus. Since it was now ready to take off, we were instructed to put our gear aboard and we would be flown to Minneapolis. This flight, being our first aboard a big bomber that had actually seen foreign combat duty, was quite interesting. Gene usually sat in the cockpit with the pilots while we had the run of the plane from one end to the other. We sat in the nose, the tail, and the other 'bubbles' where machine gunners had sat shooting real bullets at a very real enemy.

While seated in the nose of the plane, enjoying a rare, unobstructed, up-front view of the sky above, the clouds upon us and the vast farmlands below, Carl and I noticed that we were heading straight into a very dark cloud which just happened to be hovering over a very large city which we assumed to be Minneapolis, our destination. We couldn't believe that our pilot would actually enter this cloud, entwined with small streaks of lightning, but he did. The minute we hit it the plane started bouncing. Cotner looked at me and I looked at him.

"What'a you think?" I asked, sheepishly.

"I think we'd better get the hell out of here," said Carl as we both dove for the small exit.

In the main body of the plane there were no seats, no pretty stewardesses, no other comforts of modern day commercial flights; nothing but parachute packs to sit on. Eddie and Jimmie Dean were there already holding on for dear life while some of the crew ran back and forth through the airplane trying to give it balance. Naturally, it had been necessary to enter the heavy weather front because it was hanging right over Minneapolis and there was no other way to go around it without having to go off to another location.

As we circled the city awaiting a chance to land I happened to remember some instructions from my bride back home in Los Angeles. "Write me every day." With this I seated myself upon a parachute, took my pencil and paper in hand and attempted to write that day's letter. It was at that precise moment that Sergeant Autry had chosen to leave his seat in the cockpit and join the rest of his troupe here in the back. When he noticed my activity, he inquired, "Jonathan Q, what in the hell are you writing at a time like this?"

"Making out my will," I replied. At this stage of my association with Autry I had learned that he was fond of the lighthearted by-play and was quite a practical joker. To state that I was working on my will was simply the first thing that entered my head and was probably meant to imply that I might be a bit leery of the predicament in which we had now found ourselves. Maybe I was a bit edgy as a result of the plane's bouncing but I wouldn't have wanted Gene or the others to know it if it were true.

Be that as it may, Autry thought that this was about the funniest sight that he had seen. From that day forward he never let me forget the day I made out my will in a violent storm over Minneapolis. We played this area many times thereafter and each time we entered the city limits he would point toward the skies and say, "Right up there is where ole Bond made out his will."

The laughter quickly subsided when we entered the airport terminal and picked up the local newspaper, the headlines of which read: ARMY BOMBER CRASHES IN CHICAGO SUBURBS.

Our pilot then informed us that it was one of the planes in the flight he had left Fort Worth with.

"My God," said the pilot. "It could have been us."

"Maybe I had better make out my will for sure," I whistled under my breath.

♪   ♪   ♪

Sergeant Gene Autry was a model soldier. Even Colonel Smith told him that in our presence. There was one thing, however, that the Sergeant refused to do . . . he would not salute the female officers.

At our show in Indianapolis, three Waves officers invited themselves into Autry's suite at the hotel where he and the gang were going over the events of the day. They knocked on the door and were invited in to join the conversation and refreshments. I excused myself stating that I was under orders from home to write every day. Later, when I went down to the lobby to mail the letter I spotted the three leaving, apparently in a huff.

"Those gals looked a little mad as they tromped out of the hotel," I told Gene the next day. "What was wrong?"

"They got mad because I wouldn't salute them," said the Sergeant, looking over the cockpit with the pilot.

Vera Wooters, sister to Mary Lee, who was in many Autry films as well as *Melody Ranch*, showed up in Chicago in Wac uniform. Since she was not an officer there was no problem about the salute.

"I'd like for you to meet Colonel Hobby," Vera said to the Sergeant.

"Will I have to salute her?"

"Of course."

"Forget it."
No salute . . . no introduction.

♫   ♫   ♫

The tour of Army bases continued. We played several bases in the Chicago area and broadcast *The Melody Ranch Show* from the studios of the Wrigley Building. Here, we had ample time to get better acquainted with all of the Wrigley people as well as many of the powers-that-be from the CBS line-up of executives. The one Wrigley executive who was not around was Mr. P. K. Wrigley, whom we would meet on Catalina Island at a later date.*

We were flown to Florida aboard the Mary Ann, the Flying Fortress that had made history by seeing combat in the South Pacific before being featured in the Warner Brothers film *Air Force* with John Garfield.

We also took trains to Indianapolis, Louisville, Nashville and Birmingham, making up about six weeks for the tour of military camps. After the last show, we returned to Chicago for a broadcast and then it was back home where we soon received the news that we had been anticipating for quite some time . . . Sergeant Autry would be sent overseas and the Wrigley CBS *Melody Ranch* radio broadcast would go off the air for the duration.

* While setting up for a show in the Casino on Catalina Island, this carpenter in overalls kept getting in our way. He was heavily loaded with hammers and saws but continually asked if he could be of assistance to us. We said 'no.' Later Gene introduced us to the 'helper' who turned out to be Mr. P.K. Wrigley.

PART THREE
Recollections

"Life outside the Autry Organization"

Johnny was host and comic on *Hollywood Barn Dance,* 1944.

When the Trio (Wakely, Bond and Reinhart) arrived in California about June 4, 1940, we didn't go to work for Gene Autry immediately. In fact, he had since left town on tour leaving us four long months in which to wonder if his invitation to come to California was only social. We picked up odd jobs making electrical transcriptions for Standard Radio and managed to talk our way into some after-hours nightclubs.

Dick Reinhart was under contract to Okeh Records before we left Oklahoma. When Art Satherly, his producer, came to Los Angeles, Jimmy and I played guitars on a Dick Reinhart recording session. The scale per musician then was $30.00 per session per man, double for the leader. It was in this manner that we first met Uncle Art.

Satherly then recorded Autry (as he had been doing for nine years) and Jimmy and I were again hired to play guitars. We got more and more acquainted with the British gentleman. I finally approached him with the idea of recording solo for him myself. He said, "I promise to listen to you sometime." When I later reminded him of his promise, he said, "Oh, yes. I promised to record you, didn't I?" And he did. In August of 1941, I signed a recording contract with Columbia Records and had my first session for Gene Autry's label.

In the meantime Jimmy Wakely signed with Decca and we got in more record sessions. Jimmy recorded "Cimarron" and my new "I Wonder Where You Are Tonight?" on his first Decca session. By this time Autry had hired us for his *Melody Ranch Show*, and we had appeared in a number of Western movies. We really were beginning to feel we were no longer outsiders but had a solid future here Hollywood.

GENE AUTRY was the undisputed King of Western/Cowboy Music when we joined him on his CBS Radio Network show for Doublemint Gum in September of 1940. He was still one of the leading record sellers for

Columbia Records and his Republic singing Westerns had placed him as #1 in the Western polls as well as within the Top Ten of all the box office stars along with Clark Gable, Spencer Tracy, Shirley Temple and the rest. While he had had many top songs with which he was identified, it should be remembered that in 1947 he led the nation in sales highlighted by "Here Comes Santa Claus," followed two years later with "Rudolph the Red Nosed Reindeer."

Roy Rogers, who stepped into singing Westerns out of The Sons Of The Pioneers in 1937, was the number two man at Republic, before moving up a notch when Autry went into the Army in 1942. Rogers recorded for Decca initially, before signing with RCA in 1945. His radio show, *The Roy Rogers Show*, broadcast over the Mutual Network from 1945 till it moved to NBC in 1951, where it stayed till it ended in 1955, never achieved the popularity of the *Melody Ranch Show*. Although Roy would carry the mantel of "King of the Cowboys," and remain the top box office draw among the cowboy stars until the very end in the mid-50s, he never achieved the success on record that Gene or another cowboy movie star Tex Ritter did.

Tex Ritter left New York radio, stage and other activities, to enter singing Westerns for Grand National, Monogram, Columbia, Universal, and later, PRC Pictures. From 1935 to 1939, he recorded 30 songs for Decca. His popularity on screen never reached that of either Rogers or Autry and his records never quite reached the heights of Autry and others until he signed with Capitol Records as their first country artist in 1942. Three years later would see him set an all-time record by virtue of having the #1, 2 and 3 records in the Billboard Record Charts at the same time. Unlike Autry and Rogers, Ritter never made the national radio scene, even though he had been one of the most popular radio stars in New York City and the Northeast region in the early 1930s.

The first time that the Bell Boys, or Jimmy Wakely and His Roughriders, appeared in a singing Western, was while we were still with WKY. With the help of a local theater owner, we landed a small part in a Roy Rogers picture entitled, *Saga of Death Valley*, in which we sang "Song of the Bandit." After we went to work with Gene Autry, we began getting singing parts in other Westerns at various studios all over town. Singing

Westerns were very popular around the world, and producers began to introduce music even into the more popular action cowboy series.

Singing Trios of Cowboy/Western Music such as ours were all of a sudden in demand. I suppose that it could be said that The Jimmy Wakely Trio, as we were now known, was the nearest thing to the Sons Of The Pioneers available, and since that group was then under contract to Columbia Pictures, we managed to pick up film work with Autry, Rogers, Don Barry, The Range Busters, Hopalong Cassidy and others. Our biggest break came' when Universal signed us for a full series with Tex Ritter and Johnny Mack Brown.

The making of these movies gave us the opportunity to not only show our singing ability, but also that of composing Western songs as well. As stated previously, we used "Cimarron" in two pictures, then began composing new songs just in case the studios would ask us for more. Universal used my "Saddle Serenade" in a Johnny Mack Brown film *Pony Post*, which led our signing for the Brown/Ritter series.

Perhaps it should be mentioned that it was while we were appearing in the movies with other Stars that the producers and distributors began to take notice of Jimmy Wakely, resulting in his landing in a series of his own at Monogram which lasted for more than 5 years. "Saddle Serenade" was not only used in one of his movies, they used it as the title of the movie.

Stuart Hamblen (with Cliffie Stone) was playing live music on KFWB and KFVD when we hit town in 1940. His morning and afternoon shows had been going since the late twenties making him one of the leaders in the West Coast radio at that time. He was also the first radio personality to bill himself as a singing cowboy. Bert "Foreman" Phillips was heard on KRKD (now KIIS) daily. His DJ style shows (using transcriptions) were Western orientated, with a Friday night *Western Hit Parade*, to which we tuned in the hopes that one of our songs would be included.

Early in the forties, Phillips began his series of County (not Country) Barn Dances, the first being at the Santa Monica Pier, with others at the old Town Hall building in Compton and later in Baldwyn Park. The Jimmy Wakely Trio, joined with several other local groups and singers to furnish the music for the initial shows which played to ever growing crowds after the War started. In the group was a fiddle player by the name of Spade

Cooley who caught the public's fancy with his lively showmanship. When we had to take off on tour with our boss, Gene Autry, Spade was put in charge of the band and remained there for several years. After Tex Williams and Smokey Rogers came into the band, Spade made history with his unique Western Swing style. Bob Wills and Tommy Duncan also played at the pier with the Texas Playboys.

It should be mentioned here that after the war started and the Boss (Autry) entered the Army, with the changing back and forth of Dick Reinhart and Scotty Harrel in the Trio, the Trio itself disbanded. We all continued to work together in one way or another. Wakely went out on his own and I stayed with Autry after a brief hiatus. Dick Reinhart stayed with Autry for a short time and then returned to his home in Texas where he passed away suddenly in the late 1940s. Scotty Harrel worked many of the Western movies with us, but later, he too, went home, back to Oklahoma City.

In 1943, Cottonseed Clark and initiated the *Hollywood Barn Dance* on CBS Radio West Coast. This was a 30-minute, Saturday night studio show with free admission for the live audience. I began doing comedy to Clark's straight-man act. Others included Merle Travis, Cliffie Stone, Colleen Summers (Mary Ford), Andy Parker and the Plainsmen, and Foy Willing with The Riders of the Purple Sage. This show lasted until 1947. Guest stars included Ray Whitley, Tex Ritter, Bill Elliot, Jennifer Holt and many others.

PART FOUR
Thirty Years on the Road

The Melody Ranch Show officially changed its name to *The Gene Autry Show* when it was moved from Sunday to Saturday Night over the CBS network in 1948. However, it was commonly referred to *Gene Autry's Melody Ranch Show*.

CHAPTER NINE

The Mid-1940s

Or, Shed These Army Duds and Git —Back In The Saddle Again —

The mere fact that our broadcast had been closed down and that Sergeant Gene Autry was being prepared for overseas duty did not necessarily mean that we had seen the last of him during these times. Often my phone would ring and the familiar voice on the other end would say,

"Hello there, Jonathan Q, what's goin' on?"

"Well, hello there, General. When did you get in from Phoenix?"

"Oh, just blew in for a couple of days to wind up a few things." He might go on for a few minutes and then invite me down to his office where he still maintained a small staff. They ran his music publishing companies and sent out occasional press releases, keeping the name before the public.

I would drop in at the office where he would be going through the mail and dictating answers. In between paragraphs, Gene would look over at me and say,

"How's Wakely?" "How's Uncle Art?" "What'a you hear from Reinhart?" "Have you made any good records?" "Written any good songs? "What's this Hollywood Barn Dance I hear you on?" and so on.

Gene always asked about Jimmy Wakely. I told him all of the news. Dick Reinhart had left his bass fiddle with me when he left for Texas. Later he wrote me, asking me to sell it for him. I did, to Cliffie Stone, then working on KFWB radio with Stuart Hamblen.

Uncle Art was around and I had made a few records for him including the Walt Disney "Der Fueherer's Face," but my recording had been lost in the shuffle after Spike Jones came out with it. The song made Spike a star while I remained in eternal limbo. I also told Gene that Ernest Tubb had recorded two of my compositions, "Tomorrow Never Comes" and "I'll Step Aside."

"I wrote one for you," I said. "It's called "Don't Live A Lie." He later recorded it.

After filling him in on all of the local gossip, I inquired about Carl and Frankie.

"Frank's tending his juke boxes in Phoenix," Gene told me. "They got Cotner in that walking Army in the Pacific. Johnny Marvin's also in the South Pacific entertaining troupes with Joe E. Brown." I knew about Johnny Marvin, having run into him often around this same office. Unfortunately, he would pick up some kind of exotic fever over there which would cause his untimely passing within the year.

"Going to do a record session while you're here?" I asked.

"I don't know," Gene replied, still looking over his mail. "I'll call Uncle Art after a while."

I was a bit nervous over this particular subject because the Musician's Union had called a strike in 1942. I made the last session permissible under Uncle Art on July 31. I later learned that Gene had been trying to get back to Chicago to record before that ban, so I was hoping that he didn't blame me for it. Gene's last record session had been in June of 1942, when he recorded the popular "Jingle Jangle Jingle". His next session would not be until November 29, 1944, when he would record the very popular "Don't Fence Me In."

I didn't see Gene for a long time after that. I later learned that they assigned him to Air Transport Command, where he co-piloted cargo-carrying C-47s to Europe, Africa and the China-Burma-India Theater as well as into the South Pacific. He was offered a commission but turned it down, preferring the title of Flight Officer which would permit him to continue to do entertaining should those occasions arise.

Afterwards he told me,

"Don't drink any booze but Scotch."

"But I don't like Scotch."

"Learn to like it because if you ever go to Europe or anywhere else overseas that's the only whiskey you can get."

"But I don't know if I'll ever get to Europe."

"Oh, you'll get there alright. We'll take a tour over there whenever this dammed mess is over." I did get there, but not with him.

♫　♫　♫

The voice on the telephone again greeted me with,

"Jonathan Q, how're you?"

"Fine, General. How's yourself?"

"Fine. What's goin' on?"

"Nothin' much. Are you out of uniform now?"

"Not yet. You could give me a hand on that score if you want to."

"I can help you get out of the Army? How?"

"The Air Force has agreed to release me on one condition. I have to make a tour of the Pacific entertaining troupes."

"Where do I come in?"

"You still pick that damned guitar, don't you? It'll be just you and me. We'll have a ball."

"Hey! They're still shooting over there!"

"Hellfire, you're so skinny they'd never hit you."

"OK, I'm ready to go. On second thought, I doubt that my draft board will let me go."

"Why not? If the Army thinks it's important enough to send me, why wouldn't your draft board feel the same way?"

"All I know is, Spencer Tracy wanted me to go to Alaska with him. He even appeared before my draft board in person. They said I could go then, but the tour fizzled out and now, I got my doubts."

"Frig 'em. They're just a bunch of old fogies sitting behind a desk. Tell them you're going anyway."

"I told them that before. They said I might get out of the country, but I might have a little trouble getting back in."

"I'll be damned," said Flight Officer Gene Autry.

I contacted by draft board about the matter and they answer was 'definitely not.'

"We have bigger and better plans for you," the lady draft boarder said. Within a few days they sent me my notice. I took and passed the physical, but while I was packing my bags, they sent me a letter saying (in words to this effect), "Forget the notice. Don't show. Who needs you? Go on to the South Pacific with Autry. We've won the war without you."

It was too late. Gene got Rufe Davis to go with him and from that day forward, all that I heard from either of them is, "Boy, you should have been with us. Did we have a ball!?"

♪   ♪   ♪

Gene Autry was released from the service in September of 1945. Soon, we received the call that we had been waiting for. *The Melody Ranch Show* sponsored by Doublemint was going back on the air. CBS airtime was sold out, so initially they could only clear 15 minutes for the show. The show reverted to its original 30-minute schedule in the spring of 1946.

There were a few changes in the show. The Cass County Boys (Fred Martin, Jerry Scoggins and Bert Dodson) were added as the singing/playing trio, and Carl Cotner was now directing the band. My job now was to play guitar on the mike next to Gene, making it sound over the air as if it were he doing the picking. I also was required to read script, both comedy and drama, and to sing occasionally with the trio. They also added a second trio, Beulah, Eunice and Ione Kettle, whom they named The Pinafores.

Additional good news came when we learned that we would return to the New York and Boston rodeos that fall. We were, truly, "back in the saddle again."

Naturally, I was interested in knowing what was going to take place with Gene's movies, so during one of the radio broadcast rehearsals, I eased into the subject in order to try and feel him out. After all, it had been almost two years since we had done the army tours and I was well aware how some people forget.

"I read in the papers about your compromise with Republic," I said, sheepishly. I used the newspaper routine so that it wouldn't appear so much that I might be snooping.

"Yeah," Gene said, casually. "I made a deal with them. I'm going to make one more series for them, and then I'm moving over to Columbia. Gonna' make my own, in color."

"Smiley coming with you?" I asked.

"No, Smiley's been doing his own thing at Republic while I've been away. We've got Sterling Holloway for a few. Don't know how many we'll use him in. After that . . . " About that time we both were called back to rehearsal. I suppose he knew what I'd have given to be put in that comedy spot, but then, I wasn't the type to ask for it.

Neither was I the type to get it.

By the beginning of 1946, Gene was firmly back in business. He completed his agreement with Republic by turning out the required number of films then went over to Columbia Pictures where he acted as co-producer as well as the star performer. We were to find out later, by the

On October 22,1946, Gene took his show to the Kingsbridge Veterans Hospital while in New York for the rodeo. l to r: Ray Whitley (seated),JB, Carl Cotner, Fred Martin and Jerry Scoggins. Frankie Marvin is behind Cotner and Bert Dodson is playing the bass.

grapevine, that he was also responsible for much of the financing of these films.

The first Columbia release, completed in 1947, was to be named after one of his favorite songs, "The Last Roundup." Unfortunately, to the great disappointment of all concerned, this film was not shot in color, as he desired. It was explained that the demands upon the Technicolor Corporation were so great that their schedule was already years behind. Other color processes were being experimented with, but Gene didn't think that he wanted to use any of those just yet.

They had a special screening of the finished film at Columbia and all of us associated with Autry were invited to see it. It was a very good picture and we all extended our congratulations to Gene for turning out such a great movie. We just knew that Gene was now going to make bigger and better Westerns than ever before. The story line was so modern that they even employed the use of a television set in a scene or two. TV in 1947 was still new to the average patron and unheard of in Western movies.

During the cocktail party, which followed this private screening, there was much more discussion of the film as Gene, his producer and director pumped us all with questions seeking opinions.

"It's a magnificent picture," echoed the full group gathered around the room, shaking hands with one hand, holding martinis in the other.

"Did you miss old Frog?"

Some said 'yes,' some said 'no.'

"I thought the TV set was the only thing out of place," said somebody.

"That so," said Gene. "Well, that's one man's opinion."

"Shug Fisher did a fine comedy bit."

"Yeah, but Shug played a character part, not a side-kick. We're dropping the side-kick routine."

"We had much discussion and deliberation on that side-kick business."

"Well, what the hell. Tom Mix, Buck Jones Ken Maynard, those guys seldom used a side-kick."

"We almost used one but threw it out at the last minute," the producer was confiding with me in a corner.

"That right?" I said.

"Sure did. Want to know who we almost used?"

"If you want to tell me."

"Next time you look in the mirror you'll see him."

"Oh, well," I sighed. "Can't win 'em all."

There was surely much more to the conversation between the producer, as well as the director and myself, but whatever it was, those words have long since become lost in the din of the overtones coming from a room filled with big talk and loud laughter.

♫   ♫   ♫

Most of 1947 was taken up with the making of more pictures, more records, and as usual, the weekly radio broadcast. Even though I was not to appear on screen in any of the Columbia films, I was called, along with most of the radio musicians, to do the pre-recording for the songs that Gene sang in the films so I can't say that I was left out entirely.

While Gene had been away the past few years, there had been an abundance of material that had been completed before his donning of the uniform to keep the Autry name before the public, but when the 1948 list of the Top Ten Box Office Stars was released, his name was no longer there. Naturally, both Autry and Columbia Pictures were determined to regain this lost rating. Unfortunately, they never did. Although we didn't know it at the time, the days of the B Western were numbered. Within a short time television would begin saturating the market with B Westerns, 'free' entertainment, making it impractical and unprofitable for the theater owners to continue to run them. In spite of the decline in the movies, the Autry popularity continued to reign on radio, records, and later, TV, not to mention the all-important nationwide personal appearances.

The appearances at the Madison Square Garden and Boston Gardens rodeos were resumed as well as other rodeos around the country in such places as Baton Rouge, Birmingham, St. Paul, Houston, and cities of equal stature. The New York and Boston rodeos had been filled in Gene's absence with other personalities such as Tex Ritter and Roy Rogers in the Star Spotlight.

I would way that everything about these new seasons was just about the same as before with one exception. As the seasons went by we began to notice some empty seats at both matinee and night shows. The number of these vacancies would increase until the mid-'50s, when it was announced that both the Madison Square Garden and the Boston Gardens would drop the rodeos and stage something else in their place. This change in the schedule was not unexpected and did not deter the Autry camp. Gene had already instigated another form of personal appearance which we began as early as 1948, a series of extended one-night stands. We would continue to do these auditorium-type stage shows for almost 10 years. Each show ran for approximately two hours in length, was performed twice a day while on the road, and was staged in every major city within the 48 States and Canada.

CHAPTER TEN

1948

Or, Life and Love on a Greyhound Bus —
Or, What Time Does The Bus Leave? —
Or, Where Do You Go From Here? —

The light from certain stars shines on for a very, very long time while other lights go out, never to re-appear. So it is with great stars in show business. Some of their achievements live on by way of phonograph records and motion pictures, which show them and their talents as it was recorded on a given day, even though the star may have long ago faded into the wild blue yonder.

But! What about the personal appearance? This is entirely something else. The film, the record, the video can be played over and over again, but when the curtain comes down on the stage show, that is it. There is no such thing as a re-play. No re-runs possible. It lives only in the memory of those who saw it or those who participated.

It shall, therefore, be my purpose here to attempt to duplicate in words on paper, one typical show that was staged by Gene Autry and performed by those of us who were privileged to trail along.

I will try to take all of those 10 years of tours and break them down into one average, typical 24-hour day and thus, hopefully, preserve forever those exciting moments that were experienced and enjoyed by so many, both performer and spectator.

♫   ♫   ♫

Before 1948, the Autry personal appearances in which I participated were limited to rodeos, theater premieres and other special one-time functions. There were no auditorium staged shows other than those put on especially for servicemen during his stint in uniform. It was during this year (1948) that Gene called us together at this home in Studio City, California, for a conference.

"How would you folks like to hit the road for a change and maybe pick up a few extra bucks?" Gene said to us after a pleasant session of food and drink.

Naturally, there were no dissenting voices or votes.

"Well," Autry continued, smiling broadly. "We've got a couple of pictures under our belt already and it looks like we're going to have a little time on our hands before the Fall rodeos. I've been wondering if, perhaps, we shouldn't put some kind of a stage show together and take off on a tour of one-nighters."

Again, everyone echoed approval. Great idea!

"The question is, do we have enough for a full show or not?"

Each one of us looked at the other, there was no doubt in anyone's mind.

"Jonathan Q., you and me tore 'em up on those army camp shows. Do you think you can remember all of those corny jokes you told?"

"I think so," I said, happy in the thought that he cared to revive our act together. "Some of the Military material might have to be changed, left out or updated. I think I could probably dig up a few more laughs." I felt confident that material for the two of us would be plentiful, because between 1943 and 1947, I had written comedy for a CBS Show, *The Hollywood Barn Dance*, for Cottonseed Clark.

"How about you kids?" Gene directed his question towards the two trios, The Cass County Boys and The Pinafores.

"Sure, we have a bunch of songs," they all admitted.

"I know what Cotner and Marvin can do," Gene said, laughing at Carl and Frankie. "After all, we killed 'em in Boone, Iowa." This brought laughs from both Gene and Ina, as well as from Carl and Frankie, but the rest of us had not been present during those early days.

"And," Gene continued, looking around at his houseguest for the evening, "ole Big Butt (another one of Autry's nicknames: Pat Buttram) here hasn't been doing anything since both the National Barn Dance and Roy Rogers fired him. He says that he might be willing to go along for the ride."

Gene in the custom built horse trailer with dressing room and wardrobe closets.

The rest of us were convinced that we had enough for the show. "You can take up about thirty minutes or more with Champion alone," somebody said.

"Oh, I don't know about the horse," Gene said, glancing at a painting on the wall. "He's okay for rodeos, and I have had him on a theater stage before, but it's an awful lot of trouble taking a horse along. I just don't know whether I want to."

As it later turned out, Gene did take along not only Champion, but Little Champ as well. Both horses were the highlight of the show as far as the kids were concerned. When we played Lynn, Massachusetts, later, all that we could hear during the show, including Gene's songs, was, "Bring on the hosses! Bring on the hosses!" (They pronounced it with the 'ah', as in hah-ses!)

Thus it was decided. We did have enough for a show and we would take off across the country stopping in each city long enough to put on a matinee and night show, after which we would head on down the road three or four hundred miles to the next one. There were rare occasions (usually involving the radio show) that required us to remain more than one day in a given city. In the case of the Oriental Theater in Chicago and the Hippodrome in Baltimore and a few other major theaters into which Gene had been trying to get his pictures, we remained for a full week.

These one-nighters proved to be so successful that they were continued for season after season until Gene retired from performing, a little over a year after the discontinuation of the radio broadcast in 1956. The first tour of a given year usually began about the middle of January and lasted for about six weeks. Gene would return to Hollywood, make a movie or two then go out again for a few more weeks. There were very few summer tours but they did resume during the fall months, most of them winding up in New York and Boston for a big rodeo finale. We figured that during this time we were on tour almost six months out of a year.

The cast was transported by a Greyhound Bus, which Autry chartered originally, and later purchased. Gene traveled by car, station wagon, or in his own airplane flown by Herb Green, who was also in charge of booking the tour. The horses traveled by a van built especially for them, which was driven by the trainer, Jay Berry. This van also housed a dressing room for Gene, which he used on those occasions where none other was available.

Certain people participated in all of these tours while other acts were added and dropped, depending on their availability and acceptance by the audience. The permanent cast (included in all of the tours) were:

Gene Autry, who served as master of ceremonies, as well as performing
Pat Buttram, comedian.
Carl Cotner, violinist and orchestra leader.
Frankie Marvin, comedian and steel guitarist.
The Cass County Boys, a male singing/playing trio (Jerry Scoggins, guitar, Fred Martin, accordionist, Bert Dodson, bass and sometime bus driver).
Johnny Bond, guitar, singer and comedian.
Champion and *Little Champ*, the horses.

Various tours were augmented with the following acts and individuals:

The Pinafores, girl's singing trio (Ione, Beulah, and Eunice Kettle), regulars for over five years. Left the Autry organization in 1950.
Smiley Burnette, comedian/singer, made several tours in the early fifties.
Rufe Davis, comedian, was a semi-regular.
Jack and *Bobbi Knapp*, husband and wife team who did acrobatics, rope tricks with a trained dog, semi-regulars
The Strong Family, husband and wife with two young sons. They also had a trained dog while using rope tricks. Semi-regulars, alternate with Knapps.
Eddie Peabody, banjo. One tour.
The Hoosier Hotshots, comedy quartet. One tour.
Ginny Jackson, singer. She made several of the early tours.
Judy Clark, singer. A few tours.
Gail Davis, singer and actress. A few tours.
Merle Travis, singer and guitarist. A few tours.
Tony White Cloud troupe, authentic Indian dancers. Several tours.
The Candy Mountain Girls, singing trio. Two tours.
Various Dancers and Actors
A Chimpanzee, one tour.

CHAPTER ELEVEN

1948—1958
The Alarm Sounds

Or, Tell Gene I Quit
Or, Don't We Ever Get A Day Off?
Or, To Hell With It, Wichita, Here We Come

Our average tour day began early, depending on how far we had to drive to get to our next stop. A typical drive would be from 200 to 300 miles, but there were a few locals which were twice that much with a very few less; in any event, it was usually necessary to hit the road early in order to make our scheduled dates.

Only once were we allowed to sleep in due to the short jump to the next town. On that morning, Salinas, Kansas, my phone rang early as usual.

"Good morning," said the man on the desk. "It's Five O'clock."

"Five O'clock!" I said, sleepily. "I left my call for nine!"

"Oh, ha, ha!" returned the clerk. "I made a mistake. Wrong room. Ain't that funny? Ha, ha, ha!"

"Very funny."

The Autry troupe was loaded with practical jokers. On any given morning the telephone might ring quite early with a familiar voice saying,

"Good morning, Johnny."

"Good morning, Who's this?"

It might be Buttram, Scoggins, Marvin, Cotner, even Autry, who replies, "Just wanted to call and tell you that the mail just came. There wasn't any for you."

"Thanks a lot."

Whenever that alarm rang, regardless of who was on the other end of the telephone, it was up-and-at-'em on the double. Shave, shower, pack the bags, call the bellboy, check out, grab a quick cup of coffee, and fall on the bus. This was the hour of foggy minds from lack of sleep and too much celebration after last evenings show. The motor of the bus would be running, warming up the interior while white steam from the exhaust would envelop the entire area as most of the tours were made in the Northeastern part of the country in the dead of winter.

I don't recall anyone ever missing the Autry bus. A few might have been a few minutes late a time or two, but somehow, we always managed to make connections. Just to watch a bunch of tired sleepyheads wandering around in the early morning cold must have been something. Men, women, Indians; everyone trying to get awake while also making certain that all of their baggage had been carried down by bell-boys (who sometimes had to come on board in order to gain an otherwise overlooked tip).

At this hour of the morning there were few towns-people on hand to see us off. If there was one it was usually some slow-witted character just now making his way home after a long night out on the town. Many such characters over the 10-years on the road managed to stop whenever they saw the Autry name on the side of the bus.

"You Gene Autry?" many of them asked me.

"Not me."

"Where's ole Gene?"

"He's already gone," we'd say. "Did you see the show last night?"

"No, but I seen you on the radio."

"You saw us on the radio?"

"Yeah. You done good."

"Thanks a lot."

"Where do you go from here?"

This was a common question that I never quite understood. Why would they be interested in where we went next? It would have been easier to give him the honest answer but after a few weeks on the road the entire group would begin to get a little slaphappy ourselves and it became a common practice to beat around the bush. We made a pact among the full troupe; no matter where we were in the world, the next fellow that asked us were we went next, the answer was to be Seattle.

The location of Seattle failed to get much of a reaction out of the locals, that is, until we hit Jacksonville, Florida.

"How'd the show go last night," one local asked.

"Fine."

"Play again tonight?"

"Sure do."

"That so. Where 'bouts?"

"Seattle!"

"Seattle," he said, nodding his head, satisfied with his newly gained knowledge. He would look at us, then at the bus. (The swiftness of jet travel had not yet come into being.)

"Seattle"" the little man said as he stroked his bearded chin.

"Yep. Better come go with us."

"No. No thanks. Some other time." Then he turned and walked away, only to stop, turn around, look at us again and say in a voice so soft that all we could do was try our luck at lip-reading. To the best of our knowledge, he was saying . . . "Seattle!"

♪   ♪   ♪

Once the bus got under way, each of us made a vain attempt to settle back, trying to catch a few more minutes of slumber. Chatter from the few wide-awake, as well as the bumpy roads almost always prevented this. After about an hour of riding, the troupe began, one by one, began to awaken and start their usual everyday activities. That consisted of card games, poker, chess, matching coins, reading and general all-around conversation. One might request the heat to be turned up, while another could very well complain that it was too hot already. Practical jokes were plentiful; most were taken in good spirit, but others resentfully.

No matter how early the bus began to lumber out of the town, we could pretty well bet on hearing one familiar line from somebody . . . "The bar is open!"

♪   ♪   ♪

Since it would be an impossibility to describe everything unusual, funny or otherwise out of the ordinary, which took place on these tours, I will single out a few separate events throughout the narrative that stand out in memory and about which many of us recall over and over again in various social gatherings:

One of the earliest such incidents involved Champion. It seems that neither Champion nor Little Champ had been housebroken and they were continually embarrassing us all whenever they were on the stage in full view of thousands of people. When we learned that the horses were going to be a part of our stage show, Carl and Frankie hastened to alert those of us who hadn't been members of Gene's early tours to expect incidents on stage that were not part of the program.

One such incident was particularly memorable. Gene made his entrance, riding out onto the stage mounted on Champion. The two of them circled the stage a time or two while the horse went through his routine tricks and Gene devoted his attention to the fans. Champion proceeded to let it be known that he was not yet stage broken and let go to the delight of most of the patrons. Evidently Gene was unaware of this movement. Thinking the comments and cheers were for him, he concluded his Champion bit by quickly dismounting and rushing to the mike, preparing to sing his songs.

"Well, folks," Gene said amid wild applause. "Champion has done his part, now it's my turn."

♫   ♫   ♫

True to form, both horses began to decorate the stage floors regularly the minute they went into their respective routines. Soon thereafter, this subject began to float around as a main topic of conversation on the bus as we chugged along the highways.

"Somebody ought to do something about it," said one of the girls.

"Part of Jay Berry's job is to trip 'em before they go on stage," said Frankie Marvin. "Besides, the horses want some attention the same as the rest of us. Any bets as to when they'll do it next?"

That gave me an idea. Before we left we were given a mimeographed itinerary of the tour, listing the names of the cities, dates, auditoriums, as well as the hotels where we had reservations. I conceived the idea of a lottery whereby I placed the names of the upcoming towns in a hat, and for a dollar a draw, everyone bought a name of a town. The idea was whenever either of the horses let go on the stage, whoever held the name of that particular city was the winner of the jackpot. Once a winner was decided, plans were to start over and make up another jackpot. Believe it or not, from the moment of the conception of this lottery, both horses proceeded to behave themselves completely and it became necessary for me to refund the money to the bus riders for two consecutive tours.

The third time around was different. The names of the towns had been bought and paid for barely an hour before the first show when Little Champ did his thing amid hilarious screams in the audience. One of the youngest members of the Strong Family tracked me down to claim his reward.

After that, many lost interest and the lottery was discontinued.

♫   ♫   ♫

Someone asked the question, "Of all the tours you did with Gene Autry, did you ever miss a show?"

The answer is, 'no.' Not one show was missed. However, it almost happened on a tour in Canada one time. We closed Calgary and drove on to Edmonton without incident. Herb Green had warned us that we had some long jumps ahead through some wide-open country, over highways that might not quite be up to those to which we had become accustomed. It was during the drive between Edmonton, Alberta, and Saskatoon, Saskatchewan, one of our longer jumps, that the bus met with a dead end. Not only were we out in semi-primitive territory, but we were following heavy rainstorms, which had left deep puddles on the open plains on both sides of the highway. At about 3 pm, already running late, the bus came to a complete stop.

"What's up, Bert?" someone yelled out from the back off the Greyhound.

"Take a look for yourself," called back Dodson. "Look's like today is the day that we finally miss a show."

Everyone rushed forward to discover that the highway ahead of us was completely submerged by the recent rains.

"I told Autry we'd be needing a boat," said Frankie Marvin in his familiar manner of unconcern.

"Looks like this is it," I said. "Gene and Herb (who had flown ahead of us earlier) will never know what happened to us."

The situation, while appearing to be quite critical at first, was soon resolved. It was decided that we should return to the nearest town, call ahead to Saskatoon and get both Gene and Herb on the telephone and make them aware of our predicament. Herb Green, taking our number, asked for a few minutes while he did some calling on his own. When he got back to us we were directed to return to a dirt landing strip not too far from the town, which we had passed before unnoticed. We were to meet him there.

Soon after we got there, Autry's plane bounced down. Herb instructed certain members of the troupe to come with him. Since the plane only had room for three or four passengers, a shuttle plan was put in force until the heart of the stage show was flown into Saskatoon.

I was one of the first to arrive at the auditorium where we found Gene, plus several thousand eager fans awaiting curtain time. I walked up to my boss and said, Well, here we are."

"Where's your guitar?" Gene asked.

"On the bus," I said, feeling my face turn a very deep, burning red.

"Hell of a lot of good it's doing us there. Right?"

"Right."

"Listen, damn it," Gene said to me as sternly as he ever had during my then 11 years with him. No Jonathan Q this time. "If it ever gets to the point where it looks like the show might be delayed, if you can get here, bring your goddamn guitar! At least you and I can keep them entertained until the rest of the crew gets here."

"Yes, sir," I said, almost saluting Army style. I'm glad I didn't.

As it so happened, shortly after Herb flew in the second load, Bert Dodson discovered another route and the matinee went on after a slight delay.

Other than that, we never missed a show.

♫   ♫   ♫

Ordinarily, the bus did not head straight for the auditorium. In most cases, we arrived in town early enough to head straight for the hotel where we would check in before heading out for the auditorium. While one of our own crew, Bert Dodson, did drive the bus later on, it was the Greyhound Company that furnished us our drivers in the early years.

Our very first driver was a most congenial, heavyset gentleman known to us only as Mac. If Mac had any shortcomings, they were unknown to us for he certainly kept everything, including his thoughts, to himself. Oh, he

Johnny as the country bumpkin.

was friendly enough, liking everyone aboard his chartered vehicle who, in turn, thought that he was tops.

It soon became obvious to all of us that he was driving through virgin territory even though he would not admit it in so many words. To get from one town or city to another was no problem to Mac; it was after we arrived that we began to take note of the fact that he didn't know where he was going. That part was no big thing to us and we soon began to lend him a hand in trying to find our hotel and the auditorium, for had we not done so I believe that Mac would have kept on going rather than ask any one of us or some local on a street corner. Mac was definitely above this sort of time-killing stop. He preferred just to keep on driving.

While we were checking into our rooms, Mac had nothing more important to do than to make inquiries about how to get from the hotel to the auditorium. This was a simple procedure, but I guess Mac just didn't think about it.

When we finally piled into his gas eater, usually with only a very few minutes to show time, we, naturally had more things on our mind than giving directions to the driver. Never mind the fact that we didn't know anyway.

Did Mac ever once inquire as to which way he was supposed to go? Never. He just took off across town until one of us would take note of both the time and the city limit signs, hitting us over the head with the likelihood that the auditorium was back the other way.

"Hey, Mac," Buttram yelled out. "I got a sneaking suspicion that we've already passed it."

"OK," said Mac, turning around, heading back to town.

It was about a week or so after Mac had been with us that he uttered the line that has since become an eternal by-line with everyone connected with the Autry tours, from Gene on down. It was after a very long, hectic day of appearances in New Orleans that we all piled into the bus eagerly looking forward to getting back to our hotel for some much needed rest before our next show. When the bus took off, Autry, who seldom rode the bus, was laughing and joining with the gang as we lumbered through the narrow streets of the famous Southern city. After about an hour's drive, somebody said simply,

"Hey, Mac! Do you know where you're going?"

To which Mac replied slowly and calmly, "Nope, don't believe I do."

I suppose that if one of us hadn't pinned him down, Mac would still be driving, hoping that sooner or later the right street would lay itself in front of him.

Much to our sorrow, Mac only worked that one tour with us. Different seasons brought different drivers, supplied by the Greyhound Company. Eventually, Bert Dodson went to Gene and made the deal for him to drive the bus. You can imagine how many times one or more of us, after the loud conversation had died down in the interior of the bus, would yell up to Bert and say,

"Hey, Bert! Do you know where you're going?"

To which Bert, always the perfect straight man, would stare straight ahead and say,

"Nope, don't believe I do."

CHAPTER TWELVE

Our Average Tour Day Continues

Or, How Fer's It on In
Or, Whur's Ole Gene At?

Traveling between cities using either car or airplane enabled Gene to depart later and arrive at our next destination earlier than we did, sometimes before noon. There was usually some special occasion or reception pre-arranged by his advance personnel, where he would meet with the Mayor or other public servants or service organizations. Anything, anyplace or anybody that might create publicity and draw attention to the fact that Gene Autry and his show were in town for a matinee and evening show, would be utilized to the greatest extent possible.

Gene always bought newspaper and radio advertising, but it took a lot of special thinking on the part of the publicity staff to come up with ideas that would result in a front page picture story, especially in the larger cities like St. Louis, Toronto, Des Moines, Kansas city, and so on. They managed to come up with one idea that practically guaranteed this kind of coverage and that was to arrange for the Cowboy to make an unscheduled appearance at a Children's Hospital. Photographers and reporters ate up this kind of assignment and the afternoon and evening editions of almost all of the newspapers ran pictures and stories of Gene visiting the unfortunate kids.

I have a clipping from *The Atlanta Journal* dated Sunday Morning, January 25, 1948, containing a two-column photo showing Gene Autry, white hat on, down on his hands and knees making like Champion, while a small, two-year old girl rides him piggy-back. I am holding the child by the arms with hospital beds in the background to show where we are. Below the picture it says:

GENE AUTRY PLAYS HORSE FOR CRIPPLED CHILDREN

It goes on with more, even continued to an inside page.

The majority of these hospital shows were just Gene, with me along to strum the guitar for him as he strolled from ward to ward. There were occasions where more of our troupe went along, but that was rare.

Unlike the early morning departures where the pre-dawn hours kept the crowds down, a completely opposite situation prevailed as our bus pulled up to our next hotel. The townspeople all knew that their Cowboy Hero was due in and most of them not only had tickets to the show, but were now gathering at the hotel in hopes that they might get an extra view of the Cowboy as well as perhaps an autograph or souvenir. Yes, the fans were out in full force and it would be like this for the rest of the day. The mere fact that Gene Autry and Champion were in town was big news, indeed.

For us to just get off the bus, and into the lobby, would take much more time than one would imagine. We had to worm our way through hundreds of screaming mothers and children alerted by the Autry name on the side of our bus. They never believed us when we informed them that the star was not aboard, having arrived in their fair city hours earlier.

Getting through this eager crowd was always a hassle for, if you stopped to visit and sign all the autographs offered, we'd never be able to register and get ourselves ready for the matinee coming up shortly.

One loud question always greeted our ears, no matter where we were: "Where's Gene?"

Amplify that remark by several hundred local citizens whose volume seemed to increase as time went by, and you have a question that still rings in the ears of all of us who made the tours.

Once, a tall local grabbed me by the coat collar, pulled me off my feet, and shouted into my face, "Git a'holt of ole Gene. I wanna talk to that sumbitch."

Eventually, with some effort, we all managed to get into the lobby, which was also very crowded, and up to the desk. For the full troupe to sign-in usually took much longer than we thought necessary. We knew that we were in a hurry, but just you try and tell them that. This was a big day for this hotel and they weren't about to let it rush them by. The little man behind the desk would usually greet us with a big smile of welcome, pick up one card, place it in it's proper place, step back politely as he turned it around, handing the nearest one of us a pen, saying:

"There you are, sir. How do you like our fair city?"

"We just got here."

"Oh, yes, that's right. Now then, Mr. Bond, I believe that we've got you in with . . . let's see now" . . . they would always drag it out as he looked over something. "Ah, yes," the clerk continued. "You'll be sharing a room with Mr. Kettle . . . "

"She's a lady. I'm by myself."

"Oh, sure. My mistake. Sorry, we don't have any singles left. How about putting you in with Mr. Knapp?"

"Sure, put him in with Knapp," yelled Cotner or Marvin behind me. "Come on, we got a matinee to do."

"Mr. Knapp has his wife with him" I said. "I doubt if. . ."

After a while the man would have me all squared away with a room partner, which usually was Cotner, Marvin, Scoggins, Rufe Davis or Dodson. Now I could go up and do what I needed to do before the bus left for the auditorium.

In 1948 and 1949, the hotel situation was such that we had difficulty getting reservations for our large troupe. That was why we always had to double-up, not that this was any big deal. But after all of us had been crowded together on the bus and backstage for several weeks, the urge to try and gain a moment of privacy reigned supreme throughout the entire Autry bunch.

"Try and get me a single room next time," many of us told Herb Green.

"Chin up," said Herb. "Way ahead of you. In Buffalo, you can have all the single rooms you want."

With that good news tucked away in our mental lockers, everyone looked forward to Buffalo. When we finally reached that stop we learned why. This hotel was old enough for George Washington's father to have slept there. Still, most of us were content knowing that, after many weeks of doubling up, today's stop was going to be different. All of us smiled as we stood in line to register.

"Everybody going to get himself a single room?" asked Earl Lindsay, stepping out of the elevator with a very broad smile, making his way through the long line of hopefuls.

"Good old single," all said, smiling back.

"I got me one of them singles," Earl continued. "You won't like it."

"Why not?"

"Well, for openers, it's only about this big," he made motions with his hands relaying the message that the single rooms were not like the great open spaces.

"So what?"

"No bathroom either," Earl said.

"NO BATHROOM!"

"Now, they got doubles. They're nice. Large, and they got bathrooms. Cost you more, though."

"So what! I'll get me a double."

By this time I was now facing the little old lady behind the desk. True to form, she was taking her own sweet time in getting the next registration card in place.

"II understand your single rooms don't have a bath."

"That's right," said the little lady without looking up.

"Can I have a double? Provided it does have a bath."

"Certainly you can have a double. It's a large room with bath."

"Fine. I'll take it."

"Cost you more money!"

"I said I'd take it."

"Sign your name right here."

"I'm signing."

"Now, whom do you want to share your double with?" asked the little lady, not realizing what discouraging words were floating through her uppers and lowers.

"Nobody. Just me"

"I thought you said double."

"I do want a double," I said. "I don't mind paying the extra amount."

"Oh, I can't give you a double if you're alone. You'll have to settle for a single."

"But I don't want your single. I'm perfectly willing to pay the difference. Just give me my double."

"Not as long as you're alone. Two in a double. One in a single." The lady clerk was most definite in her keeping of the house rules.

"How about me and my wife," I said, utilizing some quick thinking. She didn't know the rest of us from Adam and Even.

"Oh, sure," said the lady. "You can sign in for both you and your wife."

I signed Mr. and Mrs. Johnny Bond and got my single/double that I had been promised. All of the solos behind me quickly got the message. Most of the wives back home never knew that they were "shuffling off to Buffalo."

When we got our hotel bills the following morning, Frankie Marvin and Carl Cotner inquired as to why I was tearing mine into little pieces instead of saving it for income tax purposes as was the custom.

"Well, " I said to them. "I thought about it all night. It's such a complicated situation, I doubt if I could ever explain it to Dorothy and keep a straight face. I think I'll just pass these few deductions and chalk it off as a great night of solitude."

"You got something there," said Carl and Frankie as they too tore up their Mr. and Mrs. Hotel receipts.

♪　　♪　　♪

We noticed that Tony White Cloud always registered for all four of the Indians. They called the oldest one Chief. We never knew if he was one or not. Later on Frankie pointed out to me that the Chief never signed anything; not the hotel register, not autographs.

"How come you don't sign autographs," I later asked the Chief.

"Chief no sign," was my only answer. Later Tony informed us that the Chief, the Chief's father and his grandfather were once wealthy in land and other holdings.

"They lost it all by simply signing their names."

♪　　♪　　♪

The fact that we had now been assigned our respective hotel rooms did not mean that we were finally free until the first matinee. We were usually called upon to participate in various endeavors to promote the show. There were record stores to visit to sign records. There were radio stations to visit for free plugs. Gene initially tried to touch all of these bases himself, but eventually found it to be impossible. So he brought in the rest of us.

One time a disc jockey in Cleveland got very angry because he figured Gene had called on everybody but him. When he couldn't find Autry to complain to in person, he took his wrath out on me and I have a sneaking feeling that he's never played either an Autry or Bond phonograph record since. As this sort of incident began to multiply, Herb Green came up with a brilliant idea.

"Mr. Autry," said Herb, snapping his suspenders. "Since there aren't enough hours in the day for you to visit all of the proper folks, why not bring them all to you?"

Gene bought the plan, which was immediately put into practice. From that day forward, a cocktail party was arranged in a banquet room at our hotel just prior to the day's matinee. Invitees included local show sponsors, city officials, film distributors, record distributors, disc jockeys, radio station officials, ladies aid societies, and anybody in town who might have a legitimate gripe should he be left out. Add to the list the merchants who handled the Gene Autry jeans, guns, boots, hats, etc.

Even this plan was not foolproof, for should Gene get tied up with, say, the Governor or a Senator, he might be a little late coming to his own reception. If he thought this might occur, he made sure that Carl, Frankie, The Cass County Boys and I were there to stand in for him.

On one particular occasion, when it did become necessary for us to go in his place, we discovered something; by the time we got there, the guests were already quite put out, having been waiting around for quite some time for their Star to arrive. Frankly, I'd expected all of them to be looped; but no, every one of them was cold sober.

That we were part of Autry's show made little or no impact on the locals. Our arrival meant nothing to them. We noticed the usual bar, holding every type of liquid refreshment imaginable, plus the inevitable hors d'oeuvres, all set to go; but none of these things were moving.

"How about a drink?" I said to one local citizen after introducing myself as Autry's stand-in for this occasion.

"Fat chance," the man said, indignantly. "You can't get a drink here."

"Now that's strange," I said, puzzled. "This is Gene Autry's party. He's buying. You're invited guests. There's a bar ready to roll; there's a bartender behind it with his arms folded and chin out. Who says we can't get a drink?"

"Be my guest," said Gene's guest, leading me toward the reluctant bartender who, remember, didn't know me from Adam.

"We'd like a drink!"

"Nothin' doin'," said the man, indifferently, shaking his head as if to give his refusal added emphasis.

"But this is Gene Autry's reception. He's paying for all of this . . . including your fee."

"Don't make no difference," said the bartender, closing his eyes and his mind in one full sweep.

"Well, why not?" I blurted out.

"I'm not pouring one drink until I get the OK!"

"It's OK," I said, not realizing that my voice contained so much authority.

"OK," said the bartender, unfolding his arms, scooping up the ice cubes, "Step right up and name yer pizen."

I suppose there's nothing like a servant who abides by the rules laid down to him. At any rate, everyone had a good time until finally, Gene walked in sporting his self-contained halo-like-spotlight to the jubilation of all present.

"Did the bus get in?" Autry asked me, aside.

"Everybody's checked in and ready for the show," I assured him.

"Well, I hate to tell you this, Jonathan Q, but it looks like both shows are going to be sold out."

"What! Again?"

"Yep, looks like we're going to break even today!" Autry was happy. These tours were paying off. He was probably the biggest drawing card going during these times.

"That's what you said yesterday, and the day before."

"We gotta' get 'em while we're hot," said Gene Autry, setting his glass down, shaking hands with a few more of the locals. "Well, folks, we have to go over to the auditorium and put on a show. Everybody stick around if you want to. Have fun."

"We'll be there tonight," they all yelled out. I tried to wave at the bartender, but he could care less.

"Let's get the hell out of here," Gene said to me.

CHAPTER THIRTEEN

1948—1958
The Gene Autry Show

Or, Bring On The Hosses
Or, Why Did The Curtain Have to Fall

Two two-hour shows per day. Seven days a week. Six weeks to the season, totaling out about six months per year. Three hundred thirty-six shows per year for almost ten years. That's a lot of shows.

How would you like to see one of them?

Since there is no way, or perhaps I should say, no other way, that this stage show can ever be seen as it was produced then, let me see if I can recreate it here and now, on paper.

If it is a matinee, it starts exactly at 4:30 pm on weekdays because Gene doesn't want the youngsters to miss either school or the show. If it is evening it will begin at 8:30 pm. There usually are from one to four thousand excited patrons in any one of the ordinary auditoriums around the country. However, at the Forum in Montreal on October 19, 1951, there were 25,000 in the audience.

From behind the closed curtain come the opening bars of "Back In The Saddle Again." The curtain opens, and the entire troupe of regulars, including Gene Autry, are onstage as Gene sings his famous theme song. The applause is deafening. Gene walks up to the mike and waits for the greeting to subside.

"Howdy, my name is Gene Autry." More applause.

Most headliners make you wait through the first hour or more before making an appearance. Not Gene Autry. He opens the show, introduces each and every act, does his thing with both songs and horses and will still be there two hours later when the curtain falls.

"And, folks," he continues, "that's just a sample of what you're going to hear for the next two hours."

"How long?" This voice yells out from the audience. It's Frankie Marvin, planted in the crowd making like a customer.

"I said two hours," Gene repeats.

"Oh, my lord, I can't stand it!" This remark from Marvin is followed by a gunshot. Frank fires a blank into the air, then disappears into the ladies room across the aisle from him. The show has begun with a great belly laugh.

"Well," says Gene, unconcernedly. "That's one we won't have to worry about."

This is followed by a few more jokes from Gene while the full crew sits there laughing, waiting. Gene loved to do comedy. If the fans only exposure to Gene had been through his movies, records and radio shows, most of which reflect his more serious nature, they were usually quite surprised at his ability to bring forth laughter. He spent thousands of dollars for fresh comedy material, as well as seeking out jokes from such veterans as Bob Hope, Jack Benny and others of the time. All of us on the show considered this strange when he had with him some of the funniest men in the business, Smiley Burnette, Rufe Davis, and especially Pat Buttram, among others. "Now, I realize that a lot of you folks out there may not know who I am," Gene continues. "My pictures don't play a lot of the big cities like this. As a matter of fact, my pictures usually play in towns so small Mrs. Roosevelt hasn't even been there yet." This one was good enough during the Roosevelt administration, but once Autry got hung on a gag he continued to use it, even into the 50s and 60s.

"Oh, now don't get me wrong," he continues now that he's got them going his way. "I never get mixed up in politics. As a matter of fact, I belong to no organized political party, I'm a Democrat."

We used to cringe at that old Will Rogers gag until it finally occurred to us that 99% of the folks present probably never saw Rogers on the stage or heard him on the radio.

At this point Gene introduced the first act, which varied from tour to tour, year to year. It was almost always a visual act, ropes or dancing, or both. At any rate, it would be a 'fast' act, getting the show off to a good start while the band played rousing-ly.

Behind the performers hangs a backdrop curtain that gives the stage a Western setting. This is Autry's own property that goes along with the show. It is a painting, made up to simulate the interior of a very elegant ranch house. Note the fireplace blazing, the windows revealing a Western exterior, the head of a long-horned steer so natural that it seems to protrude out into the room. Across the ceiling, giving added depth and dimension, are some huge beams so real that one could almost get up there and walk across them. All of this setting added much visually, to an otherwise musical/comedy show.

Following the opening act that draws loud applause, Autry returned to the mike. No use trying to give the act an encore; we were all warned not to expect one due to the length of the show.

"Mighty fine," says Gene, beckoning the roper to take another bow or two from the wings. As Gene begins to speak into the microphone again, a short, chubby, bald headed man dressed in cowboy attire and sporting a broad grin, waddles onto the stage. He is twirling a short rope with a very small loop at the end. Autry, who doesn't see him yet, speaks.

"You know, you folks here in Dubuque have really made us feel welcome." The little man roper, Jack Knapp, has now reached a spot on stage half way between the wings and the center where the Star stands.

"Yes, we love it here," Gene goes on, supposedly unaware of the uninvited intruder. "I could even go so far as to tell you that I was born here but that would be lying. I was born in Texas. But if it ever happens again, I aim to see that it's right here in Dubuque."

This gag of Autry's gets more laughs than he has anticipated. The audience continues to chuckle as the little fat man continues twirling his wee loop. Gene looks over the other way at the band, seemingly happy that the crowd is with us.

Suddenly, he sees the stage crasher.

"Hey, Jack!" says Gene into the mike. "What the . . . "

Jack Knapp continues to twirl his very small loop at the end of his rope while smiling on the assumption that he's really going over big. He rubs the top of his baldhead with the palm of his hand.

"What a lovely head of skin," say's Gene Autry, shaking his head in disgust.

"Hey, Jack!" Gene repeats, pointing with his forefinger that Knapp should get lost. Jack Knapp, disappointed at this reception, stops cold. His small loop falls to the end of his rope, motionless. Jack looks at the audience, woefully, then casts a disgruntled look at the M.C. and turns to waddle off the stage on his short, bowed legs. His 'dead" rope drags along behind him.

"Everybody wants to get into the act," says Gene, shaking his head. "And now, friends, let's listen to three very lovely young ladies that you all hear on our CBS Melody Ranch Doublemint Show over your local CBS Station. You're really going to love these girls . . . I've been trying to . . . " He glances at the three girls seated in the 'parlor' behind him. They are ready.

"A big hand for the three Pinafores!"

While the audience is welcoming them loudly, the three sisters rush up to the mike while the Cass County Boys step forward to accompany them.

The Pinafores open with a short, fast selection, followed by a familiar hit song of the day, then close out with another quickie. Their act is short, sweet and well received.

Eunice, Ione and Beulah Kettle joined the Autry organization to do the radio show in 1946. They remained, making several tours such as this through the 1950 season, when they departed for points unknown for personal reasons. They were lovely ladies and great troupers. The audience loved them.

The Kettle Sisters were replaced by two different groups, one for the tours and a different one for the radio show. The Candy Mountain Girls, three lovelies who sang very much in the same manner during two seasons, 1951 and 1952; and by the King Sisters on radio, augmented by a most charming lady, Norma Zimmer.

Following the girls, the Cowboy MC strode back onto the stage to introduce the next act. Once again, much to Gene's apparent displeasure, Jack Knapp waddles out again, uninvited, and begins twirling his diminutive loop at the end of his rope.

"Jack! Not now." Said the M.C.

Jack Knapp ignores Autry's remark and keeps on twirling as though he owns the show.

"Jack! We'll call you if we need you."

Knapp ignores.

With lightning speed, Gene Autry pulls his 45 and shoots directly at the little man who, with much of the simulated action of an animated cartoon, turns and scampers off the stage.

Returning his attention to the audience, Gene introduces one of the most colorful acts ever seen on the stage. For this he leaves out any attempt at comedy. It is Tony White Cloud and three other Indians. The four Red Men scamper out onto the stage amid shrill Indian War Cries heard well above the music of the band which brings them on with a loud, fast, Red Wing type of number. After the entrance the band settles back while the Native Americans take over their own act.

Naturally, they are dressed in typical, multi-colored Indian fashion, feathers and belts of beads, belled anklets and all. Tony and his troupe, who lived on the Jemez Reservation near Albuquerque, were a complete act within themselves. The older man, whom everyone tabbed as "Chief," steps to one side and begins beating upon his Tom Tom while filling the auditorium with his vocal musical chants. To this, the other three go into a series of dances. War Dances. Snake Dances. Rain Dances. The works. While audiences all over the country ate this sort of entertainment up, I am certain that they overlooked one point in the act that continued to amaze the rest of the Autry troupe each time they hit the stage. As the dances began, the very second the Indians feet hit the floor, the Chief hit the Tom Tom at the same time. This procedure continued for a long time as the dancers went through their various routines. No matter how carefully the rest of us in the wings tried to count the beats and the steps, we found it impossible to keep track of their routines. However, without fail, show after show, we learned, to our utter amazement, that the steps of the dancers and the beat of the Tom Tom always came to an abrupt end on exactly the same beat.

"One of these days the Chief is going to hit one extra beat on that damn drum, or one of the dancers is going to keep on jitterbugging for a step or two," said Jay Berry, watching in the wings with the rest of us.

The Indians act came out exact every time.

The pay-off of this interesting act was Tony White Cloud himself. For a finale, he brought out a half-a-dozen hoops, each one slightly larger than the other. Immediately, while the other three chanted, clapped their hands and Tom Tom, Tony went into his Hoop Dance.

Dancing with the hoops is best described by imagining a child jumping six ropes at a time. While Tony danced around the floor of the stage, the hoops were going in all directions, up, over, down, around and under. The fact that the hoops were all of different circumference, enabled Tony to manipulate them all, hoop within a hoop, while he, himself, seemingly entangled himself among all six. The act ended as Tony emerged from all of the hoops, coming to a dead stop the minute the last drum beat sounded. Again, the applause was deafening.

As the Indians left the stage, Gene Autry walked out applauding them with the rest of the crowd. He stepped up to the mike to give them their final tribute:

"Tony White Cloud and the Jemez Indians!"

As the applause finally dies down, Gene prepares to introduce the next act. He turns to discover Jack Knapp standing near the wings with his diminutive loop still twirling. Once more a couple of gun shots from Autry sends the little fellow scampering off stage.

Now it is my time to shine. Gene always gave me a very complimentary introduction after which I would walk out wearing old boots, levis, plaid shirt, slouch hat, carrying the guitar over my shoulder and with a piece of paper in one hand and a pencil in the other. The act began in this manner:

BOND: Thank you, Mr. Autry. I'll be with you in just a minute. First I have to finish this.

GENE: What are you doing? Making out your will?

BOND: Nope. I'm makin' up a list of names of all the guys that I can whup.

GENE: That so? (he pauses. Looks at the audience as if to be thinking, "What in the hell have we got here." I keep on scribbling) Mmmm. Let me take a look at that list. I see you have Tex Ritter Jimmy Wakely, Jack Dempsey, Hey! Just a minute there son. You've got MY name there.

BOND: (unconcerned) Certainly I got your name on there. Number one, top of the list.

GENE: Well now, looky here, son. You don't think that you can whip me, do you?

BOND: It says here that I can whup you. See that right there?

GENE: I don't care what it says there. You know you can't whip me.

BOND: (with daring confidence) I CAN'T WHUP YOU?

GENE: NO, YOU CAN'T WHIP ME!

BOND: OK! I'll just rub your name out. (erases)

GENE: That's more like it. Now, tell me why you were late.

BOND: I couldn't help it. I was out there signing some little kid's autographs.

GENE: Well, what took you so long?

BOND: I had to chase 'em three blocks 'fore they'd take it.

GENE: I don't blame them. All right, you're out here now. Sing us a song. And it better be good. (He makes his move to exit)

BOND: It will be (looking over to make certain that the Boss is gone) I'm gonna tell you something 'bout that Gene Autry. He squanders his money. Did you get a load of that fancy outfit he's wearin'? You know what he paid for that? Five hundred dollars! Five hundred bucks, and he'll wear the raggediest underwear you ever saw. (begins to strum, casually, upon the guitar)

GENE: (Re-enters, firing his six-shooter) What was that you just said?

BOND: (frightened) I didn't say nothin'.

GENE: Listen, buster. I've had just about enough of you.

BOND: You act like you're mad at me!

GENE: You're doggone right I'm mad at you.

BOND: Well, what did I do?

GENE: You know what you did.

BOND: No, what did I do?

GENE: You stole my Roy Rogers button.

BOND: (reacts silently over crowd's laughter)

GENE: What's more, I figure that it's about time that you and I had a showdown.

BOND: Showdown?

GENE: Right. I'll meet you out back in five minutes and we'll settle this thing once and for all.

BOND: (Gulps)

GENE: . . . and remember one thing. I'm not afraid. (Gene replaces his revolver in the holster. Looks at the audience, then at Bond and slowly turns to make his exit.)

BOND: (Watches him disappear into the wings. Turns slowly to the audience and says) I'm not afraid either . . . 'cause I won't be there! (sings "If You've Got The Money I've Got The Time," or "Don't Let the Stars Get in Your Eyes," or "Alabama Jubilee," or "Oklahoma Hills" depending upon which tour it is)

Following my act, Autry returned to the stage to introduce the next act, which varied from tour to tour. One tour the next act was the great Eddie Peabody. Eddie played a whole lot of Banjo and was a super showman on top of it. Eddie amazed us all when once he broke a string during one of his solos. Instructing the band to keep going, he reached in his upper pocket, produced a new string, placed it in the proper slots, turned the key until the new one was in tune with the rest, and continued to the conclusion of the number before any of us realized what had happened. It was one of the greatest acts of 're-covery' showmanship that we had ever seen. In many cases, if a musician breaks a string, it could bring on a total calamity since his act has come to a complete halt, something dreaded in live, stage entertainment.

On other tours this spot might be taken by other famous acts, such as the Hoosier Hot Shots, four guys from Chicago radio first brought to the movies by Autry. The highlight of this act was Hezzie, who played on the washboard while accompanying himself with other wild sounds such as whistles, bells, honking horns, etc.

Also in that slot could have been one of the many girl singers who were part of the ten years of touring. Ginny Jackson was the first. She lasted several tours before being replaced by a movie starlet, Judy Clark. Gloria Grey made a few tours, as did Gail Davis, who, at the time was appearing in her own TV series entitled, "Annie Oakley." Each of these beauties added much color and enrichment to the Autry stage.

Following whichever of the above acts, Gene returned to the center of the stage to give each of them their proper 'send offs'. When Jack Knapp waddles back out onto the stage again, Gene begins his motion to evict him, but on second thought, he says,

"Well, OK, Jack. It looks like you're not going to give up, so go ahead. Make it snappy and get it over with."

With that opening, little, bald, chubby Jack Knapp starts twirling his rope. The noose begins with an oval about the size of a saucer. Little by little it grows until it becomes about the size of a bicycle wheel, at which time it begins to climb up and over the little man, rolling off the top of his head so slowly that everyone wonders what keeps it together. The climax of Jack's loop trick is the growing of it until it becomes so large that the full stage becomes almost too small to prevent it from collapsing. The loop falls to the floor; the band plays a loud chord as Jack Knapp takes a bow so low that he almost rolls over like a snowball.

"Ladies and gentlemen," says Gene into the mike. "You just saw the great Jack Knapp. Now, how about a big hand for his better half . . . Bobbie Knapp!"

Bobbie Knapp runs out onto the stage, going into a series of acrobatics assisted by hubby, Jack, using ropes, whips and anything else imaginable that might go to make up a good roping/acrobatic act.

Autry always told us backstage that there was quite a story behind this Mr. and Mrs. Act. It seems that Jack Knapp was part of the old Tom Mix Rodeo Circus that toured this country and Europe. When they got to Hungary, the Circus more or less fell apart and Tom and his crew found themselves looking for a hitchhike ride back home. To make matters worse, it seems that this certain young Hungarian girl had taken a liking to this midget roper, which she had come to see and insisted that she might be of some assistance in getting them all out of the country. There was only one catch to it; she wanted to go to America. To make a long story short, there was only one way that this could be done. Marriage! So, Jack married Bobbie, the ambitious young Hungarian; Tom Mix and his Circus returned to America where Jack literally 'taught her the ropes.' Their fine act was featured also in the Madison Square Garden Rodeos as well as other great shows around the country.

In the mid-1960s, we learned to our great sorrow that Jack had passed on. In 1970, Bobbie Knapp, the little Hungarian, came to visit us on the set of our TV show, *Melody Ranch,* where we had many laughs remembering the 'good old days of touring.'

"And now, folks," said MC Gene Autry into the mike. "If I could get a few of these broken down musicians to give me a hand, I'd kind'a like to sing a little song myself."

As the crowd roared, Gene Autry began his series of songs. Gene always opened the singing part of his act with his theme song, "Back In The Saddle Again." It opened and closed every *Melody Ranch Show* broadcasts and was the title of one of his Republic Pictures made in 1941. In 1946, when he resumed his motion picture career after his army stint, Gene told us, "I wish to hell I hadn't used it as a picture title before. It would be the perfect number to use now that we're firing up again." The title of his first film after the war was *Sioux City Sue.*

Just as with the rodeos, Gene's selection of songs varied from tour to tour. Another one that he sang often was "Be Honest With Me."

Year after year on the one-nighters, Autry would change one or two songs adding a couple which might be popular at that particular time. Quite often he would include numbers that were not necessarily western or country, but were currently hits by other big time singers such as Bing Crosby, Frank Sinatra or Dick Haynes. Gene even recorded many of these 'pop' hits such as "Don't Fence Me In," "Have I told You Lately That I Love

You," "I Don't Want To Set The World On Fire," "Return To Me," and "Buttons and Bows." However, the finale of his musical act would always include what he called the Western Classics, "The Last Roundup," "Mexicali Rose," "Silver On The Sage," "South of the Border," "Tumbling Tumbleweeds," "Cool Water," "When It's Springtime in the Rockies," "Take Me Back To My Boots and Saddles," "There's A Gold Mine In The Sky," "You Are My Sunshine," "The Singing Hills," "The Call of the Canyon," "Deep In The Heart of Texas," "Jingle Jangle Jingle," "Old Faithful," "Missouri Waltz," "Riders In The Sky," plus any and all other great Western songs proven to be popular with the public.

During his many years of making phonograph records and singing on the radio, Gene Autry had either introduced or become identified with several famous songs. In 1949, he stumbled onto a song which would not only become an all-time best seller for both him and Columbia Records, it would have an impact which would even change the trend of the music business itself. I'm speaking of the famous "Rudolph, The Red Nosed Reindeer." Much to the delight of the youngsters in his audience, whenever Gene began singing this great song on the stage (regardless of the season), Frankie Marvin would dance out onto the stage in his "Rudolph" suit which had been constructed especially for this occasion.

The Gene Autry musical portion of his show has now been concluded. Amidst loud applause as Gene removes his big white hat, bowing gracefully and humbly, the curtain comes down on the first half of the Autry stage show.

— INTERMISSION —

The intermission was of the usual length, ten minutes, giving the vendors ample time to display and sell their wares, which consisted of songbooks, programs, pictures, and other Gene Autry merchandise, as well as soft drinks and cotton candy. Pat Buttram would step in front of the curtain to describe the various products by saying, "If anybody wants a souvenir to take home, the boys down here will take care of you. For fifty cents you can buy a picture of me to take home and set on your dresser. For One Dollar I'll come over and set it on your dresser in person. If it's too crowded and some of you don't get the item that you want, you can get them later as you pass out."

Many of the fans tried to gain entrance to the backstage areas to try and get to Gene, but special guards hired for this purpose restrained them. We had a lot of criticism about this, but had it not been put into effect the entire crowd would have wound up backstage bringing the proceedings to a standstill.

Intermission backstage was usually without incident. Small conferences were sometimes held in order to discuss the public address system as to it's good or bad points, or what suggestions might be made to overcome any weak points that might have shown up in the first half. Gene usually headed for his dressing room where he began his wardrobe change for the rest of the show. All of us would post ourselves nearby in case he had any last minute changes or observations. If any of us walked by the spot where Jay Berry was grooming the horses we would inquire as to whether or not they had gone to the bathroom yet. Jay would reply, "You pick your damned old guitar, I'll trip the horses."

Shortly after that, we would hear the introduction for the Cass County boys and the second half would be under way.

—THE SECOND HALF—

This portion of the show, just like the beginning, was programmed so that it would get off to another rousing start. Gene introduced the Cass County Boys, accompanying themselves playing the accordion, guitar and bass, as they sang in trio harmony. This always got the audience back into the proper mood while accompanying some of the straggling patrons back to their seats.

They would sing numbers like, "See That You're Born In Texas," "Room Full of Roses," "They Went That-A-Way," plus other lively numbers, while Bert Dodson did a show-stopping version of "El Rancho Grande."

♫　　♫　　♫

One time Carl Cotner and Frankie Marvin, while watching the Cass County Boys from backstage, noted the fact that once the Trio ran onto the stage for their act, they were stationed around the mike for a good thirty minutes while playing for, not only their own act, but the following three or four as well. There was no way that they could leave the stage, short of an earthquake. Both Cotner's and Marvin's minds were quaking. This was too good an opportunity to pass up.

Cass County Boys, Jerry
Scoggins, Fred Martin and
Bert Dodson.

During the intermission of the following show, I watched Carl and
Frankie as they strolled casually out onto the empty stage behind the closed
curtain. Since I was the only observer, they swore me to silence. Slowly
cautiously, the two began smearing the accordion, the guitar and the bass
with garlic. Keep in mind that the bass is quite large and can absorb a lot of
garlic, as can both the guitar and accordion.

When the curtain went up and Gene Autry called the three boys to the
mike, facing thousands of eager customers, you just know that they ran out
of the wings, grabbing up their instruments with the distinctive aroma
trailing along after.

By the time the boys were into their first number, they were fully aware
of what fate had bestowed upon them. They were forced to smile broadly at
the audience; however, each one of them could not resist turning to the rest
of us in the wings, displaying their great displeasure upon their faces.

When the time arrived for the three Texans to finally leave the stage for
a minute or so, you can probably guess already that just about everyone was
milling around the dressing room awaiting the anticipated reactions from

the three. For some reason, however, both Cotner and Marvin were conspicuous with their absence.

♫　　♫　　♫

Shades of garlic now forgotten, the show went on. Gene Autry strolled back to center stage ready to introduce the next act.

Carl Cotner, who ranked second only to Frankie Marvin in seniority with those of us working with Gene over the years, had joined forces with the traveling cowboy in the mid-thirties as a fiddle player. As did most of us connected with the musical part of Autry's activities, he worked the tours, the radio show, the movies and the phonograph records. Carl was the musical director and leader of the orchestra on the radio show, the records, and any other time that Gene had need of a band.

After being properly introduced, Carl ran out as a small group of players gathered around him and, without a word, went into his outstanding rendition of "Listen To The Mockingbird." His encores would be numbers such as "The Hot Canary," "Fiddling The Fiddle," or some other good old-fashioned fiddle hoedown.

The next act was a highlight that was part of the Autry Show for season after season. I'm speaking of the king of the hillbilly rubes, Rufe Davis. It would be most difficult to try to describe his act and give it full justice, so I will simply say that he did a series of imitations of birds, motor boats, tap dancing with his lips, animal sounds, all the while mugging with his rural, oval face in such a manner that the audience went into stitches immediately, staying there throughout his hilarious act. Rufe's pay-off number was a song he once used in a Bob Burns movie, "Mountain Music," a song called "Mama Don't Allow No Music Played In Here". This is the way that Rufe introduced the number.

"Now I'd like to play you a little song that I once sang in a picture featuring Betty Grable . . . and . . . that's all I remember about the picture."

Once Rufe sang the words, 'Mama don't allow no guitar or fiddle or bass or bazooka, or any other musical instrument, he would turn right around and imitate that particular instrument with his voice, making it sound exactly like the instrument. (Smiley Burnette, who wrote the song, featured it as a major part of his act for years. However, since he was an outstanding musician, he actually picked up and played each different instrument as it is mentioned. Both acts were outstanding, but obviously, only Ruff would use it if they both happened to be on the same show).

Rufe's act never failed to bring the house down.

Gene, as well as the rest of us, used to kid Rufe about the fact that his act never changed.

"When in the hell are you going to get a new act?" Gene asked Rufe with a broad smile.

"Next tour," grinned Rufe. "On the next tour I'm going to have a brand new act." It always turned out to be the same one and it never failed to get the job done.

The next two acts did not necessarily come in the order in which they are being described, but were placed in the show so that they did not follow each other too closely.

The first saw Pat Buttram and Frankie Marvin put on a hilarious comedy act. Gene would introduce Pat first, who would then come out and have a few words with the Cowboy MC. Pat would then continue with a series of jokes which would vary from tour to tour, show to show, making it difficult for me to repeat them here. I will merely say that they were *very, very* funny.

At this point Pat would pretend that he wished to sing a song but had no accompaniment. He would turn to the wings and say, "Send out that guitar player that came around telling us that he wanted a job."

Frankie Marvin would then stroll on stage wearing a hick suit, blacked out front teeth, and a silly grin that only Frankie could generate.

"Can you play that thing?" Pat asked Frankie.

Frankie would nod his head vigorously while grinning so broadly that the audience could not help laughing at him and at the discomfort that Pat seemed to be receiving from his accompanist.

OK then," continued Pat, preparing to sing. "Hit me a B-flat."

Frank would then pound upon the guitar so heavily that we often thought that it would break in two. Upon finishing his pounding, he would then smile broadly at the audience as if to say, 'ain't that the greatest thing you ever heard?'

"I said B-flat!" roared Pat. Frank's grin would disappear in less than a second. Again he would look at the audience, only this time it was a 'very hurt' look.

"Is that a B-flat?"

Frank nodded.

"Well, make it a plain B. We'll flatten it out as we go along."

Frank then hit a legitimate guitar chord.

Pat Buttram, who doesn't claim to be a singer, would mimic a grand tenor, clearing his throat as if he were going to sing an operatic aria. In this, he would hit a high falsetto note, turn to Frankie while still yodeling and say,

"That's a little too high. Will you bring it down a little?"

Frank would grin, nod, and then hit another chord. However, instead of lowering the key, he would raise it, so much so that when Pat tried to sing again it was much too high.

"A little bit lower yet," said Pat, pretending not to comprehend what Frank was doing to him.

The payoff to this bit was Pat discovering that Frank was raising the pitch instead of lowering it, forcing Pat to hit Frank over the head with his slouch hat, saying,

"You're going the wrong way."

At this statement, Frank pretended to be very hurt. Frankie Marvin could turn on and off the happy and sad face quicker than anybody. He did it in such a manner as to have the crowd going with him both ways all along.

"I don't know," said Pat, disgustedly. "I guess I shouldn't have called him out here in the first place. I oughter just sung it raw."

The Pat Buttram/Frankie Marvin act concluded with the two of them getting into a seemingly violent argument whereby Pat chased Frank around the stage with a broom. In conclusion Pat would bring him back out with a decent introduction.

"Now ladies and gentlemen, here's the fellow who you hear playing the steel guitar on all of Mr. Artery's records. Frankie Marvin playing the Steel Guitar Rag."

Frank played the number to the great satisfaction of the audience.

It might be well to add here that Frankie Marvin played both steel and standard guitar on all of Gene Autry's phonograph records from the very beginning of his recording career. At the end of some of Gene's verses, Frank would play a phrase best described as a 'singing slide." This musical interlude on Autry's records became so recognizable that those in show business who, as part of their act, imitated other great stars, would always add this 'singing slide' whenever they were imitating Gene Autry.

Frankie Marvin, 1948.

The second act, also a comedy, was Smiley 'Frog' Burnette. I am sure that Gene brought Smiley on the tours in 1952 and 1953, because he also brought Frog back in to his movies after an absence of 10 years. Whatever the reason, it was now time for Gene to introduce his old pal, Frog. This was done in Autry's most eloquent manner. He brought him on, and with no other dialog between them, Smiley began his outstanding act.

"Hi there, " said Smiley, smiling broadly at the entire audience. "How y'all? I heard someone say, 'look at that silly galoot . . . he's crazy.' Well I might be crazy, but I didn't pay nothin' to get in here. I like this place. I hope you all have fun. Clap your hands yell out as loud as you want to. Tear the place down if you care to, it don't belong to me. It's a real fine building, this. Got signs all over the place. One back there say's E-X-I-T. That's Latin for git-out the door. I saw another sign said, 'Ladies'. I went in . . . there they were. I don't feel so good today. Had an accident this morning. I was putting toilet water on my hair and the lid fell and hit me on the head.

"I see a lot of boys and girls in the audience. I'm glad of that. I just love children. I used to go to school with them. Oh, I went to school all right. I was the only kid in the third grade that could vote. I didn't want to go in the forth grade . . . my papa was in there. It's a wonder I learned anything at all in school. We had a great big fat schoolteacher and every time she turned around she erased everything off the blackboard. She looked like a bale of cotton with the center band busted. She fell down one day and rocked herself to sleep.

"That teacher was always asking me some silly question that I couldn't answer. One day she said, 'Frog, what does f double e-t spell?' I sez, 'I don't know.' She sez, "Yes you do. F-E-E-T, what does that spell?' I sez, 'I don't know.' So she sez, 'well think a minute. What's a cow got four of and I've got two of' and . . . whoooeee, did I get a whuppin'."

Smiley Bunette's jokes coupled with his magnificent delivery and power to control the audience, kept them constantly laughing.

More jokes followed after which he strapped on his accordion and sang such songs as, "It's My Lazy Day", "Hominy Grits", "The Animal Fair," plus many other showstoppers. With this great Star on the tours, the Gene Autry show reached a stature unequaled in any other live stage show during these days.

After Smiley came the closing act of the show. Gene Autry with Champion and Little Camp. Pat Buttram usually introduced this last act while Gene went backstage to mount his famous movie horse. On cue, the beautiful animal strode out to the center of the stage with the cowboy star sitting astride him waving his big white hat at the crowd. With thousands of youngsters in the audience you can well imagine the reception that this got. Hadn't they been yelling, "bring on the hosses" for two hours?

While the band played the special arrangements, Champion went through the same steps, dances and tricks that he had done in the arena at Madison Square Garden. He did the Hula, the March, the low Bows, topped by the famous End of the Trail pose. Champ was a smash. All that Gene had to do was hang on and give the appropriate cues taught Gene and horse by the great trainer Johnny Agee.

Even though the addition of Little Champ to the act was a letdown to many of us participating in the show, the kids loved him. For this part, Gene had now dismounted, taking his whip in hand while the two horses went through various routines. For the closing, Gene Autry, with Champion and Little Champ following behind, would walk up to the mike where Gene made his farewell speech.

"You might have noticed that I was having a little trouble with Champion today. Lately he's been running around with Bing Crosby's horses. Now everybody knows that Crosby's horses have never won a race, and if you have seen my pictures, you know that Champion has never lost one."

" Anyway, thanks for coming out. Thanks for watching our movies, listening to our radio show, and for buying our phonograph records. If all goes well we'll see you here again next year. In the meantime, this is Gene Autry saying, (beginning to sing) . . . "I'm Back in the Saddle Again. . ."

♪   ♪   ♪

With that, the curtain came down on one of the finest stage shows ever produced, one that played to millions of people throughout the USA and Canada. It's too bad that somebody didn't think to record one of those shows on film so, like all of his movies, records and TV shows, it could still be played over and over again.

One of the shows, in Atlanta, Georgia, was televised live during the performance but nothing was ever said about it's being recorded at the same time. In those days they only had the kinescope process and that was not the best reproduction compared to the tape that is used exclusively today.

After the two-hour dinner break, we would come back to the auditorium for the evening's performance and repeat the same show.

CHAPTER FOURTEEN

We Have Two Hours

Or, Recommended By Duncan Hines
Or, "Your deal, Gene."

The weekday matinee, having begun at 4:30pm, was over at about 6:30, giving us just enough time to scamper out past the thousands of screaming children, teenagers and parents, each of whom demanded a personal audience and autograph session with the Boss. Into the waiting bus we went; followed by a quick ride back to the hotel with just enough time for a quickie blast at the bar and an attempt to get served in the dining room before boarding the same bus headed back to the auditorium. This was always much easier said than done, for trying to worm one's way through a surging mob of excited fans while wearing our cowboy outfits was about like trying to swim the Grand Canyon's Colorado River upstream. Just how Gene always managed to get aboard the bus undetected was one more mystery about the man that we never quite figured out. And, this was about the only time that he rode the bus with us.

As the driver pulled away from the clamoring fans, somebody would yell out, "Hey Mac! Know where you're going?"

Whether or not it was now Mac driving, the answer always came back the same, "Nope, don't believe I do!"

"Looked like standing room only again today, Gene," somebody else said to the smiling Autry.

"Yeah," said the Boss. "We're gonna break even in Pittsburgh."

Anytime that we had a 'turn away' crowd, we knew that he was going to give us that 'break even' bit.

Conversation during this short ride was usually light. Little was said about the show just concluded. Sometimes the show might be running a bit long and we'd have to do something about that. Gene hardly ever commented about the quality of our individual act, pro or con. The mere fact that he had hired us to go along was about his only compliment. Occasionally, he might become dissatisfied with one of the supporting acts, in which case he simply would not include them on the next tour. One time in Tulsa, a Chimpanzee, which had been brought along for the first time, bit a little boy backstage, so there was no choice but to send the act home.

Once we reached our hotel, the entire gang scattered in all directions. Gene usually headed for his suite, taking along local dignitaries, their wives and friends, where room service was most often called for. Carl. Frankie and I would head for the bar for appetizers while ordering our supper from the menu at the same time.

♫   ♫   ♫

Out of all of the many tours we made, there is one particular dinner so outstanding that it must be told. In order to appreciate it more fully, a little bit of background is required.

As has been stated, nothing in the way of practical jokes, or the 'riding' of a fellow touring companion, was overlooked by the Autry troupe. Whenever Gene was briefed on the gag, he too would gladly join in. On this particular occasion, the joke was on Rufe Davis. Or was it?

I had learned many miles back, while riding along on the bus sitting next to Rufe, that he had a problem.

"I gotta hell of a problem" Rufe said to me confidently.

"How's That?" I asked.

"I can't seem to save up any money on these tours."

"Are you kidding?" I said. "Why Gene pays you more'n all the rest of us put together."

"Ha!"

"What I in the hell do you do with all your loot?"

"Well. I send most of it home where my wife spends it and what little I keep for myself, I spent it." Rufe was not alone on this common problem.

"You know what it costs me a week on these tours?" the Oklahoma comedian continued.

"How much?"

"Over a hundred dollars a week."

Smiley Burnette on stage.

"Wow!" I commented. On the tours we were required to pay for our own meals and hotel bill. Gene paid us well for our services and furnished the transportation.

"How much does it cost you per week?" Rufe asked. Since I felt the beginning of a sneaky opportunity coming on, I couldn't bring myself to answer Rufe truthfully. I could confess later. Right now we were in desperate need of a new gag.

I said calmly, "Oh hell. I don't spend more'n forty or fifty dollars a week on the road."

"What!" yelled Rufe above the road noise of the passing miles.

I turned to look at Carl and Frankie across the aisle. Winking at them, I said, "Hey, Carl, Frank. How much do you guys spend per week on these tours?"

Both fellows picked up the ball immediately.

"Oh, not more'n thirty or forty dollars." They both said with a straight face. Rufe Davis was the type of guy who believed anything you told him. Tell Rufe the sky's falling and he'll duck.

This question of economics was carried on for several months while Rufe searched in vain for ways around the heavy cost of touring. Finally the word got to Smiley Burnette, who loved a good gag better than anybody.

"Send Rufe to me, " Smiley said to us. "I'll lay it on him good."

Smiley, who furnished his own transportation, a house trailer, was his own cook and bottle washer. Actually, Smiley was an excellent cook, having turned out several cookbooks of his own.

"Now Rufe, you take me," Smiley told Davis with a very straight face. "Cooking my own meals on the road, hell, it don't cost me anything. These grocery stores back here don't know what high prices mean. Chicken feed. That's my expense."

"I shore gotta do something," Rufe said, shaking his head. "I'm making money, but going in the hole at the same time."

As it sometimes does, fate placed a most juicy plum in our hands. It was Monday, January 29, 1951, that we played Bowling Green, Kentucky, home of the famous food critic, Duncan Hines. Restaurants all over the country carried the advertising slogan "Recommended by Duncan Hines." Smiley and Duncan were very close friends, having much in common in the culinary arts.

"I wanna see everybody backstage between shows. Gene included," Smiley said to us during the matinee at Bowling Green. "Want you to meet a friend of mine.

Back in Frog's temporary kitchen, he proudly introduced us to his good friend, Duncan Hines." Herb Green brought in the cameras while Mr. Hines wrote out the words in large letters,

SMILEY BURNETTE'S KITCHEN: RECOMMENDED BY DUNCAN HINES

Everyone applauded. Rufe took it all in without saying a word. Up to now this event had no bearing upon his cost of living.

The next day, several of us were talking to Smiley who, seeing Rufe approaching, said, "Watch this."

Just as Rufe joined the party, Smiley said, "There it is. Take a look. Enjoy." Frog was holding up Duncan Hines business card.

"What's that?" asked Rufe.

"What's that, he sez," said Smiley, acting put out. "I got me a Duncan Hines card and all he has to say is "what's that?"

"What does it do?" asked Rufe, again.

"You see this Duncan Hines card?" said Smiley, waving the common calling card under Rufe's nose. "That means that I can eat at any restaurant anywhere, for free, as long as it is recommended by Duncan Hines."

"That I've got to see, " said Rufe. The sky was falling but he hadn't ducked yet.

"Alright, " continued Smiley. "The next time we come to a town where they have a Duncan Hines restaurant, let me know and I'll take the whole Autry troupe."

That was all that Rufe Davis needed. At the next stop Rufe rushed backstage with the news that he had just located a Duncan Hines recommended restaurant not too far from the auditorium.

"Good," said Smiley. "You and Gene and all of the musicians will be my guests for dinner tonight. I'll get the restaurant on the phone and tell 'em we're coming."

Later alone, Smiley not only called the restaurant for a reservation, he also spoke to the manager and alerted him to the full particulars of the gag.

Between shows, a large group of us including Gene, Rufe and of course Smiley Burnette, gathered at the restaurant where all of us were invited to order freely . . . cocktails, porterhouse steaks, the works. Duncan Hines was right. This was a fine restaurant and everybody was enjoying the meal, especially Rufe Davis who just knew that there was a catch to it somewhere. A bill like this? For free? Just by the showing of a card? This Rufe had to see.

As the elegant meal was about finished, Smiley called the waitress over.

"Hey, Miss," Frog said in a voice loud enough to be heard by all. "Whur's the men's room?"

She pointed it out and Smiley excused himself. However, instead of going to the men's room, he went to an area out of sight, met with the manager, paid the bill and asked the manager to meet us at the cashier's stand as we were leaving. With that chore taken car of, safe in the knowledge that each of us, Rufe excepted, would later refund our share of the bill, Smiley came back to his seat. He was beaming in the satisfaction of knowing that all of us had a wonderful dinner on Duncan Hines.

"That was a fine meal," said Gene, echoed by the rest of us. "But we have a show to do, so, what do you say we go do it?"

"Everybody follow me," Instructed Smiley. "And don't nobody go grabbing for any check. This one's on me, remember?"

All of us formed a single line as we walked by the manager who was standing back of the counter near the cash register. Smiley Burnette, always the great actor, walked slowly by with the rest of us, waving the Duncan Hines calling card close to the manager, a pretty good actor himself, who said, "Thank you, Mr. Burnette, Mr. Autry . . . you folks come back again.

We then marched out of the establishment, having consumed a dinner probably costing $50.00 or more but having all the appearance of being on the house, or as it was, "on the card."

"Well, I'll be goddamned!" said Rufe Davis as we gathered around him outside the restaurant. He shifted a toothpick from one side of his mouth to the other. "You know something. I gotta get me one of them cards."

An hour or so later, while Rufe was doing his act on the stage, several of us gathered around Smiley in his backstage kitchen, refunding to him our part of the check.

"That was some joke we pulled on Rufe, wasn't it?" I said, laughing with the rest of the gang at the smoothness in the way the gag had come off.

"Yeah, some joke on Rufe," said Gene Autry, smiling at each of us. "But he's the only one that got a free steak dinner."

So . . . the joke was on us, but we loved it.

♫   ♫   ♫

At about 8:20 the entire gang began taking their place on stage behind the drawn curtain through which we usually peeked to see if the seats were all sold out. I would guess that this would be the case about 90% of the time.

Meanwhile, behind the backdrop curtain, near the vicinity of his dressing room, Gene paced the floor awaiting his cue to open the show. Dozens of local dignitaries, their wives, children and friends, were swarming around the Star, seeking, not only autographs and souvenirs, but also any opportunity to lay hands on the Singing Cowboy. Often there would be governors, congressmen, mayors, executives with film and record distributors, and merchandisers. Then, there would be the inevitable fan club members who came from near and far, sometimes following the show for days or weeks on end. The Autry fan club was something else. It was made of thousands of loyal members, all of whom were kept up-to-date on the Cowboy's schedule by means of their bulky, monthly fan letter.

All of these fine folks were soon advised by Herb Green, using a firm but polite voice, that they should take their seats in the audience because the curtain was about to go up. As most of them filed out, there were inevitably a few young lady fan club members who would linger, hoping to spend as much time in Gene's presence as possible. I can't recall any occasion when these ladies were asked to leave.

At 8:30 on the nose, everyone was in place, gathered around the mike. On cue, a simple nod from the Boss man in the wings, Fred Martin sounded a chord on the accordion and every one of us began singing,

"He' Back in the Saddle Again . . . " After a verse or so had been sung, the full band kept on playing the rest of the song as the curtain opened, reveling a huge auditorium filled with the beaming faces of the audience, upstairs and downstairs, clapping their hands together vigorously.

Gene Autry strode across the stage and up to the mike where he waited until the applause died down.

"Howdy, my name is Gene Autry," he said for the umpteenth time.

More applause followed as we, on stage, scanned the entire audience, wondering where Frankie Marvin had posted himself this time. In the early days, there had been a few confrontations between Frankie, as the audience plant, and some of the more rugged individuals seated near him in the crowd.

"What's goin' on back of that curtain behind you?" Frankie had yelled out at the time.

"What difference does it make," Gene had yelled back at him.

"Well, there ought'a be . . . there ain't nothin' goin' on in front of it."
Seeing and hearing this stranger in their midst, the patrons had no way of
knowing this was part of the show.

"Sing the Baby Buggy Song," Frankie yelled out again as the customers
pondered their move, wondering what gives.

"How does it go?" Gene asked on the mike.

"It don't go. You have to push it."

More than once, some overgrown country boys, having come a long
way to see their movie hero in person, threatened to take Frankie outside
with the idea of teaching him some theater manners. But then, Frankie was
pretty good with the dialogue and talked his way out of it.

We all sat onstage in our respective places as Gene went though the rest
of his routine. One day, Saturday January 7, 1950, opening up in Pueblo,
Colorado, he introduced for the first time, the young lady roper/dancer. Her
name was Barbara and her act was superb. I paid no particular attention to
her first performance because I now had the opportunity to leave the stage
while the lights were down and the spotlight was thrown on both Gene and
the opening act.

Once off stage and in the wings, I was free to mosey around at will, safe
in the knowledge that I now had 30 or 40 minutes to kill before I would be
called out for my bit with the Boss.

The natural thing to do was to walk around backstage area in the
semi-darkness while listening to everything that was going on out front. All
that I could hear was the band playing for her act while the audience came
on every few minutes with scattered applause. The act sounded pretty good,
but then, there were many touring days ahead of us . . . plenty of time to get
a good look at it.

I walked by where Jay Berry was combing the horses.

"Sounds like the new act is going over great" I said to Jay who hardly
looked up. 'Better go out and take a look at it."

"You want'a grab that pitch folk and help me rake up all this horseshit?
Then we can both go take a look." His job was a rough one and we all knew
better than to get in his way.

"Match you a quarter," I said, letting him know that I was willing to
change the subject.

Jay stopped his currycombing long enough to enrich his pockets by 25
cents. I saw a good opportunity to move along and walked all the way

around to the other side of the wings. Doug Autry, Gene's brother, was standing there watching the new roper with much interest. Gene had been watching with him but was about to walk off as I approached.

"Hey, John!" said Doug. "Get a load of the new dish."

He was pointing out onto the stage where the scantily clad young dancer was going through some very fast routines with the ropes while dancing in and out of them as they twirled. She did, indeed, look very good. The fact that she was getting a lot loud response out of the paying customers made it even more interesting.

"Got a quarter you can spare?" I said to Doug as I flipped a two-bit piece in the air.

"John, "said Doug, waving me off. "Can't you see I'm busy? I gotta see this act."

"We got a lot'a shows ahead of us," I reminded him. "Lots and lots of time."

"I know, John. But you know me. I'm a fast worker. I got'a find out if she's married or not, and if not, if she wants to get married . . . you know me.

"Yeah, I know you, Doug," I said, walking away. "You will wait until she gets off stage, won't you?"

Gene was standing near his dressing room surrounded by several of the fan clubbers, signing pictures, books, anything, and something that he done for these same folks time after time. While it was his policy to permit certain members of the fan club to linger backstage if they wanted to, none of them ever got in the show free. If they chose to travel from town to town for several days in a row, they did so on their own time and expense and were never allowed to ride on the bus as some of them hoped they might be.

During the two hours required to perform the night show, Gene spent his time either on stage or in and around his dressing room, which was always situated near the stage in the wings so he could get back onstage quickly if needed. Besides Gene, there were two other people who spent a lot of time in his dressing room. One of them was Herb Green, Gene's pilot and the tour manager, who spent a great deal of time commuting between the backstage area and the ticket office up at the front of the building. The other was Colonel Eddie Hogan, a large, tall, happy individual who was in charge of the dressing room itself.

The main dressing room show was the Colonel as he rushed to and fro in one continual crisis, deep enough to cause the perspiration to flow off him like a summer rain storm. His problem? A lost shoestring, a mild spot on a newly cleaned uniform, anything out of place would get Eddie Hogan out of sorts.

If his dressing room door was closed, I stood in the wings, glancing out onto the stage from time to time (just enough to keep up with what was going on), chewing the fat with Doug, Jay and any others who lingered around. If the door was open, I would mosey nearby until I heard the invitation, "Come on in, Jonathan Q." I would enter and sit down to wait for him to finish reading the *Daily Variety* or the *Hollywood Reporter,* two trade papers that were always sent to where we were. In this manner, Gene kept up with all of the important happenings back in Hollywood. He made it a point to keep well informed.

With his door wide open, we could always hear and know exactly who and what was going on onstage. He never missed a cue. If it was Rufe, Pat or Smiley, we knew by the jokes. If it was a musical number we knew by the final song. If it was my time we would both leave together.

" O.K., Jonathan Q, its me and you. Let's go out there and stop the show. And if we can't stop it, we'll damned sure slow it down."

It is with great pride and satisfaction that I say that working as comic to Gene's 'straight man,' our act usually came off as well as any other of the great acts that he employed. With Gene Autry, how could we miss? I think he enjoyed his part as well as I did mine and his timing was about as perfect as anyone could be. He was a super showman.

Gene was very easy to work with. His disposition was always the same and he was not, as some might suppose, the temperamental type, demanding the spotlight, and such. If he had a suggestion, he made it in a gentlemanly manner, always the positive, and in a way that made us want to improve. He never put his people down. Neither did he build them up. We knew what was expected of us and were always anxious to give our all.

While Autry mulled over the trade papers, I might casually pick up a deck of cards and began shuffling them softly. In due time, depending on how interesting the Hollywood news was, he would fold the trade papers neatly, place them to his side, look at me in a sly manner and say,

"O.K., Bond. If you think you're so damned hot, deal!"

With that cue I dealt us a hand of gin rummy. Over the years, Gene and I played hundreds of hands of the game that he so dearly loved. As these games played out over the years, small, unimportant dramas unfolded near or around the door of his dressing room as we listened to the stage show progress.

The other show, usually witnessed only by Gene and myself, took place daily, town after town. One time a young mother and child, who had forced their way backstage, bypassing the police guard, rushed frantically into the dressing room. The uniformed guard, following closely on their heels, overtook them in the doorway, saying,

"I'm sorry, Mr. Autry. I tried to stop this lady . . . "

"I'm sorry too, Mr. Autry," shouted the highly nervous young woman, hanging on to her child. "But you don't know what this means to us. We just couldn't let you get out of this town without you meeting and shaking hands with my son."

The young mother, trembling with excitement, broke away from the guard's grasp, thrust her 4 or 5 year old towards Gene, who took his hand gently and said,

"Well now, I guess that's alright." He waved the officer away. "How are you Sonny?"

The child let Gene shake his hand, completely unaware of what was going on.

"Oh, Mr. Autry," the fairly good-looking mother continued, trying hard to calm herself. "You just have not idea . . . you don't know . . . why, would you believe it, when I was single, seeing you on the screen, I used to dream one day I would marry Gene Autry."

"That so?" said Gene, signing a photo for the kid, calmly handing it to him with a smile, "Well, who knows, maybe we'll get together yet."

This stopped the mother. "Well, now wait a minute. I'm already . . . what I mean is . . . that was before. . .I don't know . . . !

"There you are, young fellow, "said Gene, shaking the boy's hand gently, completely ignoring the mother. "You come back and see us again, any time."

The guard escorted the happy, but confused pair out as we resumed our gin rummy game. I neither said nor did anything throughout the entire incident. I had learned from past experience to remain in my own quiet corner until the storm subsided. It had now passed. Another would come along again tomorrow, the next day and so until the end of the tour.

"Good looking kid, that, "Gene said as he re-arranged the cards in his hand. "I wish I had a boy like that."

"I believe you could of had that 'n . . . and that mother too," I said, laughingly.

Gene merely stared at the cards in his hand. Presently, he selected a choice one, Plucked it away from the rest, then, amid a broad smile of satisfaction, he threw it, face down upon the table and said,

"Gin!"

I'd heard that so many times I really got to hate the sound of it.

♪   ♪   ♪

I don't know how or when the big fellow got there. It was quite unusual for a local stranger to be allowed to linger backstage during the show, let alone stand in the doorway of Gene's dressing room. That was a definite no-no.

This one happened to be huge; tall, country, heavy-set, gawky, shabbily dressed, and above all, totally silent. I first noticed him leaning against the open doorway while I was looking for a sucker with a quarter to lose. He was just lingering there, halfway in and halfway out of the Boss' private domain. Nobody, but nobody parked himself in that particular spot. Since I had no way of knowing, I just figured he was a friend of Gene, Herb or the Colonel. Chances are that they thought he was someone that I had invited in. In order to get in and out of the dressing room, we had to go around the brute who continued his silent vigil all during the show.

Gene and I played several hands of gin as our visitor stood there watching us.

"Well, it sounds as though I'd better get ready for the horse act," said Gene, laying his cards down, beginning to change his costume.

While Gene changed, it was my usual custom to make my exit from the Boss' room to the wings. As I squeezed past the hefty visitor standing in the doorway, I excused myself, but did not hurry on my way. Something told me that he was about to speak his first words. I was right. As Gene sought out a very fancy pair of footwear, removed the others and put the new ones upon his feet, the big country boy, shifted his excess weight from one foot to the other, cleared his throat carefully and said,

"Hey, Gene. I'll throw you fer them boots."

Had there been a larger crowd of our troupe around, Pat, Rufe, Smiley, Carl, Frankie, and some of the others, I am certain that the visitor's straight line would have received an audience type of response. As it was, I had already left the room and was technically out of range. This left Gene, and Gene alone, to hear the line and to make any comment necessary.

There was none. He put his boots on and left to do the horse act. We never saw the man anymore.

"That fellow was going to throw you for your boots," I told Gene later. Gene just looked at his cards. "Think I'll add him to my list of names," I said.

"If you do you'll have to rub his name out," said Gene Autry immediately before announcing,

"Gin!"

♫   ♫   ♫

One comment from Gene that I heard almost daily was, "Bond, you can b e replaced."

It was always uttered in jest and never meant to be serious. I tried to come up with an answer for it but never did, so the only thing left for me to do was to use it on him if the opportunity ever presented itself. It did one day in Harrisburg, Pennsylvania.

Local musical groups would often come down to the hotel hoping to see Gene in person. When they learned that he was either busy or out on the town, they usually called me hoping that they would eventually get to him that way.

"All we want to do is to audition for him," one group informed me.

"Come to the stage entrance of the auditorium this afternoon and I'll see what I can do" was my usual reply, remembering the times several years earlier when Jimmy, Scotty and I had made the same request.

The matinee was in full swing and so was our gin rummy game when I got the word that the band was outside, waiting to get in. I asked Gene if he would care to hear the boys and he said, "Sure, what the hell. Run 'em back here."

The word was sent out. Presently, here came half-a-dozen local musicians, instruments, costumes and all, ready to sing and play for Gene Autry in his dressing room.

After double-checking the show on stage to determine how much time he had, Gene told the boys to go to it while he and I continued our card game. The boys sang one song with broad grins upon their faces as they went through it,

"I'm back in the saddle again,
Out where a friend is a friend . . . "

Playing Gene's theme song for him was one thing, but deliberately trying to imitate the Star was another. The very last thing that he would want to hear was someone else who, try as they may, sounded like he did. Gene hardly looked up during the performance. When it was concluded he extended his hand to all of the members individually and thanked them, saying,

"That was real fine, fellows, real fine. Now, why don't you boys go out front and watch the rest of the show." They took the hint and left, seemingly disappointed in the fact that Gene Autry had failed to recognize his vocal stand-in.

As we resumed our game of gin, I waited through a long moment of silence to see if he was going to make any comment. He did not.

My time had come. I said, "Mr. Autry, you can be replaced."

"Yeah," he answered, still not looking up from his cards. "Who by?"

♫   ♫   ♫

Often, a lot of the traffic in and out of the Boss' dressing room was Herb Green with the local sponsors of the show discussing certain aspects of the evening's procedures. To these ins and outs, ups and downs of the business end of the show, I pretended to turn a deaf ear by concentrating on my gin rummy hand.

More than once, Herb ushered in one (or more) unhappy member of the Lion's Club or the Good Fellow Charities, members of the committee who brought the show to their particular city.

"Mr. Autry," said one disgruntled local character. "You got one hell of a show."

"Thank you, Mr. Jones," said Gene, after giving the man a cordial greeting and a comfortable chair. "We try to please."

"And we got one hell of a crowd out there."

"Looks pretty good, does it?"

"Sure, but you are making all the money, and we're standing all of the expense." Gene had heard this line before and I knew his answer already.

"How's that?" Gene asked the man.

"Well," said the almost angry Lion. "You come in here . . . get us to sponsor and push your show . . . and you give us a small percentage of the gate, out of which we have to furnish this expensive auditorium, six weeks of advertising, janitors and roustabouts, plus a whole lot of other expenses. You get the lion's share of the money and we do good if we break even. You drive one hell of a bargain, don't you, Mr. Autry?"

"You really think so?" asked Gene, laying for the man.

"I know so. What the hell. We'll do well to come out of it without going into the red, while you take a bundle of our money out of our town."

"You guys accepted the deal, didn't you? Nobody twisted your arm."

"Sure, sure! The committee is star struck. 'Let's buy the show! Who cares if we make a dime?' Well, I care. I voted against you but they overrode me."

"Let me tell you something, Mr. Jones," said Gene, laying his cards face down as I tried to turn away from the scene. "You think you fellows got a raw deal?"

"I know we did."

"Did you happen to count the number of people that I brought in here with me?" Gene asked the man, looking him squarely in the eye with a stolid face.

"Did you ever try paying Smiley Burnette's salary for a week. We got a lot of expensive people on this show. They demand a lot of money out'a me. (In my corner I nodded my head slightly) How much do you think it costs me to transport those two horses, not to mention the groom's salary? We bought one hell of a bunch of newspaper and radio advertising in your town . . . you never thought of that, did you? How many uniformed policemen do you think I had to employ? Your people! How much insurance do you think we had to take out in your city? What'a you think that Greyhound Bus costs me? With a driver, yet. How much local city taxes do you guys charge me over and above your percentage? Did it ever occur to you that I could have stayed home in Hollywood, making pictures or radio appearances with Bing Crosby or somebody and you and your committee would be sitting here around your table wondering what you could do to stir up some action? Why do you think all of those people out there turned out for this show? Why? Because you and your lazy Lions never give them any reason to get off of their lazy asses. Go along and die a slow death doing nothing, that's the motto of most of your cities back here." After that, Gene returned to his card game and let the man soak it all in.

"Now, wait a minute, Gene. I didn't mean . . ."

"I know, you just didn't think."

"I guess you have a pretty good nut here at that."

"Suppose we run into some weather and have a couple of washouts. My expense goes on just the same."

"It does at that, don't it?"

Gene concentrated on the cards while the man arose from his chair, slowly, cautiously.

"No hard feeling, Gene. I was just . . ."

"Oh, by the way," Autry interrupted him. "We'll be coming back, this way again next year. Do you guys want the show again or would you prefer that we turn it over to the Rotarians?"

"No, no!" said the man, quickly. "Don't do that. We'll take it. What the hell, we're not in business to make money. Break even! That's our motto. We'll take it. Next time I'll even vote for it myself."

The Lion went out like a Lamb while Gene and I returned to our card game.

"Gin!"

♪　　♪　　♪

Violence never erupted during any of the Autry tours, but it came close a couple of times. I had heard that Gene would sock a guy if you made him mad enough, but I only saw it happen once off the screen. The concessions, or, the selling of programs, photographs and other goodies was part of the show and, naturally, the rights belonged to Gene Autry. Before we knew what was happening, outsiders had begun to move in on the action for it was difficult for the backers themselves to know who belonged and who didn't. Whenever it was pointed out to Gene that the freeloaders were coming on with their candy and balloons, Gene took legal action to have them stopped. This was easier said than done since we were only in the town for one day and seldom can the tired arm of the law move that fast. Also, once the authorities started moving in on the bad guys, they couldn't tell a good pitchman from the others. You take a dozen or so vendors, walking up and down in front of and around a huge auditorium surrounded by thousands of local fans and face the fact . . . who's who and what's what?

Somehow, Autry finally found a way to put the pressure on the intruders, who, little by little, began to fade away. However, one particular tough guy refused to roll over and play dead and proceeded to burst into the dressing room with the information that Autry was a son-of-a bitch, depriving him of his right to make an honest living.

Words were tossed around between the two until their voices began to get louder and louder. When the villain informed Gene that he was going back outside to sell his wares, the law-be-damned, Gene pulled back and let the big fellow have it full in the face. A hard fist usually reserved for the screen's bad guys!

Needless to say, that one bothered us no more, I think the incident scared me more than it did Gene. After all, wasn't he risking an assault and battery charge? Wouldn't I be called in as star witness against my own boss and friend? It was a great relief to move on down the road to the next stop on the schedule.

♫   ♫   ♫

Some local unions are a little empire unto themselves. The mere fact that Autry paid all of his employees well above scale meant nothing to some of the city union bosses. The show came under the jurisdiction of several different unions. Many of us were musicians . . . the dancers were A.G.V.A . . . then there were stagehands . . . Jay Berry was a teamster, and so on down the line. Most of the time, whenever a local union situation came up, Herb Green or one of the other advance men settled it in advance by

Still, there were occasions where a very strong "one-man-union" might cause a minor confrontation. Almost always these things were settled peacefully, to the satisfaction of all parties concerned. Not so, the case in one Eastern City.

"Mr. Autry," said Herb Green to our boss in his dressing room immediately after we arrived and started unpacking. "It looks like we might have to hire a large orchestra here."

"I don't need a large orchestra," said Gene. Something we'd all heard him say many times over. "I have my own orchestra. They know my show. I thought you usually paid off these local Czars and let it go at that."

"Yes, sir," replied Herb, diplomatically. "However, this particular gentleman who runs the local here . . . well, I don't know how to say it, but, frankly, I don't think he likes hillbillies or screen cowboys . . . his words, you understand."

"I've seen a million of them. Tell him we're not hillbillies. We're artists."

"I've already told him that. I also told him that we were willing to allow for a certain number of stand-by musicians but that his demands were out of line. He insists that we put his men on our stage."

"You goddamned right you're going to put my men on your stage," said the union man, bursting in through Gene's dressing room door, unannounced and uninvited. "What's more, you'll have an orchestra, the likes of which you've never heard before."

"That so," said Gene to the man without formal introductions. "I suppose they've all got uniforms, too?"

"You dammed right, they have. Most all of them have their own tuxedos."

"We don't use tuxedos," said Gene. "We have our own costumes. What's more, I have my own band. Here, take this gentleman out to the box office . . . call up Petrillo if you have to . . . pay them for a logical number of standby musicians and let us put on our own show."

The man left with Herb and we prepared for our matinee. At 4:20, the union man burst into the room again.

"Didn't you get squared away with Herb?" asked Gene.

"Hell no, we didn't get squared away. My men are here and ready to go on stage with your show."

"We don't want your men," said Autry, color beginning to show in his face. "Now, you take your big orchestra and get out of our way. If you want to call a hearing before the National Board, go to it. Right now we've got a show to do."

"Are you refusing to put my men on your stage?"

"That's right," said Gene, angrily.

"Very well," said the union man. "You've made your decision. In that case I can't allow the show to go on."

"Listen here, my friend," said Gene Autry, moving his face up close to the man's. "There's several thousand people, school children, out front. They've come here and paid their money to see my show and by God, they're going to see it."

"Not without my orchestra!"

"Without your orchestra! Now get out of our way."

"You're not going to put this show on," said the man, defiantly, almost laughing in Gene's face. "I'm telling you, you're not going on."

"And I'm telling you we are," said Gene, pointing the barrel of his silver-plated revolver under the man's nose. "Our curtain is about to go up."

The man stuttered and stammered as he felt the cold-steel pressing against his face. He looked down at the gun, backed away from Gene, pointed to the firearm and said, "Y — y — you wouldn't dare!"

"There's one way to find out," said the singing cowboy.

"Well, to hell with that," said the man, turning to make his quick exit. "This job's not worth getting shot over. We'll settle this thing later." With that, he took off for parts unknown.

Gene replaced the six-shooter in his holster, turned to the few of us who had stood silently, nervously throughout the entire incident, and said, "Let's go out there and put on a show,"

We did just that. Naturally, this was not the end of the incident. It was settled later behind closed doors by the proper authorities. I was not present.

♫   ♫   ♫

Backstage during all of the one-niters, something different and unexpected was going on all the time. These are merely a few samples.

The final curtain fell anywhere between 10:30 and 11:00 P.M. Was our day over? Not by a long shot.

CHAPTER FIFTEEN

Our Day Is Ending

*Or, Did You See Gene Sock That Guy
Or, Lay That Pistol Down, Gene!*

Getting out of the auditorium and back to our hotel was an experience within itself. Practically all of the men, women, children, and single girls with a gleaming eye, who had just seen the show, were now looking for the star himself. They rushed backstage; they encircle the building, the bus, the horses trailer, making every attempt to get to him that they could possibly think of. They thought that if they couldn't locate their Hero, they could take a short cut through one of us.

Many times we would worm our way through the crowd, saying to those asking for Gene, "I think he went that-a-way!" which sometimes worked and sometimes didn't. Anything to break loose and climb aboard the bus where none of them could follow, no matter how hard they tried.

As Mac closed the bus door after calling out, "All aboard," Gene Autry might very well come out from behind the many costumes hanging in the back of the bus and say, "Let's get the hell out of here."

"I didn't see you come in here," somebody said. "How in the hell did you do it?"

"Oh, damned if I know," said the sneaky Autry, grinning like a 'possum eating pumpkin through a picket fence.' "Just get this thing on back to the hotel before that mob gets there. Hey, Mac!" Gene raised his voice. "Know where you're going?"

"Nope, don't believe I do!" came back the answer from a dozen different sources.

Once in the hotel lobby where the crowd of fans was not quite so large or boisterous, Gene would usually stop for a while, sign autographs and speak to many of the local dignitaries and their families before excusing himself after working his way to the vicinity of the elevator.

One particular entrance into a hotel lobby stands out as being so completely different from the others and gives one more example of the man's subtle character and presence of mind in the face of a very, very mild crisis.

The weather in upper New York State had been particularly atrocious that February. Carl, Frankie and I got stuck in a blizzard between Elmira and Utica. Gene and Herb had flown into the same storm, winding up with a very tricky landing. Finally, we were all in Troy but the weather still hadn't let up. While this hadn't hurt our paid attendance too much, the local folks being used to it, it had cut down on the clamoring of the fans between and after the shows.

As Gene, Carl, Herb and I, and a couple of others, strolled into the lobby of the Hendrick Hudson Hotel just after midnight, Gene turned to us with the comment that the lobby was deserted. Most unusual.

"Just look outside," said Herb. The blizzard was raging.

"Seems funny, " said Gene, looking around at the empty premises. "Its just so unusual seeing nobody in the lobby. Looks like we're the only ones here."

"Even the desk clerk is back by the stove," said Carl.

"Well, Ace," Gene said slyly. "Guess you won't be going out on the prowl tonight."

"Nope," replied Ace sheepishly. "Guess she'll just have to do without me tonight."

"Anybody for a quick bite to eat?" Gene asked, looking around some more. He could have fired his cannon.

"I could use a bite," we all said at the same time.

"I had a swell Prime Rib dinner in here between shows," Gene said, walking over toward the desk.

He found the clerk who informed him that everything was closed . . . room service included.

"I'll be damned," said Gene, walking back to our vicinity.

"Looks like they just turned off the lights in the dining room," Herb said, pointing out the several chairs having been placed upside down on some of the tables.

"Did you ever see anything more dismal than all those chair legs pointing toward the ceiling?" someone asked. All agreed.

We walked toward the entrance to the dining room, which was quite dark and seemingly deserted. A lady in the back of the room, spotting the cowboy star, walked over and opened one of the swinging doors.

"Good evening, Mr. Autry," she said, smiling at meeting the popular entertainer again.

"How are you?" Gene asked. "Understand you're closed."

"Just a few minutes ago," said the lady. "Sorry you couldn't have come in earlier."

"Well, our show ran a little long tonight."

"All of my family saw the matinee," she said. "They all enjoyed it immensely."

"Thank you," said Gene, searching for an opening. "You won't tell them that we all starved to death tonight, will you?"

"What?" the woman laughed. "Surely things aren't as bad as that. We have some all-night restaurants around town; that is, if you're really that hungry."

"Why, I wouldn't send Roy Rogers out on a night like this," Gene said, looking over toward the outside windows. We could see the driving snow coming down hard. The temperature had to be zero or lower.

"Of course," said the woman. "I wish I could help you. Everything in the kitchen is closed down. All the help is gone, the food is locked up in the refrigerator . . . I'm so sorry."

"You wouldn't let a few tired cowboys sit down at one of your tables for a minute, would you?" From the tone of Gene's voice, we could see it coming.

"You . . . sit down?" said the lady, not thinking to ask why we didn't choose the lobby sofas instead. "Why, of course you may sit here if you wish. I was just closing up. They won't be picking me up for a few minutes yet."

We sat down at a bare table with blank faces.

"May I bring you some water?" the lady asked.

"That'd help a lot," said Herb. Herb drank lots of water.

"How about some cold milk?" Gene said.

"I guess so," said the woman, walking away.

"What'a you boys want to eat?" Gene asked us, after he saw that she was out of sight.

"If we get fed here tonight, it'll be a miracle" I said.

"Don't bet against it," said Gene.

"They got some back there," smiled Gene. "I can smell it."

The lady brought us glasses of water and milk. "Both of them ought to be cold enough tonight," she said, putting it all before us.

"You wouldn't have any tomatoes hidden away in that ice box, would you?" Gene asked, smiling his sweetest smile at the lady.

"Tomatoes? You want tomatoes? Cold tomatoes?" she thought for a minute. "Well, I guess we don't heat them, do we? Sure, I could bring out some sliced tomatoes, I guess."

"What about a head of lettuce?" Gene asked. "There ought to be some of that left over."

"A head of lettuce?"

"And some mayonnaise."

The woman looked at us all, smiled and walked away toward the kitchen. It was obvious that she had never served anyone in this manner before.

"Where's that tray they keep all the Catsup crap?" asked Gene, looking around during her absence.

The tray was spotted and pointed out. Gene jumped up, ran over to it, and came back with a handful of bottles of condiments . . . catsup, A-1, Tabasco sauce, the works, setting them down in the center of our table. "Anybody see a bowl around?"

A bowl was produced from out of the darkness, as was some silverware. Gene began opening all of the bottles, pouring the contents into the one bowl.

"Here's your head of lettuce and some tomatoes," said the lady upon her return. She stopped quickly when she saw what Gene was doing. "What in the world . . . ?"

"Shhh!" said Gene, placing a finger to his lips. "Don't tell anybody! My own invention. My own concoction. A brand new salad dressing."

"Really?" the woman hesitated. I think the light at the end of the tunnel was beginning to shine through as she displayed a slight smile at all of us.

"You didn't happen to see any carrots, celery or onions when you opened that ice box door did you?" Gene asked, quite seriously.

The woman stopped cold for a brief moment, smiled again, and said, "Carrots, celery and onions coming right up." Once more she walked away.

"Give that knife," said Gene, beginning to slice the head of lettuce into equal pieces. "This is just the weather for some Icebergs, right?"

"Right!" we agreed, preparing to dig in.

"Try some of my special slumgullion on those tomatoes and lettuce," said Gene, passing it around. He even added some of the mayonnaise to it. It didn't look so hot in the dim light, but it tasted swell.

The dining room hostess returned with the rest of the requested vegetables.

"Well, I'll say one thing, Mr. Autry," she said, spreading the food around. "I've never served a midnight snack quite like this one before."

"Ever been in show business?"

"No."

"That's why," said Gene. "Stick around. You'll learn."

"I never tried cold vegetables with Catsup and Tabasco before."

"That sure was a delicious Prime Rib you served me for dinner earlier," said Gene.

"Wasn't it, though?"

"I suppose you sold out?"

"Sold out?" said the woman, slightly startled. "Why, yes . . . I mean, we sold all that was ordered . . . the rest . . . "

"You mean you've got some Prime Rib back there, too?"

"I guess so. But it would be cold. Now, don't tell me you want some cold meat too?"

Gene looked up at the woman, smiled sweetly, clasped his palms together, and said, "You wouldn't run the butt end of that old steer out here, would you?"

The lady looked at us all again. 'They're all starving maniacs,' she probably thought. At any rate, she took off again and returned with the solid hunk of meat, which was carved for us so nobly by our boss.

The midnight snack was delicious. Gene slipped the lady a greenback of some unknown denomination, thanked her on behalf of the group, after which we retired to our respective rooms.

Through our hotel room window I watched the blizzard blow across the city of Troy, New York, as certain thoughts raced through my mind. It wasn't so much the getting of the meal that enthralled me as it was the smooth manner in which it came about.

Most people, including myself, would have taken 'no' for an answer and retired unfed. Gene Autry knew that he held certain prestige and powers of persuasion in his hands. There are many big stars who would have pounded on the clerk's desk, shouting loud threats until satisfaction was achieved. In Autry's mind there had to be but one thought: results . . . and the smoothest, quietest way to get there.

I pulled my blinds and went to bed . . . well fed.

♫   ♫   ♫

Most days on the tours ended in a more routine manner. Finish the show . . . hit the sack for the few hours remaining before the early alarm sounds signaling that it is time to start all over again. Another town, another show, more adventures backstage and around the bus.

If the weather permitted, Ace usually grabbed a couple of the other musicians and went out on the town to take in a bit of the local nightlife. Full reports were forthcoming on the bus the following day. No matter what Ace told us, we never quite believed it all.

"I sure hope she doesn't write me at home," Ace would say, trying to make up for some lost sleep along the way.

During the later years of the tours, Gene began inviting the full troupe to his hotel suite after the last show. Here we would be treated to food and drink as we engaged in a lot of small talk. Gene loved all of his people and seemed to want us around him more and more. Unlike a lot of other headliners, Gene never 'rode' his people about their act. These occasions were always happy ones and that was the way he made us all feel.

We, in turn, made it a point to try and make him feel good. This was often done by pointing out that his show continued to 'turn them away' at the box office.

"Yep," he would always say, smiling. "I think we broke even today."

One night, after a late show in Cleveland, Ohio, Gene, Carl, Frankie and I were walking down a side street. A wino, lingering in the shadows, seeing the Cowboy in a big white hat, spoke up in an insulting manner.

"Well, well. Looky who's here? If it ain't the old purty boy, hisself." He continued his chatter with more uncomplimentary remarks until Gene had to stop and confront him face to face.

"You got something to say to me, mister?"

"Yeah!" said the bum. "You're the great Gene Autry, ain't you?"

"What about it?"

"You know sumthin'? You can't sing. You can't act. You can't even play the guitar."

"That's right, my friend," said Gene, his face getting redder in the faint light. "I admit it. I can't act. I can't sing. I can't play the guitar . . . and I've got twenty-five million dollars to prove it."

Gene pushed the bum gently back into his shadows after which we continued on to our hotel.

♫   ♫   ♫

During all of his touring years, there were at least a half-a-dozen occasions which required the cowboy to leave immediately after the night show for some type of business meeting in another city. More than once, Herb Green came to me, asking me not to check into the hotel where the troupe was staying.

"The Boss has to fly out for Chicago tonight and we'd like for you to come along with us. Bring your guitar."

This change of routine almost always met with my approval, for it was interesting to learn what he might have up his sleeve next. I knew that he was talking television to the Wrigley people, and some of us in the group had been bending his ear a bit to try and get him to book some of his tours in places where we hadn't played so much. Canada, Hawaii, Mexico . . . London!

Also, I knew that it would probably be just Gene, Herb and myself, which meant another opportunity to talk to the man, just the two of us.

Once we got in the air. . .Herb up front, piloting Gene's plane, the boss and I would lean back while I looked around for a deck of cards. They were always there. So was his portable bar from which he would pour a couple as we sailed along.

"Well, Jonathan Q," he would most often begin. "What do you think about the overall situation?"

"I think we broke even again today," I said, beating him to the line. After he nodded his agreement, I continued, "Think you'll ever get tired of this grind?"

"Oh, hell, we're young. We can take it."

I always knew that one was coming.

"Besides," Gene continued, indicating that I should go ahead and deal the cards. "I can't afford to let these tours tire me out. I know a lot of the guys are beginning to complain about them, but what would they be doing back home? I do these tours because I like them. A fellow has to get it while he can. When you cool off, you're a long time cold! Remember that. Another thing. I need the cash to pay my income taxes. I make eight pictures a year, that's only sixteen weeks of work, well, what the hell, I'm not about to sit around Hollywood and starve to death." (I have repeated this 'starve to death' conversation to a few people in confidence over the years. It never fails to get a laugh since few people can even comprehend the thought that the popular Gene Autry might go out that way.)

These private conversations with the Boss were especially interesting to me since Gene was usually not one to let his hair down and talk much along these lines. It was only after the few slugs that we poured for each other that he began to open up.

"You take Tom Mix," Autry said. "He and Buck Jones, Art Acord, Ken Maynard and a lot of other western actors . . . they made money but they all died broke. That's not going to happen to me. I was born broke and I stayed that way all of my early life. I don't like it and I don't plan on going back to it. (He tapped on the table). I've got me a way of making money now and I aim to make all I can . . . while I can. Money is the only thing that people respect in the world and I enjoy commanding respect." As he paused to rearrange his gin rummy hand, I remained silent to see if he was finished. "Besides, all of you bastards are making good money too, don't you ever forget that!

"Money talks, alright. No doubt about that," I said. What else was there to say?

"One thing's for certain, though," Gene continued. "I've got to make a lot of changes in this show." This revelation startled me since it was the first time that this type of thinking had been mentioned. "We're going to have to put a little more class into the show. I don't want us to stay corny like that damn Grand Ole Opry bunch. Why they're still wearing those hick costumes, straw hats, corncob pipes, same sort of stuff they've been doing since the twenties. They never improve. We've got to keep up with the times. Now you take that stuff that Pat Buttram and Frankie Marvin are doing. . .that's just a plain old hillbilly act, too damn corny. I might have to have them change that. I've asked Frankie to get rid of that washboard time after time.

"While we're on the subject of costumes," I said. "You know, I'm still wearing the hick shirt and slouch hat. I'll be glad to change them if you want me to."

"OK," Gene said. "Why don't you switch to a regular western costume?"

"I'll do it tomorrow," I told him. "I've been wanting to drop the hillbilly character anyway."

"Sure. We can still do the same routine."

On through the night we soared toward Chicago, where he closed the deal to begin his TV show. One thing about those films . . . they would have class. Gene always told us, "For a little bit more, you can go first class."

♪   ♪   ♪

Only on rare occasions, perhaps once or twice per tour, were we subjected to an all-night ride on the bus. As mentioned earlier, one of our schedules has us opening in Pueblo, Colorado, January 7, 1950. (This was where Doug Autry spied the pretty young dancer/roper doing her thing on stage.) The following stop was Denver where we were instructed not to check in a hotel because Hutchinson, Kansas, next on the list, was too far away, making it necessary for us to leave immediately after the show in Denver.

During the two shows in Denver, Doug continued his admiration of the new act, calling several of us to the wings to see if we agreed with his opinion. We did.

After closing that night, we all wormed our was through the crowd of fans, boarded the bus and saluted the driver with our familiar "know where you're going, Mac?"

"Shore do," came the answer. "Goin' to Hutchinson, Kansas and its one hell of a long way. Goodnight, everybody."

Just because we got the 'goodnight' salutation from the driver didn't necessarily mean that everybody was going to start sawing logs immediately. Up and down the aisle of the Greyhound, several small worlds began to take shape.

In the far rear, Carl, Frankie, Rufe and I, along with one or two others managed to construct a poker table, which would fit between the backs of the two seats, stretching across the aisle where the cards were out and the chips were down. This game would last until the wee hours, long after the border of Kansas had come and gone beneath our wheels.

Doug Autry was most conspicuous with his absence from the game. Usually, he was one of the first to sit down. It wasn't long until we discovered the reason for this.

A seat or two ahead of us, Fred Martin and a couple of the Pinafores engaged in small talk while trying to catch up on their reading. The Indians, the Strongs and the Knapps were usually the first to turn out their lights and try for slumber.

There were several new members on this particular tour; our old stage hand quit and we were now in the process of getting acquainted with his replacement, Sid. Sid had situated himself in one of the seats near the poker game where he was an observer but not a participant. In the seats directly ahead of him were two more newcomers, identical twin sisters who put on a very colorful dance act. I think Sid must have pulled the curls of the one for we saw her turn around and give him a few discouraging words. To this Sid only smiled and played dumb as if he knew not what was bugging the girl.

We soon noted that the other newcomer, Barbara, had taken the very front seat directly behind the driver. In the same seat, close to her side, we discovered Doug Autry.

"I wondered what had happened to Doug," said a poker player.

"It was too dark up front to see Doug, but I did recognize his overcoat."

"Doesn't he ever take that thing off?"

"Shut up and deal."

"I'll open and bet twenty that he never takes the coat off."

"How do you know?"

"Don't it look slept in?"

"I raise."

"You might know he's be sitting next to the new rope act."

"How do you think he'll make out?"

"Doug's a fast worker . . . we ought a know pretty soon."

It must have been between two and three in the morning when one of the twins nearby turned and slapped Sid full on the face. About that same time the entire bus was shaken halfway off the road by a blood-curdling scream from up front.

"Looks like Doug's working a little slower than usual," remarked one of the poker players.

"How can you talk like that when it sounds as though somebody was screaming bloody murder?"

It was the new girl, Barbara, who had given out with the loud expression of displeasure. Lights came on in the bus and the driver inquired if he should stop or not.

"Hell no, don't stop," Doug said, standing up, turning around to adjust his overcoat. "Hells fire, she's not hurt."

The girl continued her hysterics as Doug walked down the aisle to the poker game.

"What'd you do to that pore girl?"

"Nothing."

"How come she's so loud?"

"Well you know women."

Later, her version was that she had taken one of the few vacant front seats and had tried to get some sleep when, according to her, Doug had seated himself beside her, uninvited, and proceeded to get familiar with both hands and dialog. Three or four times she claimed that she had commanded him to behave but that he had persisted. In fact, he got so familiar that she could no longer put up with these advances and, thus, the loud screams.

After several of us came up to console her, the young lady calmed down. Doug denied any out-of-the-way maneuvers. The remainder of the bus ride brought no further disturbances. Afterwards, we learned that she had gone straight to Gene with her complaints when we pulled up to the auditorium in Hutchison. She was so nervous and upset that she missed a couple of shows. His brother, of course called Doug, on the carpet.

As the bus rolled on down the highways, day after day, week after week, Barbara continued to give Doug the cold shoulder while he searched for a new and warmer approach. Little by little, we could see the icicles beginning to melt. After about two weeks, they were sharing the front seat again.

Things between Sid and the twin sister got much worse before they got better. The names that they called him in our presence would be cut from an "X" rated movie, let alone this narrative. Still, there eventually came a thaw there as well as the bus moved on into upper New England where the weather got colder and the bus interior got warmer.

We had a saying that anything can happen on a warm bus. Ace got a letter from home informing him of his impending divorce.

"I told that broad not to write me at home," said Ace, disgustedly.

"Serves you right for foolin' around with an educated woman," said Frankie, leaning on Carl.

On February 13, 1950 in Bangor, Maine, same tour, the entire Autry troupe was handed invitations to a wedding to take place immediately after the last show. Doug and Barbara made a beautiful couple. During the ceremonies, Sid and the twin announced that they, too, would soon be tying the knot.

Several years later poor Doug died of TB in the Veteran's Hospital in the San Fernando Valley. His widow, Barbara Autry, continued performing her roping/dancing act for a number of years.

And the bus rolled on.

What else can I say?

It was quite a day.

And tomorrow it would be done all over again.

And again,

And again!

For almost 10 years.

CHAPTER SIXTEEN

Jingle, Jingle, Jingle

Or, ". . . too many reindeer flying around now."
Or, "Boy, Was His Nose Red!"

The wide popularity of Gene Autry on photograph records dates back to October 9, 1929, when he recorded his very first discs for Victor. Two years and twenty-five recording sessions later he turned out his first big hit, "That Silver Haired Daddy of Mine," in New York under the direction of Uncle Art Satherly. This record enjoyed best-seller status in spite of the fact that it was released and sold during the depression hard times.

My first opportunity to play guitar for him on one of his recording sessions came on June 18, 1941 in the CBS Studios of Hollywood, California. That day he recorded "You Are My Sunshine," "It Makes No Difference Now," "After Tomorrow" and "A Year Ago Tonight." This was almost a year after we had been hired for his radio show. From that date forward, I was called for almost all of his subsequent sessions as long as he continued to record.

In 1947, he released his first big Christmas hit, "Here Comes Santa Clause," which became even more popular the following year after the song had been 'covered' by such popular recording artists as Bing Crosby, The Andrew Sisters, Doris Day, Red Foley and many others.

In 1949, a young New Yorker by the name of Johnny Marks wrote a Christmas song and mailed it out to Gene in Hollywood. This number not only would enhance the record career of the Singing Cowboy, it would change the course of the music industry itself concerning Holiday Music and recordings.

Songwriters all over the country were bringing and mailing their manuscripts and demonstration records to the singer who must have considered hundreds of Christmas songs during the summer of 1949. His policy was to take them home where he could study them carefully with his wife, Ina Mae, whose opinion he respected greatly.

When the time approached for him to record another Christmas song, we learned that he had two songs that he wrote which he was quite fond of, "Santa, Santa, Santa" and "He's a Chubby Little Fellow." Another he was considering was entitled, "If It Doesn't Snow On Christmas." If, on the recording session, there were time to get in the traditional fourth song, he would record the Johnny Marks composition, "Rudolph The Red Nosed Reindeer."

Autry has often admitted in public that he had some misgivings about recording "Rudolph . . . "

"What the hell," he is supposed to have said privately. "There's too many reindeer flying around now. How many kids can get further than Dancer and Prancer? Who say's we need another reindeer?"

"Look at it this way," said Ina Mae, tactfully. "Think about the old story of the Ugly Duckling. The others kicked him around, drawing sympathy in his direction. Rudolph is the underdog. I think you ought to give it a try."

In the meantime, something was taking place at Columbia Records that would have had a serious bearing upon both Gene and Rudolph. Long Playing Records had now come into being, and Gene's two-year sales of "Here Comes Santa Clause," had prompted Columbia to put his records into two different categories — the straight country ballads to be produced by another producer. They wanted the Cowboy to record a ten-inch Long Playing record called "Stampede" for the 1949 Holiday Season. This was a story with songs and sound effects on the same order of the skits he was still doing on the *Melody Ranch* Broadcast. This would be the follow-up to "Here Comes Santa Clause"

We were alerted to stand by for at least three sessions with our Boss in June and August of 1949. In the first session, the Christmas session, everything came off to Gene's satisfaction except Rudolph and the new producer. "Stampede" was put down successfully. However, "He's a Chubby Little Fellow" and "Santa, Santa, Santa," were recorded over and over again. We thought we would never get the 'takes' to the producer's satisfaction, but finally we did.

Much of the allotted time was given to these two numbers. Then, with time running out and a pending feud brewing between the singer and the new producer, we began to wonder if we were going to even complete this session at all. There were still two songs to go with little time in which to do them. "If It Doesn't Snow On Christmas" was tried next and came off beautifully. Then the dam almost broke. Gene and the new producer got into some kind of an argument causing the Star to almost walk out. A second man from Columbia, being present, persuaded the producer to leave and the session proceeded. The thing was, we only had fifteen to twenty minutes left. Not nearly enough time to make a good take, but too much time to leave unused. (They never like to go over-time if they could help it.)

"What the hell," said Gene, trying to shrug off his little spat with the New Yorker recently departed. "It's only that Rudolph thing. Let's run it through once for size. You can even record the rehearsal if you want to."

"Rudolph The Red Nosed Reindeer" was a first 'take'. Ordinarily, as in the case of most other favorite songs, it should have been re-recorded several times due to certain technicalities as far as music balance and voicing is concerned.

"That's it!" came our instructions over the studio control room speaker. "Wrap it up." (No overtime today)

This then is the manner in which Rudolph was first discovered and recorded. He almost didn't make it on the wax. The neon-snouted, long-horned quadruped was almost stranded at the North Pole for the duration.

"Stampede" was released on a Long Playing Special record since there was nothing in it to confine it to the Holiday Season ahead. On September 19, 1949, "Rudolph The Red Nosed Reindeer" was coupled with "If It Doesn't Snow On Christmas," while Gene's favorites, "He's a Chubby Little Fellow" and "Santa, Santa, Santa" were coupled back to back on a separate release. A few accomplishments:

1. Gene Autry's version sold over 8 million copies in the first 25 years.
2. Over four hundred other artists have recorded it.
3. Over one hundred millions records by all artists were sold around the world in the first 25 years.
4. It was the only record ever to be number one simultaneously on Pop, Country and Most Played DJ record charts in trade magazines.

It seems ironical to note that within seven years, in spite of this and many other sensational records sales that Gene Autry had with Columbia Records during his twenty-five years in their camp, his option would be allowed to drop for, shall we say, lack of sales?

"Oh well," as Gene would often say. "That's the way the old ball bounces."

CHAPTER SEVENTEEN

The Sailing Fifties

Or, Top of the Mountain,
Or, Where Do We Go From Here?

It was during the years 1950, 1951 and 1952 that Gene Autry reached the pinnacle of his success. If he wasn't a household name prior to the birth and rapid development of "Rudolph The Red Nosed Reindeer, he was now. As everyone knows, Santa Claus visits every home everywhere. Both Gene and the new addition to Santa's sleigh were welcome guests in homes scattered throughout the four corners.

He had been turning out hit records for more than 20 years. Now, with the advent of the Long Playing Records (developed by Columbia Records), long forgotten masters recorded by Gene in days gone by were now being re-released and some early hits re-recorded using the new and better sound that these unbreakable discs produced.

Nor was Rudolph the only new addition to the attractions of the Holidays. "Peter Cottontail" was born, adding to the soaring record sales by Gene Autry. A new trend came along and the world loved every groove of it. A touch of this newfound prosperity rubbed off on me in a roundabout way. When Gene recorded "Peter Cottontail," he came to me with the request for a song to put on the "B" Side. (In these years the record industry would send their new single releases to radio disc jockeys on a 45 record, the anticipated "hit" on the "A" Side, another song on the "B" Side. In the business, the "B" Side was referred to as a 'free ride,' since the song sold as many records as the "A" Side, even though it usually remained relatively obscure.) He even suggested a title to write up, which I did on the bus as we sped along the icy highways. "The Funny Little Bunny With the Powder Puff Tail," unknown, unheralded and even

February 17, 1951, Gene on stage at the *Prince Albert Grand Ole Opry*.
Left to right: Ernie Newton, bass; Augie Clevenger, accordion; Merle Travis; Tommy
Vaden, fiddle; Gene Autry; Johnny Bond; Carl Smith; Grant Turner, Opry announcer; and
Jack Stapp, Program Director.

unsung, save the one time performance by Gene, in order to get me the
coupling, earned me considerable royalties despite the fact that our
powder puff tail wagged in very few homes. (By the way, what ever
happened to Rudolph's "B" side, "If It Doesn't Snow On Christmas?"

Gene re-recorded his first hit, "That Silver Haired Daddy of Mine,"
using Bert Dodson singing the Jimmy Long part. When Columbia presented
Autry with his Gold Record for this number, there were so many Gold
Records on the Autry's mantle already, who is going to notice?

"Where are you going to put all of those Gold Records?" we asked of our
Boss.

"Melt 'em down! What else?"

Still, many of us associated with the Cowboy find it difficult to get over
the fact that he was later dismissed from the company for lack of sales.

♪   ♪   ♪

While he was no longer listed in the top ten moneymakers in films, he was still turning out eight pictures a year for Columbia. In addition to these, he had 60 other films still showing around the world, including the one film he made on loan-out to 20th Century-Fox, *Shooting High* with Jane Withers. Most of those pictures were in the process of being leased to television.

Gene had by now formed his own movie production company and was in complete charge of his product. Contrary to his plans and dreams of years ago, the cost of making color Westerns proved to be so expensive he had to give up and return to the original black and white process. Even though his movies were in production and showing around the world, the winds of change were blowing in, threatening to sweep the little "B" Western movies out of production. After that they would be TV bait, then . . . collector's items.

The immediate success of the Lone Ranger and Cisco Kid on television prompted the Wrigley Company to broaden their broadcast ventures into television by sponsoring the *Gene Autry Show*. This turned out to be a 30-minute action film, in which he sang one song, produced by his own Flying-A Productions. Not only was he making his own TV shows but others as well.

It can safely be said that the advent of television, assisted so ably by "Rudolph The Red Nosed Reindeer" and "Peter Cottontail," on records, had given the Singing Cowboy's career a shot in the arm that was to send him to newer heights, indeed.

In 1950, Gene Autry's Melody Ranch Show, still broadcast on CBS and still sponsored by Doublemint, was now over the ten-year mark and doing well. They enlarged the orchestra, hired more writers, singers and actors, and even put Gene's own publicity man, Bev Barnett, to work publicizing the show in order to offset any loss of listeners to television. Here too, another change had come . . . wire and tape recordings were now being used in radio, which, heretofore, had been 'live'. This solved several problems for both stars and producers. By taping a broadcast, many mistakes and slips of the tongue could be remedied by going back and re-recording the segments as photograph records had been able to do all along. Also, the star could tape one or more appearances in advance. For the Autry road show, it saved us the trouble of having to interrupt our schedule of "one nighters" in order to do a broadcast away from Hollywood. Instead, when the show hit the air, it was another Hollywood Studio Production with much better sound than the boondocks afforded.

Strangely enough, it turned out that everybody preferred the taped broadcast except the Wrigley people.

"But, this way we can cut out the mistakes!"

"To hell with that!" was the answer. "Some of the mistakes are the best parts of the show. It proves that you're human, after all. Put a few of those mistakes back in."

Even so, everyone, from Gene on down, strove for perfection. And, while Autry had, from the beginning of his career, taken his talents to the public in person, he was doing so more and more in the early Fifties. He was a popular entertainer. Even though he was seen and heard in all mediums, he was still a "draw." The crowds continued to turn out in large numbers.

And the bus rolled on!

♫   ♫   ♫

Gene Autry was one of the first stars to lend his name to commercial products such as wrist watches, rubber and leather boots, toy pistols, hats, belts, dolls and the one that was probably the most famous of the bunch, the Gene Autry Jeans, which were similar to the traditional Levis. On these products he merely allowed his name to be used on a license and royalty basis.

"Operate on the other fellow's money," Gene always advised us. Try it sometime! You'll find it easier said than done.

While waiting for that bus that would take us to an auditorium one time, Gene and I stepped into a drug store next to the hotel lobby and looked around. We noted a toy Dick Tracy wristwatch with which the famous detective was supposed to communicate with his assistants. Gene picked up the watch and gave it the once over; then he had me take another, in 'walkie talkie' fashion, to the other side of the store to determine if it would work or not. Naturally, it didn't.

"Boy," he said. "If we could get something like that going we'd all get rich."

Even still, it is our understanding that the merchandising business was quite lucrative for him for many years.

Gene Autry was not in the habit of divulging the details of his outside interests and investments. Neither were we, his musical aggregation, especially interested in trying to eavesdrop. There were, however, certain tidbits of dialogue and information such as the pending recording of a certain Christmas song that might come along either during radio rehearsals or backstage at the auditorium. Many of his business transactions were reported in newspapers and the trade papers; information that was available to any and all, provided they had learned to read..

One day after wrapping a recording session at Radio Recorders in Hollywood, Gene invited everyone to stop by his office at the corner of Sunset Boulevard and Orange Street. Once we were all seated around his plush upstairs quarters, the bar door swung open and it was every man for himself. While the rest of us were discussing the quality of the music just put down, Gene sat at his desk thumbing though the Daily Variety. All of a sudden he said to Mitch Hamilburg, "Hey Mitch! It says here that KMPC is up for sale."

"Damn good station," said Mitch. "50,000 watts now." Gene was well aware of the difficulties that the former owner had gone through with the FCC. All of the local newspapers had reported on that subject thoroughly, and now the man had died and the widow, seemingly, had no interest in running a radio station.

'What'a you say we pawn something and buy it," Gene continued, smiling more broadly than ever. He could smell a bargain a million miles away.

'Might as well." said Mitch. The rest of us sipped on our grape squeezing and wondered when the next tour would begin.

That was it. The next thing we knew he was the owner of the station. The newspaper quoted the selling price at just over $800,000. Four years later Gene told us that he had turned down four million for it.

I'd say . . . good buy!

It became common talk in the industry that he gave 12 million cash for TV station KTLA, Channel 5, across the street from KMPC. However, after we went to work at the station we learned that there were slight differences in the rumor. The amount was a few dollars under the 12 million reported, and someone else in the organization signed the check.

"They framed the cancelled check and hung it on the wall."

Now let's talk about oil.

Texas Millionaires loved Gene Autry. All they wanted to do, so it seemed to us, was just to hob-knob and rub elbows with the Cowboy Star. Oh, and sure, they brought along their wives, kids, friends, neighbors, everybody from back home who got autographs and signed photos galore.

When we were doing the Madison Square Garden Rodeos we got the impression that half of the people present were Texas millionaires who found no difficulty whatsoever in getting backstage and into Gene's dressing room. Perhaps he knew them, perhaps not. We just figured that they were there so that they could brag to the folks back home that they had been present when Gene was changing his jeans.

There's one thing about a Texan, especially a rich one . . . they talk loud and long.

"Hey, Gene!" said one man from Wichita Falls. "I'm just about to sink 20 wells. How about you and Jack Dempsey here coming in with me?"

Nobody turned to us and said, "You guys, too. Get aboard the Gravy Train!" I guess the fact that we were holding guitars and fiddles gave an indication of our own bank balances.

The Texan later paid our way to Wichita Falls to do a benefit for some local charity. While I was standing around in the hotel lobby, Gene, Jack Dempsey, Pat Buttram, and the Stetson topped Texan emerged from the elevator.

"Gonna bring in a bunch of oil wells! Come see!"

I hopped aboard the man's plane with the rest and before long we were flying over the Red River. I tried to spot my hometown of Marietta in the distance.

When the plane sat down on Oklahoma soil, I noted a small reception committee . . . but saw no oil wells. I soon learned that they do it differently than they do when they blow high and wild like in the movies. Everyone gathered around a little pipe sticking out of the ground while several people with movie cameras adjusted their lenses and light settings in order to begin grinding away at the big event. To me, it appeared that they were all a bunch of 16mm home movie cameras for I didn't see any call letters of television stations or movie newsreel companies.

Anyway, the oilman pulled Gene, Jack Dempsey, Buttram and a few others into the scene while I stood by wondering what I was doing here. On cue from somebody, the cameras started whirling as the man gave the signal . . . somebody turned a little knob on the pipe and lo and behold, here came a big bunch of oil spurting up in to the air.

I had been reared in this part of the country, oil country, and this was the first time that I'd ever witnessed the bringing in of an oil strike. It was nothing like *Boom Town* where Clark Cable and Spencer Tracy got themselves drenched as the crude spewed up though the derrick. Neither Gene nor any of the Texas men got one little droplet on their while hats.

"What'll they think of next?"

Flying back to Wichita Falls in the oilman's plane, Pat Buttram leaned across the aisle and said in my ear, "What in the hell were you and I doing out there?"

"Damn if I know," I replied. There weren't many people around there that day, so I suppose they just wanted to augment the crowd.

That Christmas Season, when the Autry's gave their annual party, inviting all of their friends in for drinks, supper and a nice evening of conversation, topped with a few songs from all of us, we were given an added treat... home movies. The Texas Oilman and his clan were there with sound home movies. As we sat there watching the glorious Kodachrome scenes, we were pleased to witness the blowing of well after well after well, of glorious black oil, that is.

♪   ♪   ♪

There is no aspect of the entertainment business that Gene did not enter into. For music publishing, he formed Western Music Co. in the early forties and began collecting hit songs immediately. Later, he formed Golden West Music Co. and it, too, gained its share of moneymaking copyrights.

In years to come he purchased several music-publishing companies. Some he sold, others he kept. Also, he would start a couple of record companies. Shortly after the forming of Challenge Records, they had a million record seller called, "Tequila." One of the first records released on his Republic Records label was another hit entitled, "Hot Rod Lincoln."

In the mid-50's, Gene's stardom and his entertainment career would begin it's slow decline. However, his life as a big businessman would take just the opposite course.

In the Old West, whenever a lone cowboy or Indian needed to take a long and important journey by horseback, it was customary for him to ride one horse while leading another. When the mount he was riding began to tire, instead of stopping for extended rest, he merely slipped the saddle onto the second horse, rotating the two, and rode on.

So it was with Gene Autry. Ten years earlier, on the sleeper jump from Phoenix to Los Angeles, he had hinted to me that he had already begun preparation for such a situation. He knew that stars do not shine forever but that the dollar remains supreme and important as long as we shall live.

Like the Boy Scout . . . Gene Autry would be prepared.

CHAPTER EIGHTEEN

Exit and Re-Entry

Or, If You Hitch Your Wagon To A Star,
Or, What If He Cuts You Loose?

In 1953, I resigned my job with Gene Autry for personal reasons. I will re-late the highlights of that event here, not to try and gain sympathy for my-self, but to give an insight in to his reactions, both on my leaving and upon my return soon thereafter.

In 1948, I was receiving second billing on the radio broadcast. They gave me comedy lines in the early part of the show and as well as in the dramatic sketch. I was sometimes the 'sidekick', riding in and out of trouble with the Star. By 1949, my billing had slipped to the third spot and my role on the show had diminished considerably. When we learned that Gene would go on television, I was so naïve as to believe that they would simply being the TV camera into the radio broadcast and shoot it in that manner. How wrong I was.

One day I asked Frankie Marvin when he thought they would begin the TV shows.

"Are you kidding? They've already made a bunch of them," was his answer.

Add to this bit of discouragement the fact that the long, long tours of one-nighters were now beginning to become more work than play. For years well meaning friends and relatives had been trying to persuade me to leave the shadow of the big Star and go on my own. Before "Here Comes Santa Clause," and "Rudolph The Red Nosed Reindeer," even some people at Columbia Records whispered in my ear that my records were selling almost as good as his.

"Hellfire son! You can sing twice as good as Gene."

"Jimmy Wakely left . . . he's doin' okay!"

"Eddie Dean left . . . he's doing okay!"

"And now, ladies and gentlemen, " shouted Harry Smythe, the owner and MC of Buck Lake Ranch in Angola, Indiana. "It gives me great pleasure to introduce to you a man with great talent, but he ain't never gonna get no-where in this world as long as he stands in the shadow of a great Star like Gene Autry!" That was my introduction after which I did my thing.

There were good and definite reasons why I didn't want to leave Gene. I liked the man. I liked the job. He was easy to work for and paid well. His paycheck? It hasn't bounced yet! I was happy there, but cold winds were blowing in my ear.

"Did you hear the news? We're going to London!" That settled that. I was getting tired of opening every tour in Wichita and moving on down the icy road to Omaha. I wanted to go London.

My jubilation was short lived, however when it was rumored that not everyone would be going on the particular tour. Since I had on fairly good authority that I was one of those to be left behind, I phoned Gene for a meeting at his office.

"Gene, I understand that not everyone will be going to London with you."

"Well," he said, sitting back with his cowboy boots up on the desk. "The transportation is so steep and our show is so big it's just impossible to take everyone along."

"I understand. So I'd like to say this. True, I'd like to go, however, if you find that you have to leave me behind I want you to know that it's okay and I really do understand the reasons. However, I would like to have some advance notice so that I can line up some things in your absence."

"That's fair enough," he assured me and left it at that. While awaiting word on this matter, my part in the radio broadcast went by. The payoff came at a routine rehearsal when I discovered that I had no lines of dialog in the script for a show for the first time in over ten years.

"Hellfire, son! You ain't nuthin' but a guitar picker on the show. The only reason he keeps you on is so he can hear the bass runs and won't come in on the wrong beat!"

Then during the same rehearsal Herb Green called the Cass County Boys aside, but their talk was too low to hear. And, it was a dark corner.

"What are they doing?"

"He's telling them to go down and get their passports."

"Have they told you to?'

"No. Have they told you to?"

"No."

The next day I made it a point to run into Herb at the Plaza Bar where all of us hung out from time to time, especially around noon time. Herb was there, admiring an olive in an empty martini glass. I asked Herb to level with me.

"Just tell me the truth. I can take it."

Herb told me the truth and I found that I couldn't take it. After all of those hectic tours that I'd made . . . now here was the **one** that I really wanted. Too, I'd seen others parts in Autry's lineup of talent grow smaller and smaller as they neared the open door leading out into the cold.

What to do? The realization of where I stood was too much. I went to the producer of the radio show, Bill Burch, told him my problem, and then resigned.

"I want to leave as of this minute . . . not two weeks!"

"Got yourself a deal," he said so quickly that I almost let it go by me. "Have you told the Old Man?"

"No."

"I haven't got the nerve to face him."

"He's going to call you the minute I tell him."

That night Gene called.

"That you, Jonathan Q?"

"Yeah. How you, Mister A."

"Burch tells me you quit."

"That's right."

"What's up?"

"Mmmmm, I don't know."

"Well, if I've done anything or said anything that I shouldn't have, you know I didn't mean it."

I was in no mood to go into detail on the phone so I told him that I'd come in to see him soon, which I did.

"Gene," I told him in his office, just the two of us. "You know yourself that there comes a time in every man's life when he has to make a big decision and take a giant step." I was beating around the bush and he knew it. I wasn't about to ask him to take me to London. He was within his rights, although that was small consolation to me.

"So true" Gene said. "I've taken a many of them. Some worked, some didn't."

"I think that time has come for me." I was 38 years old and a day late and a dollar short when it came to stepping out into the wide world of show business alone.

"O.K, if you think so. I'll just say this . . . I hate to lose you and if you ever want to come back the door is always open."

"Can't beat that with a stick," I said, getting to my feet, extending my hand. It was obvious that we both were avoiding the main reason for the parting. At any rate, he didn't offer me the London tour. Neither had I asked for it. That had to be a standoff of some sort.

I concluded the meeting with these parting words: "Gene, I want you to know one thing. This has been a helluva job and I've enjoyed very minute of it. It came along at a time in my life when I needed it bad and it has done a lot for me. Frankly, I don't know what I'd done without it."

All through my magnanimous oratory he nodded his head as if to say, "Don't worry about a thing. School's gonna keep."

♫   ♫   ♫

That was it. I wished him well and he wished me well. We shook hands and I left his office. Soon after that the Autry bus (with wings added) took off for England. I took my wife and two daughters to visit relatives in Oklahoma. I later took a job in Dallas on radio WFAA. Bert Dodson came through a short time after and gave me the name and address of the place they were playing to that I could drop Gene a note just to let him know that there were no hard feelings.

Fate is tricky, fickle lady. That summer I spent in Dallas was the hottest in years with the temperature going up to about 108 during the day and way down to 98 at night.

In London, I later learned, the few who turned out for the Autry show were very vocal with expressing their displeasure. Americans, especially show people, were not the most popular folks in the world that day.

Two months later my family and I headed back to California where the temperature was closer to 70 day, and below 50 at night. Fan my brow! I joined a TV show and dance called Town Hall Party, then sat back and waited for my overseas traveling buddies to come home. Before the end of

1953, I was back on the radio show but in a little bit different capacity. I was doing just about the same things that I had done before, except for the extra duties of the cross-country tours. In other words, I worked the show while it was in town and not those on the road. At the same time I was working with another close friend, also a Singing Cowboy, Tex Ritter, on Town Hall Party.

The one big thing, to me at least, was the manner in which Gene accepted my return. Not once did he ask me to explain or go into any detail as to what happened here and in Dallas. While Kotner and some of the others were quizzing me deeply, Gene never asked. Mum's the word and sometimes that can mean more than one might think. Especially when you have a real good job up your sleeve (or make it, in the bag)!

PART FIVE
Recollections

"The nervous 1950s, the decline and re-birth
of country music"

Johnny on a rare tour without Gene.

It was said that the advent of television had been purposely delayed by World War II, and that great conflict with its restrictions had caused the powers-that-be to hold off until about 1946 or 1947, or the duration. In 1939, The Bell Boys had participated in TV experiments in Oklahoma City. Nobody at that time thought too much of it, so radio continued to flourish and great live shows were being beamed coast to coast with such stars as Bob Hope and Jack Benny, with the *Grand Ole Opry, The National Barn Dance* and *Gene Autry's Melody Ranch* being added to the list, signifying that our type of music was holding its own side by side with the rest. It seemed to us that in 1947, they ushered in both TV sets and programs simultaneously, almost overnight. As a result, those of us in radio got very nervous.

"What's going to happen to us?"

Our first impulse was assume that they might just bring in their cameras, place them alongside our radio microphones, and let us proceed with that which we had been doing all along. Indeed, a few programs, such as Arthur Godfrey's daily CBS morning show out of New York City, were handled in this very manner for a brief period, beginning in 1948. About the time that TV was in a position to begin to dominate, Jimmy Wakely and I happened to be in Oklahoma City visiting with our old sponsor, the Bell Clothing Company. The owner informed us that, in his opinion, radio was finished. He was buying no more radio advertising and had switched to television. He proved correct, as one by one, each of the network shows began to fold, including *Prince Albert's Grand Ole Opry* and *Gene Autry's Melody Ranch*, which was one of the last to leave the air on May 13, 1956. I was there.

Up until that time almost every town and city throughout the country large enough to support a radio station, enjoyed its own live, local radio programs and personalities. Now these were to be no more.

Where once it had been prohibited to play a commercial phonograph record on the air, now that's about all we were going to get.

In 1952, William Wagnon, Jr., who had been booking Bob Wills, Tex Ritter and others into his dance clubs up and down the San Joaquin Valley from Bakersfield to Sacramento, moved into the L. A. area and took over from Foreman Phillips the old Town Hall building in Compton, near Long Beach. Wagnon's first move was to experiment with ballroom dancing.

When the initial shows failed to pay off, it was decided to switch to the old-fashioned 'barn dance' format. The resulting show was called *Town Hall Party*. Almost all of the C&W artists who were based in the Las Angeles area were hired to be permanent members of the cast. Wesley Tuttle was hired as a performer as well as writer/talent coordinator; Eddie Dean and I were to co-host; Lefty Frizzell, Eddie Kirk, Les 'Carrot Top' Anderson, Joe and Rose Maphis, Merle Travis, and others made up the cast of what was to become the biggest and most successful of all the West Coast County Music Shows.

Wagnon's next step was to contact Los Angeles TV station KFI, Channel 13, who was finding it difficult to sellout their Friday and Saturday night's schedules and therefore had plenty of sustaining airtime available. These KFI shows from Town Hall were then fed to NBC West Coast and later, after Wagnon hired Tex Ritter to become a regular cast member, it was fed to the full NBC Network with Ritter as host. When NBC canceled the show after a couple of years, a new TV station, KTTV, Channel 11 in Los Angeles, was then contacted and two hours of the show were then telecast live from the stage. A few weeks later, when KTTV informed Mr. Wagnon that they were on the verge of cancellation, Wagnon implored them to increase their show time to three hours. Ritter agreed to return to the permanent cast, and this three hour live broadcast (10:00 PM to 1:00 AM) continued until the end of 1960. I was hired to write the show as well as to perform with all of my good buddies that I'd known so long.

Town Hall Party was different from either the *National Barn Dance* or the *Grand Ole Opry* in so far as it was a combination show and dance. While the artists were performing, half of the crowd was seated while the other half was dancing. It should be added that not every customer was lucky enough to find a seat and many had to stand during the entire evenings performance. We were under strict instructions from our boss not to program any song that couldn't be danced to. Jay Stewart (later of Let's Make A Deal fame) was the MC, while Tex Ritter was considered to be the premier Star. Big name recording artists were brought in from Nashville, as guest Stars, and for two or three years *Town Hall Party* did a turn-away business at the box office.

Then, in the mid-50s, like a bolt from the blue, something drastic happened down in Memphis, Tennessee. Sam Phillips started up his Sun Records and changed the whole course of the music industry and almost brought C&W Music to a standstill. A series of Rock and Roll records with Elvis Presley turning out a new beat; and sounds like "Blue Suede Shoes" from Carl Perkins and an incredible energy from Jerry Lee Lewis. It was as though the entire country had stopped whatever it was doing and turned all eyes and ears toward Memphis. Had it not been for a fourth artist, Johnny Cash, who managed to keep the keel leveled with his Country records, the boat may very well have capsized. Radio stations everywhere began programming Rock and Roll.

"Country is dead!" the weak hearted began to cry out. One of country's best, Marty Robbins, recorded "That's All Right Mama," but it wasn't all right because it practically confirmed what many were saying. The Friday night Town Hall Party was turned into a Rock & Roll Show and the rest of us really began to get nervous. After a few weeks however, the manager admitted that he was trying to mix 'oil and water' and dropped the Friday night altogether. Radio stations began dropping their C&W format.

Hank Snow came through after playing several West Coast venues, said to me, "Johnny, what's happened to the West Coast?"

Ferlin Husky came to town and informed us that half the people on the Grand Ole Opry were changing their country costumes and had begun to wear sport coats and carnations. "When we go on the road anymore, where once we used to advertise a *Grand Ole Opry*, now we don't dare mention it."

Country was dead. Through. Finished! So many of us believed it. Still, somewhere there had to be a lifeguard. In Washington, D. C., Connie B. Gay, who owned several radio stations that played C&W music, had been staging a series of live shows; some on riverboat cruises. He came to *Town Hall Party* to view the format. We discussed the situation at length. Mr. Gay and a group of dedicated people in Nashville got together and formed the Country Music Association with the idea of not only saving Country Music, but to try and see if they couldn't get it going again more than ever.

Little by little the boat was steadied and we woke up to the realization that Rock & Roll and Country could live together in harmony. Let them do their thing and we would do ours. Some of the Country recording stars began putting a little Rock into their records and some of the R&R Stars began putting a little Country in theirs, the result being a somewhat short lived style called Rock-a-Billy. By and by things leveled off and Rock-a-Billy was integrated into Country. A new Rhythm and Blues was born, eliminating much of the hard Rock. The old "Race" records were no more as the Black Artists began calling their music "Soul." The trends and categories were changing and continue to change today.

Town Hall Party was soon back on track and continued to expand. Armed Forces Television filmed 90 minutes of every Saturday night's show and sent it to their stations around the world. A daily show was instituted on Channel, 13, between the hours of 4:00 to 6:00 in the afternoon. This newfound energy carried us for another five years, but in December of 1960, KTTV gave notice that they could no longer carry the show. Union scales began to rise, causing the talent budget to soar. The novelty of TV began to wear off and the box office receipts began to fall. With the coming of new and better shows on television, many of our viewers began switching channels causing our ratings to drop.

On January 14. 1961. we played our last dance at *Town Hall Party*, making it fall my lot to be present for the conclusion of two great shows, *Melody Ranch* and *Town Hall Party*.

It was fun while it lasted!

PART SIX
Thirty Years on the Road

The last Christmas on the *Melody Ranch Show*, 1970.

CHAPTER NINETEEN

The Big Shutdown Of The Fifties

Or, The Last Picture Show
Or, The Last TV Show
Or, The Last Radio Show

They tell me that a person can stand in the eye of a Hurricane, completely overcome by the stillness therein, and, yet, be unaware of the raging winds surrounding him. So can it be with the tornado-like winds of show business. They are quite easy to see and feel afterwards, but during the time they are talking place, they may not necessarily blow so cold.

Still, if we had only stopped, looked and listened, those of us the Autry musical camp might have noticed certain trends in those winds. Or, perhaps we saw and felt them but didn't want to admit it. The closing curtain always falls hardest upon those who were on the stage. In 1953, I had been so preoccupied with my own personal dilemmas that I failed to hear the closing of a very large door. The silence connected with it's closing was quite deafening.

Gene Autry starred in his last movie! Ironically it was titled, *Last of the Pony Riders*. Since my participation in both the movies and TV shows was so minute, I was not in that company when they shut them down.

♫ ♫ ♫

Once, not too long after his last movie was out of the theaters, Gene invited me back to his office after a recording session. As we sat sipping the sipping stuff in the wee hours of the morning, we talked and talked on various subjects, one of which was that of the singing Western movies.

"They're dead. Deader 'n a door nail! Singing Westerns are through, finished, deader'n Kelsey's! And that's pretty damn dead."

"What was it?" I actually was curious. "Was it television, or what?"

"Yeah, well, that and a bunch of other things. Cost too damn much anymore. In the silent days they could make a Western for practically nothing . . . very low budget. We made our pictures in the thirties, they thought mine were costing too much, but, hell, we had to have good songs. That's where most of them made their mistakes. They just wouldn't pay for good songs. They think all you had to do was sing "Red River Valley" in each picture and the fans would flood the box office. They didn't have unions then. Now, production, music, musicians, everything costs more and I had to scrape up all the money over at Columbia. To hell with it. Just don't pay off no more. Can't even make back your nut."

He rambled on in detail about the cost of making a movie.

"I got sore at old man Yates at Republic. I sued him for release, I sued him to keep my films off TV, and Rogers sued him. We called Yates every name we could think of, but I'm going to tell you one thing about the bald headed son-of-a-bitch . . . every time we made a picture he picked up the tab, every dime of it and he didn't bat an eyelash. He put up the dough-ray-me!"

"Do you think you'd have been better off staying with Republic," this question had come up in so many quarters that I thought I'd lay it on him again for his reaction.

"Oh, hell! I don't know," he answered, shrugging his shoulders. "Who does know? They're not making any more either. The little B Western, singing or otherwise, is dead. Only Duke Wayne and a few more of his type are doing the Westerns. It's either a multi-million dollar budget, or nothing."

♫　　♫　　♫

Radio? That's a different thing. As the home folks began watching more and more television, the popular radio shows of such stars as Jack Benny, Bob Hope, Bing Crosby and others, began to fall by the wayside one by one.

Not so the Autry *Melody Ranch* broadcast. We had been led to believe that Mr. Wrigley judged our show by the Doublemint we sold and not by the ratings we were losing.

Even so, the trend-winds did sweep over us. The first thing they whisked away was our large orchestra. Before we knew it, the *Melody Ranch* Band was the same one used on most of his tours, a skeleton crew in comparison

The cut down Melody Ranch Band, led by Carl Kotner.

to the one heard on radio and recordings over the previous several years. With most of the strings gone, for consolation they hired Buddy Cole to play the pipe organ. That helped a little.

The next thing they did was to take us out of the big studio (which CBS was converting into a TV Studio) and put us in one of the smaller studios; that meant no live audience. Since shows were now being recorded at irregular hours, anytime during the week, those of us on the show hardly noticed. The one move that caught our attention however was that they started recycling the scripts instead of hiring writers to bring in new and fresh material as they had been doing for the first fifteen years. No doubt about it, austerity was in full swing in radio as television captured more and more of the listeners.

Gene's TV Shows were broadcast nationwide weekly, but production had ended and they were in their second time around. Although I was no longer making the tours, disturbing whispers began coming my way. Carl told me that Gene missed a couple of cues, fell off his horse in Omaha, and in general, was not the same as he had been and as I had known him to be.

"I remember him saying how much he dreaded getting up early and making those western movies and TV shows just before they shut down." I reminded him.

"One good thing about radio and records . . . they're easy to do. No sweat!

That last statement of Carl's proved to be not so true after all. One morning we gathered in the little studio at CBS to rehearse the show for the taping a few hours later. It was customary for the Star to arrive a little late if he so desired, but this day's example was so unlike the Boss. After waiting as long as we could Bill Burch put in a telephone call. When Gene did show up we could soon tell that he was in no shape to do his usual, outstanding job. He was in good enough sprits and quite his old jolly self, but we soon noted that he was having difficulty reading his lines and singing his songs. Initially, this was not too important to us for we knew that he had been advised to get reading glasses. He just didn't want to resort to them . . . yet.

Of course, the voice was something else. "Maybe he did have a drink or two," said Ace.

Autry's singing voice had always been straight and clear. Suddenly it was wavering somewhat with a noticeable tremolo. With the assistance of much coffee and patience, the rehearsal and taping of the show was completed. A couple of scenes and songs had to be re-recorded, but then, that's one of the beauties of tape recording.

That radio show was in the bag now and everyone breathed easier. However, a trend was in the making. All through the second half of 1955 this condition prevailed, two or three tapings might go without a hitch, and then the situation would repeat itself to a point where earlier taped shows might have to be broadcast (re-runs were practically unheard of those days).

The sponsor and the advertising agency evidently saw no cause for alarm and all of us were told to go ahead and do the best we could. When all was going well we would tape several shows ahead, these being made just in case. As time went by more and more of those shows would be needed, in fact every now and then an old one would have to be re-run.

After repeating old shows was done several times, the sponsors came out from Chicago to see first hand what the problem was. They had private meetings with Autry and Burch, but we soon got the message; this sort of thing could go on for just so long before something would have to be done. Still, the situation had not improved. We began to get the impression that the Boss had lost interest in the show. What with the movies shut down and the TV shows in re-run, maybe he felt that his radio career had had it too.

Listeners to the show were beginning to notice the change in the voice. Also a few items of unfavorable publicity were beginning to appear in print, the result of some of the tour capers.

All of this lasted until the middle of 1956. Both Wrigley and CBS, as patient as they were, sent word that no more 'old' shows were to be substituted. (This appears to be contradictory inasmuch as they were the ones who had insisted on the recycling of old scripts. Now they were calling for those same old stories to be taped as new shows.)

On May 6, 1956, the Boss was not able to go on. His voice was shaky and so were his hands. An old tape was run at broadcast time. On Monday morning, Bud Offield of the Wrigley Company was in town and we all got the news. *The Melody Ranch Show*, which had been on the CBS network since 1939, was finished. A final show was prepared and broadcast on May 13, 1956. Gene Autry was not present, but the rest of us carried on.

The show opened as usual while several of us did musical numbers. Pat Buttram and Charles Lydon pretended to go look for Gene. Some of his recordings were played and the show ended with an invitation from the Wrigley Company for him to return anytime that he chose.

He never did!

Pat Buttram went to Chicago and hosted a show using a different format, 15 minutes daily, sponsored by Wrigley. It was broadcast over the CBS Radio Network for three years.

With the cancellation of the radio show, my employment and association with Autry, naturally, changed. We continued to make phonograph records together. We were social friends as well as coworkers; so a few parties, lunches and other types of meetings were not entirely out of order. At first, he would go into detail about why he was glad to be relieved of the burden of the radio show, and he was beginning to complain about the tours.

In May 1958, Gene contacted Merle Travis and me inquiring if we could get away from Town Hall Party for a weekend and accompany him to Milwaukee for a rodeo. We agreed to go and flew with him and Herb in his plane, along with Casey Tibbs, the famous rodeo rider. Arriving in town a few days early, we all went out to County Stadium to watch the Milwaukee Braves play the St. Louis Cardinals. Gene was in great shape, enjoyed the game and took us back to the dressing rooms afterward. The Dodgers were now in Los Angles and we shared a few games together there also.

Back at the hotel, the parties and cocktails began in earnest. When it came time for the rodeo, we were wondering if any of us were going to be in any shape to perform at our best.

Keep in mind that I hadn't made a tour with Gene for about four years and I was prepared for a few changes if they came along. The first thing I noticed was, it wasn't "Gene Autry Day" in town as it would likely have been 10 years earlier. Empty seats were conspicuous around the arena but there were improvements in his act, especially with the horses. He had added a wireless microphone so that he could talk to patrons while riding Champion around the ring. The lighting was improved for his act and he didn't fall off his horse. People don't realize that things like that do happen occasionally to anybody. However, let it happen to a Cowboy Movie Star and fans never let him forget it.

"Ride hard and fast ten million miles and they expect it. Fall off once and you've had it," I surmised.

At the end of the day in Milwaukee, Gene retired to his suite. Merle and I thought best to stay away.

Back in Los Angeles again, Gene made two separate guest appearances on Town Hall Party. This show was a different format from the type of program that he had been accustomed to doing. It was a combination variety show and dance, which was simulcast on both local radio and television. Gene's first time there broke the house attendance record, turning fans away in droves. The second time was almost as successful and far better than the average attendance we were accustomed to having. Tex Ritter was present and introduced Autry both times. The two of were always close friends. It was a treat to see Gene get out of the office and back in the saddle.

In March of 1959, he called for another rodeo, this time in South Texas down close to the Mexican border. Business was good but we had to admit to ourselves that it was not quite the same.

"Well, Jonathan Q," Gene said as we dined in a special restaurant just across the Rio Grande. "This is not the old Madison Square Garden, but it's a living."

"Just like old times, Mr. Agent," I said. Merle Travis had told Gene some joke that ended up wherein the punch line referred to a 'Mr. Agent.' The two of them had laughed at it so much that many of us just naturally took up the term.

"Who you recording for these days?" Gene asked as we sipped Tequila.

"Nobody. Since Columbia dropped me, I'm between hits!"

"Me, too. I'll tell you what. I have some ideas so let's get together when we get back home."

"Got yourself a deal," I assured him.

Again, we never thought too much about it at the time, but it turned out that the 1950s were the 'gone' years. The Western was gone, the TV show was gone, The *Melody Ranch Show* was gone, the Grand Tours of one-nighters were gone, and then I learned that on May 3, 1957, Gene had recorded one last song for Columbia Records while in New York. It was called "Johnny Reb and Billy Yank." It was no Rudolph

♫   ♫   ♫

Just before Columbia Records dropped me, the A&R man (not Uncle Art Satherly) said to me,

"You know how many records Gene sold of his latest release?"

"No, how many?"

"Not very many."

"Yeah, but he sold plenty on Rudolph and a bunch of others."

"Perhaps so, but you know the show business motto."

"No, what is it?"

"What have you done for me lately!" (I could never get that saying out of my mind, so I wrote a song by that title a few years later!)

The Columbia Record's contract was gone. However, the curtain hadn't fallen on us yet.

CHAPTER TWENTY

Big Deal, Little Deal, No Deal

Or, Let's Do Something Even If It's Wrong.

During the summer of 1959 Gene and I met many times for lunch at the Plaza Hotel, Hollywood and Vine Streets in Hollywood. Most of the time we actually drank our lunch while we discussed a wide variety of subjects. He loved to reminisce so we would talk over humorous incidents that had happened on past tours or even about the personal problems of some of the old gang.

"Somebody ought to write a book about our travels," I said, thinking ahead.

"Whoever writes it up will make a fortune," Gene said. "Hell, I'll buy 'em all myself just to stifle some of the news."

"Oh, we weren't that bad," I said. "By the way, I read in the Variety where you sold Challenge Records." I always mentioned the trades or newspapers on stuff like this; otherwise he might think I was prying into his business affairs.

"Sure did," he verified the news. He didn't mention the price and neither did I.

"And you just had a hit record on Challenge Records with "Tequila." I reminded him about the name of his record label. (He had wanted to name the record company Champion, but that name was registered so he had to settle for Challenge).

"That's the time to sell, when you have a hit. Once you cool off you're deader'n Kelsey's."

"Knowing you, you'll probably start another record company," I was fishing on that one and he knew it.

"Exactly what I want to talk to you about," Gene seemed pleased that the subject was brought up.

"You wanna talk to me about the records business?"

"Certainly, both of us are available. It's about time you and me made some more hits."

"You want me in the company?" I had always worked for Gene but never had we gone into a business together.

"Sure, with your brains and my money, what can we lose?"

"Are you sure you want me to answer that?" I asked.

"No, better not. Let's have another drink instead."

We had several drinks and several meetings. Each time this same subject was brought up about forming another record company.

"What do you plan on calling this company?" I asked on a later meeting.

"Republic!"

"Republic? What will Mr. Yates say to that?"

"I already got the old fart's blessing."

"I think there's already a company down in Nashville by that name. I heard they got some old Pat Boone masters."

"I know all about that," said Autry. "I've got Troy Martin on it and I think we can buy the name, the company, and the masters."

"Well," I said. "That name was certainly good for you in the past. Might just be a lucky charm."

"Name's awful important," said Gene Autry, whose name was still magic all over the world.

The meetings and the talk continued for weeks and months but little or no action was taking place, so I decided that I'd better try and catch him at his office rather than the Plaza Bar. He had a fairly large office staff where a lot of activity took place every day with many people waiting to see him. Several of the secretary's faces were familiar since some of them were former fan club members who had now graduated to Hollywood.

When I did get in and tried to discuss these subjects, he would avoid them by saying, "Okay, let's get together for lunch tomorrow and talk about it some more."

I was beginning to get the message. For almost 20 years I had been working *for* Gene Autry, but not necessarily *with* him. He was going to take his own time and do it his way and nobody was going to rush him. Another thing that I began to realize was he talked one way over the suds and another way in the office. Cotner had warned me about this but I had to find it out for myself. Town Hall Party was failing fast and I had no records out on the market. Soon, it appeared that I might be out in the cold altogether so I felt that I had to make a move fast. I signed with a record company called 20th Century-Fox.

"You're making a big mistake," Autry said when I broke the news to him later.

I made a BIG mistake, all right, but pretty soon my ole buddy, Gene, would come to my rescue. He would give me my biggest record up until that time.

CHAPTER TWENTY-ONE

Second Class Touring

Or, Where Have All The Neighbors Gone?
Or, Whatta Helluva Way To Make a Living

From August to October of 1959, Gene Autry booked a series of tours that were quite different from any we used to do. They were in smaller towns and at state fairs where we would appear in the Grandstand. Of all the types of show business we had experienced, I believe that these were the hardest to play. First of all, you're stationed on a temporary constructed stage at the center of a racetrack. The audience is so far from you that the echo of your voice bounces back from the loud speakers five or six seconds after a word is spoken. That doesn't seem like so long a time, but have you ever tried to pronounce the word "Mississippi" when the old man river starts flooding out your ear drums even before you're finished saying the word? Ruff! Add to that the outdoor noises from the rest of the Fair Exhibits and you find yourself the center of much confusion. Gene and I tried to do our comedy bit that had always gone over so well, but out here in the open we found ourselves competing with the popcorn salesmen, and soon learned that it was the visual acts on the trampoline and high wires that got the applause. They usually did quiet down for his songs and Champion, but the rest of us were really hurting.

To offset the fact that we were now playing smaller towns in New York, we stopped off in the Big City for a few days, visiting with old business acquaintances just to get the feeling that we were still in the big time. Being with old friends becomes occasion for a party, so out came the bottles and we all had a swinging time of it in Autry's suite.

When we got to the first date in Middletown, New York, all of us were still celebrating and we began to wonder whether we really wanted to put on a show or not. After Ina Mae arrived a day or two later, out of respect for her, we all straightened up and got down to business. She stayed for the rest of the tour, so from then on, it was just like the good old days.

Another big difference in these tours was that we didn't have a full crew like we'd had before. He it was just Autry, myself, Merle Travis, and Carl Cotner leading a local band, plus a few circus-type acts brought in just for this tour. It was mostly an outdoor affair giving us all the feeling that we were now in Carnival, sometimes considered to be second-class show business. This smaller show coupled with the smaller crowds made it obvious to all that the end was well within sight.

"Wait'll we get to Albany," someone said. "They loved us in Albany! Remember those big turn-a-way crowds we had there? Come on, Albany!"

Albany, New York, like so many other cities, had turned out big for Autry tours in the past so it was a welcome sight when we saw it on our schedule. This time we played a baseball park instead of the auditorium. They constructed a crude stage over the pitcher's mound facing in the direction of the many bleachers that surrounded us. The only people to turn out for the show were a few of his fan club members that were still around.

"Looks like we have them outnumbered," Gene said, laughing it off.

"Maybe they didn't know what team was playing today," we all said.

"What the hell," Gene shrugged his shoulders. "It's all a part of touring. Win a few, lose a few . . . "

Mother Nature was kind to us that afternoon when she tore the heavens open, drenching us all with a cloudburst and giving us a legitimate excuse to call the show off. That night the folks couldn't come out to the show since I guess we hadn't issued rain checks.

Goodbye to Albany! It's been Grande!

During the terrific rainstorm that afternoon, Merle Travis and I were standing next to each other on the unprotected, sheltered bandstand. Gene was up front on the mike trying to sing a song or two before calling a halt. All us were soaking wet while our electric guitars were shocking us a full 100 volts. I leaned over close to Merle and said, "Hey, Travis!"

"Yeah, what?" said Merle, trying to keep his composure even in the rain.

"I've got me a raincoat."

"You have. Where?"

"W-A-Y over yonder in the dugout dressing room."

Merle Travis looked at me through the raindrops falling on our heads and penetrating to the skin. Then he slowly looked in the direction of the dugout, about 30 yards away, then back at me.

"May I congratulate you, John!" he finally said, trying to play while the electric sparks flew.

♫　　♫　　♫

Sedalia, Missouri was next, then Wichita, Kansas. (I might have known we couldn't book an Autry tour without finding Wichita on the schedule.) Lots of people here turned out for the Fair, but not everyone came into the Grandstand.

Louisville, Richmond and Nashville were the last three dates in 1959. Turnouts were just about the same as the previous stops, so everybody was happy when Hurricane Gracie blew us out of town. Not only were our careers crashing down around our heads, but the elements as well showed no mercy.

Still, I don't know why I seemed to be feeling sorry for Gene Autry as I recall the 1950s coming to a close. Riding in his plane, just the two of us in the passenger compartment, we both settled back to do some reading. I picked up a magazine while he scanned the *Daily Variety*. As he thumbed through the pages, silently, I happened to glance at the headlines on Page One. It said,

AUTRY SELLS TV RE-RUNS FOR FIVE MILLION.

CHAPTER TWENTY-TWO

1960
It Was A Very Good Year

or, Weren't They All?
or, Maybe It'll Never End.

From the way things seemed so final as the 1950s drew to a close, I had just about come to the conclusion that my business association with Gene Autry would soon end also. Not so. Exciting things were in store for the both of us.

My record deal with 20th Century-Fox had stalled at the starting gate so they granted my request for a release from my contract. During three successive days, May 23, 24, and 25, 1960, things broke fast and hot. On May 23, I got the release; on May 24, Gene called me:

"Hi, Jonathan Q! What's goin' on?"

"Nothing but the rent, Mr. Agent. What's with you?"

"Who you recording for?"

"As of this moment I happen to be between hits. Free as a breeze."

"How'd you like to cut a record for Republic?"

"Hail! The Republic! I'll get my hat and go with you."

On the following day, May 25, 1960, we recorded a song, which he published, called "Hot Rod Lincoln." Even though neither of us knew it at the time, it turned out to be the biggest seller that I'd had up to that time, and I am sure that it was also Republic's biggest seller, so it can be said that Gene and I shared a hit record together. Still, all of this did not happen overnight. A month later, when he called me to accompany him for a one-night stand to Philadelphia, I went into great detail to why and how we had made a big mistake by recording the song with a semi-rock background.

When he called about the Philly date he explained that just he and I would go, pick up a small local band, play one show, pick up the loot and come home. It was all so simple, on paper. As it turned out, it became a major production.

For one thing we flew on a commercial airplane. When it was time for us to board the plane, Gene didn't lead me to the same line with rest of the passengers. He escorted me instead to a certain door at the terminal, showed somebody some kind of a card, after which we were ushered aboard the plane well ahead of the rest of the cash customers. Once we were seated I inquired about this, to which he replied.

"It all depends on who you know, Jonathan Q," he said with a big grin settling back in his seat. "If you want'a get out in front you gotta take that extra step. Once you get there, the big question is, can you stay there?"

"Hear! Hear!" I said, adjusting my seat belt.

"Now, Gene, there's something we gotta have squared away." By that time we had reached cruising altitude where the stewardess interrupted us with her routines.

"Oh! Are you Mr. Autry?" she almost shouted. She obviously hasn't seen me yet.

"That's what they tell me, honey!"

"You know something?" She was now on her knees in the aisle, leaning in closer to him. "I love you!"

"You hear that Jonathan? She loves us!"

"I heard what she said. Tell her we love her too."

"John says we love you too."

She carried on briefly then left to finish her chores. Before long she was back again, pushing her cart and serving cocktails. We each had a couple of drinks as our young admirer took advantage of every trip up and down the aisle, stopping each time to make further amorous comments.

Our plane had been scheduled to Washington, D.C., where Herb Green picked us up and took Gene over to the Capitol Building. They went inside and chewed the fat with some Senators and Congressmen, after which Gene and I took the train on to Philadelphia. This time, Herb met us at the Sheraton Hotel in Philadelphia. While Gene was signing the register, Herb called me aside.

"I wonder if you'll give me a big hand, John? After all, you haven't been out with us for some time now."

"Anything you say." I assured Gene's pilot and right hand man. Herb had probably booked this tour and had come East early in order to make sure that everything was in order.

"The Boss's getting more and more difficult to handle lately . . . keeping his mind on the show, know what I mean. Anyway, this is a very important date and it's going to be rough on me trying to keep an eye on him, while at the same time making certain that the show is set up right."

I shrugged my shoulders. I'd already volunteered my co-operation.

"He missed a couple of shows in New York recently," Herb went on. "We can't afford to let him miss this one."

"Help me keep him occupied . . . away from the Vodka. We have a large suite on the top floor with several bedrooms. Instead of you checking into a separate room, I'd sure like for you to stay in there with us. Between the both of us, I think we can swing it."

"Well," I told Herb. "I'll do anything I can. But you gotta remember, I'm working for the guy."

"So am I. But if we both level with him I think he'll listen."

I agreed to this arrangement and we all checked in. It was a nice big suite . . . drawing room, several bedrooms, enough baths to keep an army clean, color television, something not quite so common in early 1960. And, of course, a wet bar.

I had to get on the phone immediately in order to get a band together. I called two friends, Rusty Kieefer and Jack Howard, who pitched in and helped us get the proper musicians who could play Autry's type of music. After holding a couple of rehearsals with the group, one with me singing Gene's part and the other with Gene (where he pronounced everything satisfactorily- no bad effects from the jet ride), I felt that everything was under control. So I took the time to run an errand of my own. I had the crew drive me by the home of local C&W disc jockey, Pete Taylor of WKDN, Camden, New Jersey. He listened to my new record of "Hot Rod Lincoln."

"Well," Pete said. "It's not what we'd expect from Johnny Bond. Gotta awful lot of rock background to it. Course, we'll play it for you and Gene, but . . ."

Back at the hotel, I informed Autry of Pete's impression as the two of us settled back for our first relaxing session since the jet ride. Tomorrow was the big day.

"Gene," I said, nervously, not knowing exactly how to approach the subject. "I think we have made one helluva mistake. A boo-boo to end all blunders."

"How's that, Jonathan Q?" said Gene.

"This "Hot Rod Lincoln" we made."

"What about it?"

"The country jocks aren't going to play it."

"Oh?"

"And the pop jocks aren't going to play a Johnny Bond record. That's for sure."

"Because, that's the way the business is. You know that."

"Trends change, Jonathan Q. Hell, you never know."

"You know what I think?"

"I think you need a drink."

In my despair over the record, I had completely forgotten my deal with Herb. Both Gene and I were nipping on the night before the big moment.

"I think we'd better get back in the studio and come up with a country record, quick."

"Whattever you say, my boy. You do whatever you think best."

"I think I'd better . . . "

" I think you'd both better lay off the celebrating," said a disgruntled Herb Green, entering the Autry suite.

"Oh hi, Herb," said I, beginning to remember our arrangement.

"Come on in, Herb," said the Boss. "Jonathan and I were just catching our second wind."

Herb lay some fatherly dialog on the both of us, reminding one and all of the majestic importance of an A-1 performance on the morrow. It seems that the affair was some kind of important civic doings and the place had been sold out for weeks.

"Fine," Gene said, pouring. "We'll give 'em a show they'll never forget."

"Oh, yeah. Herb's right, Gene," I broke in, somewhat embarrassed that I had allowed my perceived record problem to overshadow the situation at hand. "Why don't we wait until after the show and have a real celebration?"

"Heck, gimmie a couple of good blasts, along with a lungful of pure oxygen, and I can sing better than ever."

"Gentlemen," said Herb, going around collecting all of the spirits from the wet bar. "I feel a certain responsibility for this show tomorrow. I've been meeting with the folks from Philly for days now, and I have assured them that we will uphold our end of the show." He began to walk out of the room carrying all of the celebration material.

"Oh, I know Herb's right," said Gene, agreeably. Herb beckoned me aside.

"Now, since I can't be here all of the time," Herb said. "I'll tell you what I've done so you can take it from there. I've instructed room service not to bring up any more booze! I think things are all set for now. They'll deliver food and soft drinks, but that's all."

I really felt quite helpless but I said, "O.K., like I told you. I'll stick to my guns." Then Herb left Gene and I alone. We had supper; then I went off to my room to watch television. When I discovered that the Phillies were playing baseball on one of the channels, I hastened back to inform Gene, only to see that he already had the game on. However, he didn't seem to be watching. Instead, I found him dressed in his night robe, bare feet resting on top of the desk while he leaned back with the telephone receiver to his ear. The expression on his face was one of displeasure.

" . . . I don't care what anybody said," he roared into the mouthpiece. "I placed that order over an hour ago. Now, where is it?" Obviously guess the order.

He replaced the telephone, continued to stare at it while swearing under his breath. "Damn room service!"

"I see you got the game on," I said.

"You got anything in your suitcase, Jonathan Q?"

"Nothing but some wool socks and three guitar picks."

He laughed a little. "Doug told me you always keep a little anti-freeze in your suitcase . . . just in case."

"I don't think we'd . . . I'd better not have any more until after the show. Herb said . . . what I mean is . . . " I was no good at this sort of thing and we both knew it.

"That damn show's almost 24 hours away!" Gene said, getting to his feet, coming to a stop in front of the TV set.

"Mind if I watch the game with you?"

We watched for a while, during which time he called room service a few more times. Each call produced the same negative results. When he dozed off in his easy chair, I stole out of his room and into mine where I switched channels. They had been advertising the film, *For Whom the Bell Tolls* and

I was anxious to see it again in color. I had always liked the book, Gary Cooper, and especially the Victor Young musical score. Every now and then I would tiptoe to an area where I could see him still dozing. I wanted to awaken him and suggest that he go to bed but still considered this out of my line of duty. Besides, I didn't know how.

The next time I looked in, he was sitting up, wide awake, watching the movie, with a glass in his hand. On the table beside him, pointing majestically skyward, was a quart bottle containing a water-clear liquid.

"Come on in!" Help yourself!" He motioned toward the bottle.

Five years from this date, I would record a song telling how I picked up the bottle and poured the contents down the sink. I won't go so far as to say that this is where I got the idea . . . but, if I told you now that I did the very same thing with that bottle this night, would you accuse me of prevarication? You'd be right!

"Where'd you get that?"

"Jonathan Q, I'm going to tell you something that you already know," he said, pouring himself another light one. "You know that there's more'n one way to skin a bob-cat!"

"Where'd you get it?"

"Ever heard of delivery service?" He pointed toward the Yellow Pages open on the desk. "Anything you want? Just get on the phone. It'll be here before you can say, 'screw the Sheraton's room service.'" The arrival of Herb Green a short time later saved the day . . . or the night, whichever. Calamity was avoided. Sleep well!

♪   ♪   ♪

On Saturday, June 25, 1960, the city of Philadelphia staged a giant THRILL SHOW with Gene Autry as the star attraction amid a wild lineup of racing cars, trapeze acts and a lot of other visual entertainment with a small number of city politicians thrown in. Two policemen drove us over and stayed with us throughout the entire proceedings.

We were assigned no dressing room so the only thing left for us to do was to linger by the police car until it came time for us to run onto the field.

Herb and I wandered away for a moment while Gene chewed the fat with the two policemen. Soon Herb noticed that one of the uniformed men started to move away at some request that the boss had probably made of him. We rushed over just in the time to hear Gene say, "Oh, on second thought Officer, maybe a cup of coffee instead."

"Sure thing, Mr. Autry," said one of Philadelphia's finest. "Whatever you say."

We learned from the papers next day that there were exactly 88, 223 people in the audience that night. When Gene was introduced, they gave out with a roar of approval, the likes of which I don't believe I had ever heard before. He sang his songs with tones so golden I was beginning to believe that he had swallowed all of those gold records hanging on the wall. The band played well and I was as proud to be standing by his side as I had ever been.

All of us waved our hats upon conclusion, while the crowed echoed its appreciation for several long minutes.

On the way back to the hotel Gene was giving Herb and me the horselaugh.

"You two bastards were worried as hell, weren't you? Didn't think I was going to make it, did you?"

"You were great!" we told him, disguising our sighs of relief.

♫   ♫   ♫

Those next 24 hours in Philadelphia were the longest that I can recall experiencing. Herb escorted us back to our suite where he retrieved a lost bottle, held it up, and said, "Gentlemen, that was a great show. That calls for a little drink."

"We'll all drink to that!"

While Gene and I kicked off our boots after turning on the TV, searching for another baseball game, Herb bade us farewell with this one last bit of instruction,

"When I ordered your tickets I left the return open. I would suggest that you decide now when you would like to return to the coast and I'll call and make the reservations."

"Oh, hell, Herb," Gene said, indulging. "You go ahead. Me and ole Jonathan Q here are not in any hurry. Are we, Jonathan?"

"Just so I get home for Christmas."

"I always had you home for Christmas and you know it. You go ahead, Herb, we'll call the airlines."

"Alright," said Herb. "I'll go. I might stop in once or twice on my way out. Good show, gentlemen." Herb Green shook hands with us and left the room. Now it was just Gene and I, with loads and loads of private conversation ahead of us.

"Well, my boy," Gene said. "I think we broke even tonight. Do you know how many people we had out there?"

"Looked like a full house to me."

"Over 88,000. That's a lot of bodies."

"That broke our Montreal record," I reminded him.

"Yeah, and Madison Square Garden too. Who said the old man was finished?"

"I never heard anybody say you were finished."

"Ninety thousand people," Gene mumbled over the rim.

It was more than obvious that he was pleased with the date. He had a right to be. We had a couple of blasts and talked about ordering dinner sent up. I brought up making the return reservation but he would have none of it. He passed it off by reminiscing about old times. They're not forgotten.

"Hell, I remember when I couldn't get a booking in a town like this one. We had to play the hick joints. That's what we called them. Once you're in the chips, though, then everyone loves you."

"They loved us tonight, alright," I said, going along with this line. I love to recall good times too.

"Did I ever tell you about the time me'n Smiley and Frank and Carl was playing this little place back somewhere? There was this theater over here, and then there was this little old store next door, and we had to go upstairs into the attic. That was our dressing room." He had told it many times, as had both Carl and Frank, but I wasn't about to stop him.

"Well, there wasn't any bathroom up there in that attic so one of us discovered a rusty old coal bucket. West Virginia, that's where it was, I guess. Anyway, that old coal bucket was our latrine while were playing this joint. Pretty soon we heard somebody calling out from downstairs,

"Hey! Turn the water off up there! It's running down in my Post Toasties!"

Gene laughed loud and long after telling that one for the hundredth time. Smiley, Carl and Frank also told it continuously, but I'll say one thing for their telling of it . . . they always told it the same way. We both laughed at that and other stories about the early days as we sipped our sipping stuff.

"Me 'n Smiley and Carl and Frank . . . boy, you oughta see some of the dumps we played."

It made me think for a minute. I had missed out on those tours of the mid to late 1930s. All the places that I had I had played with him had been tops. 'For a little bit more you can go first class!' Gene had always told us. I looked around our hotel suite. Super first class!

I let him ramble on through more cocktails. We were only having appetizers. Pretty soon we were going to order dinner sent up. Cocktails for two! How about that?

The telephone rang; so, while Gene was talking, I stole away into my own quarters where I called home only to learn from my wife that Mrs. Autry had been calling wanting to know if she had news of our return. I told my wife we had not yet made our return reservations but I would call back the minute we did and she, in turn, could call Ina Mae and give her the news.

After more cocktails and confab with the mellow boss, we ordered dinner, of which we ate very little. We were too engrossed in the past. Laughter was the name of the evening's game, but I finally begged off and went to bed.

Sleep was not for me this night . . . not by a long shot. It must have been a little after midnight when I woke from a short nap. I heard voices . . . or rather a voice! When I got to the door of Gene's bedroom I saw that he was flat of his back on his bed, in the raw, he always slept in the raw, ranting into the telephone receiver which was resting upon his face without assistance from either hand. Those were both on the ends of outstretched arms.

I took it upon myself to throw a blanket over him whereby he turned his head a bit, noticing for the first time that I was there.

"That you, Jonathan Q" he mumbled.

"It's only me from over the sea, said Barnacle Bill The Sailor!" I always tried to throw a little humor back at him.

"Old Carson J. Robinson did that one."

"Are you alright?"

"Oh hell yes. I was just talking to . . . who was I talking to? He spoke into the phone several times then hung up. "Whoever it was ain't there no more."

He got up and walked over to the table where he helped himself, offering one to me. I refused this time. I'd had my share. I was floating now.

"What the hell," he said. "Let's drink to the dawn of a new day."

I shook my head, "I'm on intermission."

"This is all I'm gonna have," he said, returning to his bed. 'After all . . . gotta a show to do. This one's gonna be a big one.

I looked at him. Was he serious?

This was my first realization of the fact that his memory had begun to play tricks on him.

"We've already done the show," I reminded him. 'There were almost 90,000 people out there tonight."

"Oh sure. Now I remember. That's almost a hundred thousand. That's a lot of bodies. Speaking of bodies, did you ever take a good look at . . . " He stopped for a moment, and then continued. "No, I guess you didn't. The only thing I ever saw you look at was *The Saturday Evening Post*."

I bade him goodnight again. Out of the corner of my eye I noted that he returned to the telephone again.

Leaving my light on, just in case, I tried to doze off again and probably did; but the next thing I knew he was walking around my bedroom.

"Looking for something?" I asked.

"What in the hell did you do with my jug?"

"I didn't touch it."

"I bet that damn Herb come in and swiped it."

"I don't think so. He'd have knocked."

I got up and helped him look for the lost item but it was nowhere to be found. We looked all over the suite.

"Gimme the Bell Captain," he said into the telephone after a surrender iced with cuss words. "Hello! This is Gene Autry. How about a refill up here in my suite? That's right, the same as the last time. Thanks. Goodbye!"

When I told him that I planned on retuning to slumberland, he turned around and went back to his quarters, mumbling under his breath. When the bellman brought up his order, he knocked on my door instead of Gene's, so I had to get up again. At the same time, Autry, hearing the conversation, rushed in, signed the bill, then sat down in my room and began to partake of the goods in question. He offered me a sip but I turned my head. Not at this hour!

"I been worrying about you, Jonathan Q."

"Worrying about me? Why?"

"Your record. Didn't you tell me that we'd made a big mistake? Didn't you tell me that you didn't want to be a rock and roller? Now, I want you to quit worrying about that record, cause they're gonna play it. I'll even let'em play it on KMPC and other stations. What the hell! I don't even let them play my records on my stations. Maybe on Christmas, they can play Rudolph, and on Easter they can play "Peter Cottontail," but that's all. Now, if the public demanded it, well, I doubt that. But your record . . . I'll get on the phone to come guys I know. I'll plug this record myself. What's the name of it again?"

"Hot Rod Lincoln."

"That's it. "Hot Rod Lincoln"! Hadn't been for me you wouldn't have done it. Remember, I called you on it?"

"I remember."

"I'll even get'em to play it on KMPC. Well, now, wait just a minute. I almost forgot. We don't play Country and we don't play Rock."

"Lot of people thinks it's funny, you're not playing the kind of music that made you. I said, seeing a good opening to get one in. Many people had asked me about that situation.

"Well . . . I don't know," he drawled it out. "You can't make the money playing Country that you can playing good music . . . Pop music. We give 'em music, news, and sports and what's more, we're all sold out. 24 hours a day, sold out. Can't do that with Country."

"Fine thing, I said, I decided to see how far I could go with this. "I make a record for Gene Autry and he won't play it."

"No, but I'll plug it, though," I was glad that he took no offense. "I'll get everybody else to play it. I'll book a tour and plug it in person. I got Troy Martin working for me in Nashville, I'll get him on it. Hey! Let's call up old Troy. Whatta you say?"

"At this hour of the morning?"

"What the hell. Troy don't ever go to bed. Let's call him." He picked up the phone again and had the operator get Troy Martin at the James Robertson Hotel in Nashville.

"Hello, Troy! You old sumbutch! What'n hell are you doing? . . . What? Sleeping? . . . Whatta you mean sleeping on the job. Why'n hell ain't you over there on that all night show on WSM?" Gene was having a big laugh over this phone call.

"Hey, Troy!" When we going back to the penitentiary and pick up another "Walking in the Rain"?

Gene placed his hand over the receiver and said, "Me'n old Troy went out to the Nashville penitentiary and found that song."

"I know. I was there with you." (Well, didn't exactly just walk up to the prison gate, knock, and say we came out looking for a song!).

"Hey, you know who's up here with me? Ole Bond. Yeah ... Jonathan Q. Bond. Ain't he an old bastard though? What? Where are we? Why ... Where are we, John ... Pittsburg ... no, what the hell ... We're in Philadelphia! Hell yes, me'n old Bond, we pulled in a hundred thousand people ... You damn right we did ... Did they love us? How do you like that ... don't they always?"

"Tell him about my record."

"Say, Troy, Bond cut a record for me. Hot Rod Cadillac! I mean, Lincoln. I get them two mixed up. Anyway, we want you to plug it on WSM. Oh, you already got it in. Too much Rock! Well, what the hell, I told ole Bond he could go back in the studio and cut another. This time we'll try to get you a hit to plug. You gotta do something to earn your money, you ole bastard!"

They talk on and on. Finally, Troy suggested that we come back through Nashville instead of going straight home.

"Troy wants us to come to Nashville. What about it, Jonathan ... Yeah, Troy. John's the boss. He's sez you got yourself a deal. We'll see you there ... When? Hellsfire! We don't know when. Fool with us we may never leave here."

With that question not fully answered, Gene hung up, took a long swig, then slowly stood and returned to his room, supposedly to bed. I tried for some sleep but didn't get much. The rest of the time, both the early morning hours as well as the next day were kind of blurred.

He would sleep for a little while, talk on the telephone until his voice got so rumbled that it wasn't understandable; get up, look for his jug, go back to bed, get up for the bathroom and so on, hour after hour. I would wake up to find him wandering throughout the rooms of the suite. Finally, it got to the point that whenever I would speak to him, he wouldn't even notice or respond. He just kept wandering, muttering while moving on back to his room.

The dawn of the second morning came through my windows, so I decided that this night had had it. I got up, showered, shaved, dressed and ordered a big breakfast for two with lots of coffee. I hoped that this might help snap us both out of it. Standing by his bed I began calling his name softly. Had he been asleep I would have left him alone, but he was tossing and stammering, trying to say something, so I thought it best to try and get him up, at least, for some coffee. Shortly afterward I gave it up as a lost cause and went back to my room, sat down in front of the TV and dozed off.

Gene woke me up. He was standing over me, laughing and holding a cup of coffee in each hand.

"Bond, you old bastard," he laughed. "Don't you ever dare tell anybody that I served you breakfast in bed." That did it. A new day had come forth. Herb Green came in again, suggesting that we both knock it off, head for the airport, and go on back home.

"Herb's right," I agreed. "Let's go home."

"Home! Home? What 'n hells your hurry? You know the trouble with you, Jonathan Q, you're always in a hurry to go home. Now, whatta you wanna go home for? Don't you remember what I always told you? You go home when you can't go no place else. Oh, all right. Wait'll I finish my coffee. I need a little stimulant in mine. Herb hid my stimulant . . . will you help me find it?"

"Fine, fine. You finish the coffee and I'll look for the lost dutchman."

Going through the rooms carefully, I began to find half-filled bottles in the most out-of-the-way places; behind curtains, under sofas, between the mattresses, buried in waste paper baskets. Gene had hidden his own. I decided to leave them where they were just about the time that Herb returned.

"How's everything?" Herb asked me in a soft voice not knowing if the boss was up yet or not.

"See for yourself," I said. I told him about the Nashville idea but he talked me out of it.

"Don't you think you'd both be better off going straight home?"

I agreed and made call to the airlines. We could get out on a mid-afternoon jet and get home by dark. Then I called home and instructed my wife to relay the information on to Mrs. Autry. Now all I had to do was to keep him occupied until leaving time.

Between Herb and myself, we talked him into shaving and showering and even got him to eat something. Some of his local fan club members helped save the bulk of the day for us by coming and interviewing for their club paper. He liked his fan club and was always willing to co-operate with them on their projects.

I kept my eye on my watch and felt a great relief as leaving time approached. We were now packed and ready to fly. Herb escorted the club members out gracefully and bade Gene and me goodbye by saying that he would meet us in Los Angeles later. I assumed that he was flying Gene's plane alone.

"Do I look O.K.?" Gene asked as he stood before me in the center of the spacious room. We were waiting for the bellboy to get our luggage.

"You never looked better," I assured him. It was true. He had put on a newly pressed combination business and cowboy suit, not loud, just enough of a Western touch with subdued colors. Only the boots showed where the trousers came down around the tops to the ankles. To some, the white Stetson might be considered loud, but to those of us who had been close to him for so long he looked quite natural. Without the hat and boots he might be considered undressed.

There was a big smile on his flushed face as he said, "Let's get the hell out of here, Jonathan Q."

"We've done all the damage here that we can," I said, following the luggage carrier out. "I guess the maids can look for the buried treasure now."

"Hell yes. Remember what I always told you guys. Let HER mother worry!"

I didn't get the connection, but who cares. We headed for the elevator and made a smooth landing at the lobby level. The doors opened. The lobby was full. Oh! Oh! I thought. This is not going to be as smooth as I'd figured.

To the several bystanders who knew that he was in town for the big event, he was as recognizable as the Statue of Liberty. One by one they either spoke or approached him. The public made it a point to talk up to Gene Autry whenever they saw him. They wanted autographs, the chance to shake his hand; they just wanted to be near him and to touch him. Right now, I didn't want anyone to come close, for once they did, they would discover that which would be better kept secret. Still, on they came and it wouldn't have been proper for me to try and keep them away, so I just tried to keep him moving out of the lobby toward the taxicab stand.

Even though our walk was a bit unsteady (who's going to notice me with him around?), we kept our forward momentum going pretty good. He spoke and shook hands with several people as we proceeded over the plush carpets of the Sheraton lobby. The expressions on their faces was hard to watch as it went from that of elation to one of dejection in a matter of seconds once they discovered that we had been indulging, something that cowboys never did on the screen.

"Why, he's drunk!" said one woman, turning to shout at me.

"So what, Lady?" I shouted back. "I am too."

I pushed us on through while she stared as though we had both un-dressed in the middle of the lobby. The woman couldn't wait to spread the news to the rest of the folks in the lobby. Today, she was Paul Revere spreading the news!

We reached the taxicab stand, entered one and drove away toward the Philadelphia sunset, still a few hours away.

At the Airport Terminal the situation was no better than the Sheraton lobby. After all, everybody recognized Gene Autry and many had probably attended the show. Now was their chance to get a close-up. Men, women, and children all approached their screen and TV hero only to be filled with disillusionment once they discovered the obvious. To make matters worse, he would stop and converse with them at length while I was trying to get him to hurry along, stating aloud that our plane was ready to take off at any moment. The payoff, the low point of the day was yet to come.

As we reached the gate, he showed the V.I.P. card to a man who led us out a certain door. Presently, we found ourselves outdoors in the bright sunlight, just about 25 yards from the huge jet, which was standing out in a most conspicuous area, all by itself. As we staggered, weaving freely, walking briskly toward the plane, content in the assumption that we would soon be safely aboard and out of the reach of the public, we were greeted with a wild, loud huzza, cheers and jeers from behind us. Both of us stopped and turned around to behold hundreds and hundreds of people standing on the observation platform, all over the place, having come to observe the new jets, greet new arrivals, say goodbye to those of us who hoped to be leaving soon.

Gene and I were in the spotlight again; all by our lonesome.

"Boy!" Would I like to be able to dig myself a hole," I said aloud.

The crowd was now witnessing a sight that they had not expected to see. However, none of it seemed to bother the Singing Cowboy who smiled and waved his big white hat at them. I did the same.

Now the unpleasant remarks began darting in our direction from many who had cheered us earlier.

"What did you do? Fall off your horse?"

"Better pour yourselves back in the bottle."

At least he seemed not to notice so much as he continued to smile, wave and bow to them all. But to me it was most humiliating. I shook my fist at them and sent back a few adverbs of my own. It all seemed so strange; I almost couldn't believe they were coming from me.

"Alright, you so and so's!" I yelled at the top of my voice. "Let me tell you something. Go on, ridicule the man who has done more for you . . . "

The deafening sounds of a huge jet engulfed my superlatives and sent them flinging into the four winds. We turned and walked up the ramp to the empty airliner where we found comfort and seclusion deep down low within our seats.

"Didn't I tell you, Jonathan Q.," he said to me while waving out the window at his fickle fans. "They love us in the City of Brotherly Love."

"Sure! What have you done for the world lately?"

"What was that?" he asked.

"Nothing," I said. "I was just trying to figure people out."

"When you whip that one let me know."

♫   ♫   ♫

On schedule, the plane took off and soon reached the cruising altitude of about 35,000 feet. When the glorified waitresses came around, and I decided that now we could both get a little higher ourselves without fear of being scolded by the offspring of William Penn. Pretty soon we were both sailing in more ways than one.

At that particular moment, I was no longer in his employ so I thought I would take the role of being more of a 'frank' friend with the man instead of the 'I' man that I had been as a faithful and trusted employee. I was going to see if I could get a couple of questions answered that had been on my mind for a long time.

"Gene, why did you do it?"

"Do what?"

"Take on so much of that stuff? Me, I don't count. You're Gene Autry and you're always in the spotlight, like out there on the runway just now."

"Hell, I was alright. I know what I'm doing."

"I don't want you to think I'm nagging you or trying to tell you what to do, but I remember the short Scotch and the tall glass. You even told us that we'd better learn to like Scotch because if we ever went to Europe we'd have a hard time getting good bourbon. Remember?"

"Over there it's mostly wine and beer."

"What I'm getting at is this. This Vodka stuff. I've tried it and it addles my brain. Why did you switch to Vodka?"

He leaned toward me. By this time his 'sailing' point was equal to that of any time during the past 24 hours at the hotel suite. He placed his hand close to the side of his mouth indicating a confidential message of great importance. I leaned over, putting my ear as close as called for. Then, in a voice half way between a two and three decibel whisper, he said,

"Because, it leaves you breathless!"

You ask a question — you get answer!

We finished our cocktails. I would have thought that he would have tried to get more than the traditional two servings, carrying the weight that he did, but he made no effort to get the girls to break any rules. I waited to see if he wanted to talk or to try and fall asleep.

"Well sir, Jonathan Q." he said, answering that question too. "We sure broke even in Philly."

"Turned 'em away again," I said.

"One hundred thousand people. That's a lot of bodies."

"How'd you happen to latch on to that show?" It was unusual that I would make this bold inquiry, but, as I mentioned previously, I was now a little older and bolder.

"Oh, they called me, asking if I'd come up. Said Ten Thousand was all they could pay, what the hell, I wasn't doing anything."

"That comes to about two thousand per song. Not bad. Anyway, I'm glad you asked me to go along."

"Well, whenever I have to use a strange, pickup band, I feel better with either you or Carl there to show 'em the holts." (*A term we commonly used to indicate guitar keys and chords.*)

"I take it Herb paid the band."

"Oh, sure. You can always depend on Herb to take care of details. Incidentally, how much do I owe you for this jaunt?"

Of all our jobs and tours in the past, I guess this one was the first and only one of it's kind where no payment had been mentioned in advance."

"Oh, just send me a check whenever you get back in the office. Anything you send will be O.K. I've had a ball." (What a ball!)

"To hell with that," he said, reaching into his pocket, producing a roll of one-hundred-dollar bills that would have choked Little Champ. What the hay! It might have even choked Champ, Senor.

"Say when," he said, peeling off a bunch of the cabbage.

"Whoa! You're gone too far already." I stopped him as he handed me a handful of greenbacks. I never counted them until I got home. There were five of them and he would have made it more had I not stopped him. (I mention this merely to show how he had changed towards money matters. Fifteen years ago he would not have brought up this subject in full view of a planeload of travelers. Ordinarily, a job of this duration would have called for much less.)

"You ask me why I drink . . . Vodka," said my paymaster. "Well, I'm gonna tell you, Jonathan Q. I drink it because I like it. It makes me feel good. I think I can afford a drink. I don't smoke; don't like to hunt or fish. Hell's fire! A man ought to be entitled to one little vice, don't you think? Besides, business is being taken care of in the office. I gotta pretty good staff. Sometimes I even get the idea that they don't even need me around. All I have to do is walk through ever now and then . . . look at the books and be on my way."

"Just walk in, count the money and walk out, that it?"

"Well now, I wouldn't put it exactly that way. Not quite that simple. But I'll tell you one thing, when you have money, you're O.K. If you're broke, nobody loves you . . . it's that simple."

"They tell me that a man can have money one day and lose it all the next," I said, wondering if he'd comment on that one.

"That's true. Now, you take ole (he mentioned the name of a prominent Texas Millionaire) down there. He's supposed to have millions. Still, he's making the rounds trying to borrow money. He'll wind up broke . . . you wait and see."

"Easy come, easy go."

"Anyway, it goes easy," the Cowboy Star corrected me. "But I'm going to tell you a little secret, Jonathan Q . . . and you better not tell it because if you do, I'll deny the fire out of it."

"I won't tell," I told him. "That is, I won't tell anybody now. Someday I might write a book about all this. I can tell it then, can't I?"

"Oh, hell. By that time I won't give a damn and neither will anybody else."

"O.K., what's the secret?"

"I don't intend to die broke. I've got over a hundred thousand stashed away where nobody knows where it is. They can take everything I've got but they won't know where to look for it."

"You can tell me, old Pal. Where is it?"

He looked at me, grinning royally over the rim of his martini glass, "Screw you, Jonathan Q. I just forgot."

We both laughed loud and long over that one. During all of this conversation we were not necessarily alone. The stewardesses walked back and forth, up and down the aisle, stopping whenever they reached the vicinity of the movie star. Everyone in our immediate area knew who it was that was sitting there. Glances in our direction were not uncommon. People in the rear of the plane walked up front to the lounge for no other reason than to be able to turn around and walk back to get a look at the celebrity. Sometimes he would nod his head politely at them, other times he would look out his window between sips. This would also give me some extra sipping time.

"Hey!" I just thought of something. "If you've got all that loot salted away, suppose this old jet flunked out and you and me wound up all over the desert down there . . . what about that?"

"If that happens, I won't be needing it."

Money talk continued on and on. I enjoyed it especially knowing this was one subject that would have been strictly taboo in the past. After a while we got to the subject of all of the gang that had worked for him over the years.

"Oh, they all borrowed money," Gene continued. "Now, you take old Ace. He spends every dime he makes. He's made a fortune with me, still he comes around now and then . . . borrows money all the time. I don't actually know how much he does owe me, but, what the hell!"

"Sure, it's deductible."

"Deductible, my ass. That deductible crap is a big bunch of baloney. Anyway, I guess everybody that ever worked for me owes me a bunch of money. Every mother's son of 'em. All owe me money."

"Everrrrrybody?" I asked, drawing it out slowly.

"Yeah, everybody . . ." he stopped for a moment, turned around to look at me through his grinning eyes. "You, you old miser bastard . . . hell, you got the first dime I ever paid you. You're the only one of the bunch that never borrowed any money from me."

"I was wondering if you noticed."

"I've noticed alright. And, I've often wondered why."

"You wanna know why?"

"Yes," said Gene. "I'd really like to know why."

"I planned it that way."

All through our seven-mile-high dinner and cocktail hour, the subject of ten-mile-high finance continued.

"You mentioned about what might happen if this plane hit the dirt, reminds me of the time that I took Rufe Davis over to the South Pacific with me. Now, you talk about a man with a dime, that's old Rufe. Anyway, here we were, flying this damned slow B-17 Flying Fortress over the wide Pacific . . . nothing down there but water."

"Water, water everywhere and not a drop to drink."

"That's the place," Gene continued, laughing at what was to come. He'd told it many times but I was not about to stop him.

"Anyway, I said to Rufe, 'Hey Rufe! How much money have you got on you?' and Rufe, he pats his coat pocket a couple of times, 'Oh,' he say, 'I brought along a few hundred in cash.' 'What?' I says, 'you got cash on you . . . up here in this blamed thing? What if we fall in the ocean and are never found . . . what then?' Well, anyway, ole Rufe, he worries and worries about it for a long time, then he comes to me with the money in his hand. 'Here,' he says. 'I sure wouldn't want to lose this if we hit the drink . . . will you keep it for me?' So Rufe gave me all of his money for safe keeping in case the plane went down.'"

Again, the laughter was two to three decibels above that of the pitch of the jet engines propelling us across the Great Mojave Desert far below. I took my 8mm movie camera around to all of the windows to film the sight for prosperity. It's too bad I didn't have a sound camera in order that I might have recorded much of our mirth in the same manner.

"Bond, I want a full report from you," Autry always told me and the other boys regardless of what he considered the subject to be.

♪   ♪   ♪

When we landed in Los Angeles, we stopped in at one of the private rooms and, while he was having one for the road, I called my wife informing her of our arrival. I asked her to call Mrs. Autry so the two of them could pick us up separately at Gene's office, which was then on Riverside Drive in Toluca Lake near the Warner Brother's Studios. When Gene saw me on the phone, he grabbed my arm, but my conversation had been completed.

"Don't tell them we're back," he said, shushing me with a finger to his lips.

"Too late, they already know."

"Oh, hell! Well don't tell them where we are just yet."

We had a couple of blasts, then grabbed a taxi for the long ride to his office. Once inside, he turned on the lights, walked around a bit, swaying (as was I), probed here and there in inconspicuous places until he located a pinch, which he offered to me.

"Oh, boy," I said, shaking my head. "I'm afraid you're got me under the table for this trip."

"I didn't get much sleep last night," he said, walking over to the couch, stretching out.

"May I use your phone to call my wife?" I asked.

"Go ahead, live dangerously," he waved his free hand.

I placed my call, asking her to pick me up, then said to Gene, "Now, may I use your phone to call your wife?"

He waved that one hand back and forth vigorously, "Dang you, Bond. You're about the most eager bastard I ever took to Philadelphia. What'ta you want to tell them where we are for? Give 'em time. They'll see us soon enough. Get off the damn phone."

"My wife will be picking me up any minute now."

"Fine! Go on home. Let me sleep a little. Just don't tell Ina Mae I'm back yet."

"She already knows," I said, dialing his home number. I felt obligated to do what I was doing since both of them did know that we were in town. When I held the receiver out to him, indicating that she was on the line, he did something that amazed me. He jumped to his feet, stood straight as a string, donned a smile that stretched from ear to ear, and in a voice as clear as a bell, said, "Hello, there Miss Ina Mae. Guess what, me'n Jonathan Q made it back. Now whatta you think of that?"

While their conversation continued, I got my things together and prepared for my lift home. As soon as he hung up he headed back to his couch, returning to his previous position.

So ends my Philadelphia story. It was one mile over and two miles back.
If I omit this chapter, who'll know the difference?

It's the tough decisions that get us down!

Anyway, I can still hear the cheers . . . all 88,000 of them.

They loved us in Philly!

CHAPTER TWENTY-THREE

Hot Rod Lincoln

Or, 'Son, You're Gonna Drive Me to Drinkin'
Or, We Give Up, Where'd You Hide the Goodies

Sixteen days after our return from Philadelphia, Gene called to tell me that "Hot Rod Lincoln" was a hit. After a slow start, the whole country was going to 'lay on it' both Pop and Country. Naturally, I was overjoyed. We got together and made plans for more recording sessions with the big problem being what to follow it with?

In the meantime, he was planning what turned out to be his final tour. Actually, it was two tours with a short layoff in between.

The cities were Knoxville, Tennessee; Reading, Pennsylvania; Trenton, New Jersey; (then ten days off) then stops in New Orleans and Baton Rouge, Louisiana, with the last date being Shreveport.

All of these engagements were State or Country Fairs, where we played the grandstands again. Much of our show was made up of circus type acts brought in from other sources. Of the Autry musical troupe, there were some old time regulars such as Rufe Davis, Merle Travis, with Betty Johnson taking the early dates followed by Anita Bryant taking the rest. Carl Cotner and the band missed this one, so we had to use local musicians.

Gone were the huge crowds of old and business was not good on these final tours. It was disheartening to look out at a huge grandstand full of empty seats where once there were thousands of cheering fans.

Mrs. Autry came along on these trips, as did Mrs. Herb Green. The five of us flew in Gene's plane as we journeyed from one town to the next. As we began the trip, the Boss came to me with a small box in his hand, showing the contents to everyone around.

"You see, Jonathan Q", he said, smiling proudly. "Here's twenty-five of your records ("Hot Rod Lincoln"). Since I'm the publisher and own the record company, it's no more than right that I should promote this record in person. I will hand them out to the disc jockeys, to the newspapermen, anybody that can help us sell a record. And, if these run out, there's more where they came from. I'm going to personally see to it that your record, your "Hot Rod Lincoln", is a smash hit. How do you like them apples?"

"Well, Boss, I'll tell you. Naturally, I'm very pleased," I assured him. "It's not only an honor to have a hit on your label but to know that you're promoting it yourself, well, I'm overwhelmed. What else can I say?"

With Mrs. Autry along, Gene was in pretty good shape, making all performances with a good voice and steady walk. Only once, in Trenton, was it obvious he must have been sneaking a few drinks on the side, for he made one serious blunder on the mike. Even so, his cover-up wasn't too bad at all.

This show was planned so that, after about an hour of various acts, on cue, Gene would announce loudly into the mike, "Now, if I can get a few of these musicians to gather around me, I'd like to sing a few songs myself."

Because of his memory lapses, he had a small piece of paper hidden in the palm of his hand that listed the show's line-up. As one act was ending he would refer to this list, making certain that he announced the next act correctly.

So it was in the proper place, but with a somewhat shaky voice, he gave the cue for us to step forward. He had a little difficulty getting through his songs this time, but, as most always, he made it. The crowd was polite, asking for more, but he waved them off by informing them that we had a lot more show yet to come.

With nothing to do for an hour, I wandered across the racetrack into the grandstand where a few people were gathering down front. Back behind the seats was the mid-way, where many folks wandered to and fro among merry-go-rounds and Ferris wheels, not to mention hot dog stands. By sticking close to the grandstand, I could hear the loud speakers while having a fairly good view of the stage itself. In this manner, I knew just about where they were in the show and when I should return for the wrap-up, his act with Champion and Little Champ.

As one act would finish amid usual applause, Gene, still announcing each and every act, would glance at his list and bring on the next performer. There were several yet to go. While I was putting mustard on my hot dog, trying to hold my mug of beer, I heard his say something over the loud-speakers that sounded quite strange to my eardrums:

"AND NOW, IF I CAN GET A FEW OF THESE MUSICIANS TO GATHER UP AROUND ME, I'D LIKE TO SING A FEW SONGS MYSELF."

What the hell! He just got through singing, not ten minutes ago. He had lost his place on the line-up and forgotten that he'd already sung his songs. I rushed over to the fence, looking toward the stage. It would have taken me too long to try to get backstage to remind him of his error.

"Johnny Bond!" he called again into the mike, looking to one side of the stage then the other. "Where in the . . . heck are my musicians?"

Just as I had done, the band had scattered to the winds, secure in the knowledge that the time to come forward was not for some time yet.

After he called a couple of more times, a very ticklish spot to be in for both him and me, he spotted me at the fence directly across the track from him, waving frantically at him for the proper cueing. He got the message. He looked at me, then back at his list and said, sheepishly, into the mike. "Oh!"

With that he processed to introduce the next act. It was the first and only time that I ever saw him make such an error.

"I wonder where he's hiding the jug?" I asked making certain that he was not within earshot. Herb said, "There's none in his dressing room, I've seen to that."

Jay Berry said, "Ain't none around the horse's van. He won't have any in his room at the hotel, not under the circumstances."

"But, he's obviously got himself a little jewel staked out somewhere," we all nodded in agreement.

"I wonder where in the hell it is."

Between performances as I passed by his dressing room, Gene called me in.

"Well, John," he said. "I might have missed a cue out there this after-noon, but what the hell, I've been so busy plugging your damned record here . . . " he patted the top of the box of 45 r.p.m. records. "We just have to keep this hit going, that's all there is to it."

I didn't remind him that the record had peaked in July and we were now in September, with sales tapering off. Where a "Silver Haired Daddy of Mine" or "Rudolph The Red Nosed Reindeer" might go on forever, a record of this sort is just like the hot rod it sings about, it can run out of gas. Still, if he wants to promote it, who am I to throw cold water on his plan.

Everywhere we went he carried the box of records with him. In the car; in the hotel lobby; even on the plane, always, "Hot Rod Lincoln."

Flying to the next date, (there were the usual five of us abroad—Herb, and Kitty Green, Gene, Ina Mae and myself—quite a five-some), Herb told us that arrangements had been made where the press would meet us at the airport, along with a group of youngsters and their parents who would be wanting autographs. There was to be a short ceremony of shaking hands and picture taking, things that would be making the next editions as publicity was badly needed on this trip.

As the plane landed, everyone on board began gathering their belongings.

"Eddie Hogan will be there with the station wagon to meet us." Gene said, reaching for the small box of records. "Just take those things that you need and he'll bring the rest."

I stepped out of the plane first so I could give assistance to the others as they came down the awkward steps. Gene followed after me, saying, "Here, Jonathan Q; take these records and put them in the back of the station wagon."

"O.K.," I said. "Give me the box and I'll just toss it to . . . "

"DON'T THROW IT!!!" Gene shouted into my ear in a loud whisper while rolling his eyes to one side, then the other in order to be sure that no one could hear.

"Records are unbreakable," I said.

"Dang you . . . " he continued, lowering his voice even more. "I've got my booze under those records. Didn't you know that?"

"Hell no, I didn't know that. What the heck do I know? I've been told that I don't know nothing." All this time I actually thought that he was plugging my record. He was merely using the box as his hiding place. Under the records.

Oh, well! Where there's a thirst, there's a way. Twelve years later Gene played "Hot Rod Lincoln" in his office for Jimmy Wakley and me.

"You know something," he said to us. "That's one hell of a juke box record."

"Makes a swell hiding place," I said.

"What do you mean by that? Wakely asked, not knowing. Gene and I just grinned at each other. The Lincoln finally ran out of gas.

CHAPTER TWENTY-FOUR

The Last Roundup

Or, The Final Tours Go Out In A Deafening Whisper
Or, Wrap It Up, Fellows, It's Been Grande
Or, How'n The Hell Did We Stand Up Under The Strain?

Monday, October 17, 1960, was a day of mixed emotions for me. We opened in Columbia, South Carolina, to a good crowd for a change, on the same day that "Hot Rod Lincoln." dropped out of the charts for good. It wasn't a total loss in my mind since we had what we thought was a good follow-up release already in the works. Gene hadn't yet informed me if he planned to promote this one personally. Even if he didn't, I would. I'd go to all of the radio stations in Carolina and Louisiana.

From Columbia we flew into New Orleans where we had a couple of days off. While Gene and Herb took their wives through the French Quarter, I went knocking on the doors of radio stations WNOE and WTIX trying to drum up spins for my new record, "X-15".

"Who're you?" said one young man, standing in the doorway of the station. He had evidently forgotten his 'southern' hospitality' since he didn't invite me in.

"I'm Johnny Bond. Didn't you play my "Hot Rod Lincoln."?

He turned around and yelled back at someone, "Hey, Joe! Have we been playing "Hot Rod Lincoln" by Johnny Bond?" I guess he got some kind of a positive answer for he turned back to me and said, "Yeah!"

"Well, I got a brand new release. Here it is, "X-15." You'll be the first to have it."

The man looked at the record but didn't offer to take it. Instead, he called the other man in and told him to 'take care of this guy.' He took the record, reluctantly, and left. He had the same look on his face that Clark Gable had when he told Scarlett goodbye at the Southern Plantation.

After encountering a similar reception at the other station I returned to the Roosevelt Hotel where I related the sad news to Gene, Ina, Herb and Kitty.

"Cheer up, Johnny," Gene said. "Remember. You make the records, I'll do the promoting."

"Besides," said Ina Mae, sympathetically. "We just made reservations for all of us for dinner this evening."

"Come on, Jonathan Q," Gene said to me during the lovely dinner. "Snap out of it. Why, those radio stations didn't know who you were. You didn't make the right approach. You should have had me call them first to let them know that you're coming."

You know something? That hadn't occurred to me.

The dinner at Antoine's was grand — but it was interrupted. The waiter came over informing us that somebody in the Autry party was wanted on the telephone.

"Who do they want?" Gene asked.

"Somebody named Vaughn? Pond," the man said.

"Oh, that's you, Johnny. Johnny Bond!"

"That's the one," said the waiter.

"Can't be me," I said. "Nobody knows I'm here."

"I'll get it for you," said Herb Green, jumping up from his seat. Gene, Ina, Kitty and I continued our dinner while my curiosity overcame my appetite.

Herb rushed back to our table. "It was WNOE. They want Johnny Bond over there immediately with a bunch of his new records of the X-15."

"Me! X-15?"

"Better get your ass over there right quick," said Gene, seemingly as excited as I was. "Have you got the record with you?"

"Record? No, not here."

"Hell of a recording star I've got under contract," said Gene, wrestling with his lobster.

"I left them all back at the hotel."

"Now if it was my record," said Gene. "I'd have a box right under my arm at all times."

"They asked that you come right over," said Herb, seriously.

"Hey!" I said, jumping up, preparing to leave my one and only dinner at Antoinnes. "Y'all can have my Brandy. I'll get, cab, grab the records and get over there. They're gonna play my X-15!"

"Sit down, Johnny," said Mrs. Autry as Gene and Herb tried to hide the expressions on their faces.

"What?"

"These two are pulling your leg."

Snickers went around the table as I meekly returned to my seat.

Oh, well. It wasn't a total loss. I finally had dinner at what's-his-name's.

The fact that I'd just come off a hit with "Hot Rod Lincoln" held no weight with the radio stations with "X-15." Some of them played it once or twice then dropped it for good.

Years later I made a suggestion to the manager of Republic Records. Why not re-release my record of the "Hot Rod Lincoln."? A whole new generation of teen-agers had grown up who may not have heard it.

They couldn't find the master.

I gave them mine but they decided not to release it again.

But, in 1972, "Hot Rod Lincoln" was an even bigger hit than before.

For Commander Cody!

Still, it was fun while it lasted.

I didn't quit. It quit.

♫   ♫   ♫

On the way to what turned out to be our final date in Shreveport, we landed at Baton Rouge and had lunch with Governor Jimmie Davis and his wife at the Mansion. Both Gene and I had been friends and business associates with Governor Davis for a long time. In their early recording days both Gene and the Governor had imitated the style of Jimmie Rodgers only to find out that they didn't need it. They both developed highly commercial styles of their own. The song "You Are My Sunshine" had been one of Davis's most successful compositions and Gene sang it often with great success.

Most of the talk around the table concerned Civil Rights that were one of the Governor's most pressing problems at the moment and they key issue in his recent re-election campaign. After over 30 years as a public servant, he still had occasional problems with doubters who had trouble separating Jimmie Davis, the entertainer from Jimmy Davis, the public servant. Even when he had first run for the office many years earlier, he had used a band playing and singing Country songs on his campaign tours, bringing much criticism from opponents.

"They wanted me to cut out the hillbilly music," said the Governor. "But I told 'em like it was. I said that Country music had fed me when I was hungry and clothed me when I was ragged. Before I'll cut it out, I'll cut myself out of the race. I won the first term with it, laid off politics because I couldn't succeed myself, and then ran again. Later on, if I feel like it, what the hell, I'm liable to try it again."

He also told us in confidence that he had been the target of a couple of sniper shots recently and that sort off carryings on could have a bearing on his future decisions.

Other discussions around the luncheon within the walls of the most colorful mansion concerned the current Presidential Campaign in which we were all interested. Both Gene and Ina supported Richard Nixon and I figured that the Governor, being a Democrat, would be supporting John F. Kennedy. Soon the conversation drifted toward their older songs and records, as well as the changing trends in the business.

"Johnny, how about yourself?" said the Governor with whom I had once collaborated on a song entitled, "Don't You Cry Over Me." I didn't have the heart to tell him that I was currently crying on the inside over a crippled X-15. "What have you had out on records lately?"

"You mean you didn't hear my "Hot Rod Lincoln"?

"Hot Rod Lincoln," drawled the Southern Governor.

"Mama, didn't we hear something about a Hot Rod car there awhile back. Was that you, Johnny?"

"That was ole Jonathan Q. at the wheel," said Gene, laughing.

"What you got coming out next?"

"If I'm smart I'll go home and cut "You Are My Sunshine" and couple it with "Don't You Cry Over Me.""

"Johnny's got a new record," said Gene. "But I think he might have dumped them all in the Gulf back there in New Orleans."

A most delightful, informal meeting was concluded after which we said our goodbyes and flew out to Shreveport where Mr. Davis had launched his political career.

One of the interesting sidelights of this particular tour were the constant discussions about the John Kennedy—Richard Nixon Presidential race of 1960. Practically all of the conversation in the plane was on this subject as we were all watching the debates between the two on television at our various stops. Sometimes we would have a special gathering of the entire

Autry troupe at which time we would have our own debates after the TV ones were concluded.

Both Gene and Ina Mae were very strong Nixon supporters and most definitely anti-Kennedy. They were most outspoken in their views and went into lengthy detail, especially with me when there was no one else around, about how tragic it would be for the country if Kennedy got elected. I began to feel like a 'one-man-captured' audience, but I enjoyed it and will confess that their arguments seemed valid. That year both my wife and I voted for Richard Nixon, but confess that we think John Kennedy was a very good President.

Four years later, they were just as supportive of Barry Goldwater and wanted no part of Lyndon Johnson. However, a day or two after the election, which Johnson won, they accepted an invitation to come to his Texas Ranch. The Autrys always took a deep interest in politics and were guests at the White House many times.

♫   ♫   ♫

The Shreveport, Louisiana, date was also a State Fair. However, instead of our appearing in the usual outdoor grandstand, we held fourth in one of the newer buildings, which was constructed along the same lines as some of the more popular arenas around the country. While it was a pleasure to work, the absence of the turn-away-crowds of years gone by put a small damper on the appearance. When we closed in Shreveport, on October 30, 1960, we did not know that this was the final show of the last tour. Had we known, I am certain that Gene would have called for some kind of a celebration. For more than 30, Gene Autry had been touring continuously, taking his talents and that of many, many others, to those who had no way to come to him.

This is not meant to imply that Gene had hung up his spurs and guitar completely. It was just the conclusion of another phase of his life. When any one of us mentioned to him that he should plan a grand 'farewell' tour, he merely shook his head and said, "Frankly, I think we've already had it."

While Autry was involving himself in the newest phase of his career, trying to get the new American League Baseball Franchise, I didn't see him around the usual haunts very much. So, I busied myself with my own problems, namely, trying to come up with another hit record on Republic and watching our once famous Town Hall Party close its doors.

I did manage to corner him one day and pointed out to him that Republic's brief splurge had just about splurged out, at least as far as my part of it was concerned. He not only gave me the green light to go with another record company, but he also gave his permission for me to use some of the Republic masters on the other label. I believe it is safe to say that few, if any other record company would be so lenient.

It is hard to realize that so many interesting things could have happened in one year, especially at this stage of the game. We had good luck, mediocre luck, and bad luck as we passed another milestone in his career.

I had been a part of a great transition in his life, his evolving from an Iconic Star of the entertainment field, to that of a respected, nationally known big businessman.

CHAPTER TWENTY-FIVE

1961—1964
The Lean Years,

Or, Where Have All The Cowboys Gone?
Or, Come On, Gene, Sing Us One More Song.

Where we had been in almost constant contact during the year 1960, the following four years turned out just the opposite. I still drew royalties from his music publishing companies as well as from Republic Records, but these were from past performances.

We did see each other on rare occasions; at a baseball game or accidental meeting at one of the Hollywood retreats, Brown Derby, Plaza Bar, and such. He was generally easy to find if needed. A call to his office was enough to determine if he was in town. I made it a point to bump into him accidentally now and then if, for no other reason, just to keep in contact and to let him know that I was still among the breathing.

There was another way that we could keep up with our former Boss without contact. Newspapers! Every so often we would note a small paragraph on some of the back pages where he had been stopped for a violation, stating that he had been driving while under . . .

He had been advised not to drive anymore even though they reported him as saying that most of these drives were just down to the corner for the evening paper. He might have made the papers more had it not been for the fact that on many occasions, the officers recognized the famous personality and chose to escort him to his home nearby rather than make out a ticket. It seems that, according to one daily, he had made contact with another automobile carrying youngsters and a huge lawsuit was filed.

"Well, I see where your suit was settled out of court," I said to him at the Plaza.

"That so?" Gene said, casually.

"Yes, well, it was in this morning's paper."

"I didn't see it. What did it say?"

"It just said that it was settled for a whole lot less than the original suit. I figured that you knew more about it than anybody."

"No, the lawyers . . . they handle all of that stuff. Let's have a snort."

He went on to say that he now knew he was going to have to get himself a chauffeur. Colonel Eddie Hogan drove him for a while. He even used both Carl and me on certain short journeys; but, after conferring with Carl in private, we both agreed that we were not quite ready for this type of regular employment. After a while he got a young driver who assisted him in other ways as well, sort of a driver-valet-and-constant companion.

Carl Cotner invested in and began operating a recording studio on Sunset Boulevard near Gene's radio station, where he maintained his offices. Carl and I talked about the advanced recording techniques wondered if Gene was aware of all the new techniques available.

"Let's get him in here for another session! Make an album, re-do many of his great hits in Living Stereo."

On January 22, 1962 we began a four-day recording session. Despite the fact that his voice was quite shaky and his tremolo was broader that ever, we were able to complete the sessions successfully. He even admitted to Jim Reeves, whom I had invited over one day to pay his respects, that where once recording used to be a simple task, now it was a tough job. All of his close friends were aware that he was in good condition at certain times, while at other times he might not be available for anything in the way of business.

However, the LP was completed after many over-dubs and released on RCA Victor (LPM/LSP 2623). It enjoyed considerable success, proving that, even after 32 years of recording, there were still plenty of fans around with money in hand to purchase a Gene Autry record.

This, then, would constitute the final recording sessions where Gene engaged in singing on phonograph records. He made two sides in 1964, a session in which I was not present. These were spoken recitations, the sermon, "One Solitary Life" (also known as "Here Was A Man"), and the traditional favorite, "A Cowboy's Prayer."

Another milestone transcended!

Of all facets of Gene Autry's show business career, it was the recording of phonograph records that was the first and the last on a steady basis. Now it took its place in line with the celluloid, the radio mike, and the empty stage. Show business for Gene Autry was definitely coming to a close.

By the end of 1964 I was beginning to wonder if my business association with Gene might have run its course. No so. Not yet. It was near the end of that year that I learned that *Melody Ranch* was to be revived.

This renewed association would take us well into 1970.

Thirty years!

CHAPTER TWENTY-SIX

"Take Five! — "

or, Playing Ketchup!
or, Cowboys Do Play Baseball,
or, Careful Sliding Into Third Base!

Let's talk baseball for while.

I once overheard Gene telling a radio interviewer that he had, at one time, played some semi-professional baseball. He didn't go into detail on the subject but I did run across other references in my research.

The first time that he invited me to a game was during the service tours when he was in uniform. Prior to that, I was aware of his excitement during the World Series, but that was strictly radio broadcasts, usually with the Yankees, and I was too engrossed in looking up at tall buildings and buying Brooklyn Bridges to notice what else might be going on around me.

We spent some time in Chicago in 1943, so when he caught Dorothy (my wife) and myself in the lobby of the Sherman Hotel one noon, he said, "You folks come along if you want to. We're going out to Wrigley Field to watch the Dodgers play the Cubs."

Captain Deke Holgate and our radio director, Brad Browne, were along as we watched the Cubs lose. We thought little about the outing even though I did take a few 8mm home movies of the event. Still, we were working for the owner of the Cubs, so I figured that it was for that reason alone that he had decided to go to the game.

Each fall thereafter, whenever we hit New York City, the World Series came into closer focus as there were then a few television sets around some of the local pubs. I knew Gene and some of the guys attended a few games, matinees permitting, but they never asked me to go along and I thought little about it. Who cares about New York's Yankees, or Giants, or Dodgers? If I had the chance, I'd much rather see *Oklahoma* on

Broadway. That evening around the dressing rooms backstage at the rodeo, most of the discussion was about the afternoon's game while Ace talked about broads.

Back home in Los Angeles, there was the Pacific Coast League, which had two local teams, the LA Angels and the Hollywood Stars. I went a few times but only became really interested when they put both teams on local TV. That was when I noticed that Gene spent a lot of time at the games. Sometimes the announcer would invite him over to the booth and have him call an inning or two just for kicks. He really was interested in baseball . . . I finally realized it. Don't have to hit me over the head with a Louisville Slugger. Not more'n once.

In 1958, the Dodgers came to Los Angeles and immediately fell into last place in the standings. Another cowboy movie star, Tex Ritter, being a great baseball fan, prompted me to start going to Dodger games. We went but soon discovered that, while we were sitting way beyond the outfielders, ole Gene was up front there close enough to hold hands with the batter, the catcher and the umpire. You might know that he'd have a season ticket right behind home plate.

Gene's radio station, KMPC, carried the Dodger games the first two years, so I guess that might have been the main reason he was up close while Tex and I were hanging over the far side of the Coliseum. I complained to Gene that I had tried to buy some better seats but the crowds were so large that all of the best seats were taken on a season basis. That did it. From then on, he or Ina Mae would call whenever they couldn't attend a game, so we got to use their box seats quite often.

In May of 1958, he booked a rodeo in Milwaukee and invited Merle Travis and me to go along. We had no more than hit town when the phone rang inviting us out to County Stadium for a game between the Braves and the Cards. We saw two games before our shows, and after each game Gene took us into the dressing rooms, introducing us to all of the players standing around in their complete nothings, either heading to or coming from the showers. (If anyone ever tells you that all men are created equal . . . don't believe it.)

By now I got the feeling that we were getting down to the business of baseball in earnest. It was obvious that he had something up his sleeve. At the time we knew not what.

The 1959 season began; he extended an invitation to share his box, and on many occasions, he and I went together. In August, he booked a tour of State Fairs where, again, Merle Travis and I were hired to go along. Dizzy Dean was then announcing the TV *Game of The Week,* so each Saturday of the tour, we would gather in Autry's suite to watch the action. The Dodgers were beginning to make some noise now so the interest by our part really began to increase.

"I'll bet he'll buy a team of his own," I said to Merle as the two of us left Gene's suite after watching a TV game.

"Sorta like you'n me buying a set of guitar strings," Merle said.

On September 19, 1959, while in Louisville playing a Fair, Gene came running to us with his transistor in hand.

"The Dodgers are tied for first place. They just took a double header from the Giants, 4 to 1 and 5 to 3," he shouted with just as much excitement as he would later show for the Angels. From that moment it was baseball as the tour took a back seat.

Near pandemonium broke out on September 27 when, on the last day of the season, the Dodgers tied the Braves for the pennant. We were in Richmond, Virginia and Gene's birthday was two days away. We all wanted to see the playoffs but we were working. No TV sets were available to us at the fairgrounds! What to do? We got our heads together and gave him his present early . . . a portable TV set on which we watched our team take the first game of the best 2 out of 3. That was on the 28th. On his 52nd birthday, September 29, 1959, we watched the Dodgers defeat Milwaukee to win the pennant in 12 innings, all this on his TV set. From the excitement in and around the Autry camp at the fairgrounds, a person would have thought that our names were O'Malley or Alston (owner and manager of the Dodgers).

On Tuesday, October 1, we gathered in Gene's suite to watch the first game of the World Series from Chicago. The White Sox skunked us 11 to 0. It wasn't the end of the world, though, for they played the next day as we again gathered around the TV, Dodgers 4 to 3.

Hurricane Gracie swept up from the Gulf and hit Richmond hard, washing out the last of our tour, so, late that afternoon, Gene and Herb gathered several of us into his plane and we took off for Los Angeles.

"Ever been to a World Series, Jonathan Q?" Gene asked along the all-night flight.

"Never have," I informed him.

"Next time we land for gas, call Dorothy and have her meet us at the Lockheed Airport. Tell her to have her baseball clothes on because we're all going."

He didn't have to tell me twice. I followed his instructions. Upon landing, Gene called me aside to hand me tickets for the three games in the Coliseum. This was a great thrill for us as we watched our Dodgers go from last place a year ago, to World Champs.

There were other Autry employees seated near us who had received their tickets the same as I had. I said to Billy Baukam, "I think I'll pay Gene for these tickets," to which Billy replied over the roar of the crowd, "Are you kidding, these tickets didn't cost him anything. Company seats. None of us plan on paying him for them."

A few days later I had occasion to meet Gene at his office on other business. I had the exact amount of the six tickets in my hand. At least I was going to make the offer.

"Thanks for the tickets, Gene," I said, handing him the loot.

"You're mighty welcome, Jonathan Q," said the Cowboy, taking the money.

After that he relayed the sad news to me.

"O'Malley has pulled his broadcasts away from us," he said, shaking his head. "Moving over to KFI."

"Sorry to hear it. Why don't you carry the Giants games?"

"Well," he drawled it out. "You can't do that." I should have known that the Giant's broadcasting rights would not allow their game to come into the Dodger's territorial rights. But he didn't go into detail.

"Only one thing left for you to do," I said, jokingly.

"What's that?"

"Get your own baseball team and put 'em on your station."

"I might just do that," he answered. And he did.

On December 9, 1960, he was awarded the new American League franchise, which he promptly named the Los Angeles Angels after the Pacific Coast Angels who had gone out of existence when the Dodgers and the National League had moved in. In April of the following year, his Angels opened on the road, beating Baltimore 7 to 2. Years later I heard him confess that that win was his greatest thrill in baseball.

When they opened at home in the old Wrigley Field against the Minnesota Twins, we were there watching and listening to KMPC on our small transistors. Once again he had a baseball broadcast on his radio station.

Later, the Angels played in Dodger Stadium for a season, while Angels Stadium was being built in Anaheim. On the way home from one of the games at Dodger Stadium he observed some vacant property near Warner Brother's Studios.

"That would make a fine location for a baseball stadium," he said, pointing as we drove by.

"Don't you like using Dodger Stadium?"

"Hell, O'Malley gets all the parking and the concessions. We can't make any money." He left out the fact that the crowds were not turning out for the Angels like they were for the World Champions. According to the newspaper accounts, the City of Anaheim built the present Stadium. All that he and his Angels had to do was move in.

They invited us to many games once they were the California Angels, but only once did we sit in the upstairs box especially built and reserved for the owners of the team. This was a very exciting game for, if the Angels could beat Minnesota on this night, they would tie for first place.

Gene escorted Dorothy and me into the room, saying, "And sit down anywhere you like. That is, anywhere except right here."

He pointed out a special seat behind a desk with a telephone. That was where he sat during the entire game. Not once did he call out, neither did it ring. For several innings the game was scoreless and excitement ran high all over the stadium. Mrs. Autry was there as were several of their closest friends. Somewhere along in the game the Angels managed to get on the scoreboard.

"Tonight we go into a first place tie!"

But then, the Twins got some hits, the Angels made a couple of booboos, and it soon appeared that there would be no tie for tonight. Gloom spread through the stadium while all was quiet in the Autry box.

When the Angels came up in the bottom of the ninth, needing a run to tie or two to win, I leaned over to Gene and said, " I think you'd better get on that telephone."

"Whatta you mean?"

"Well, that is a direct line to God, isn't it?"

Eventually it wasn't for the Twins retained first place that night and the Angels lost ground for the rest of the season.

The California Angels have been somewhat a disappointment in the standings as well as at the gate. Many, many people are pulling for them, hoping for a pennant, if for no other reason . . . ole Gene's sake.

CHAPTER TWENTY-SEVEN

Charity on the Q.T.

Or, "It didn't cost much."
Or, "It's a deal, but make the check out to . . ."

Ray Hodge was a sick boy. That was obvious by just looking at him. I am not sure of the name or extent of his ailment, but I would guess that it was something related to cerebral palsy. Merle Travis called it 'spastic.'

Ray was a Western Music fan, a Gene Autry fan. He loved us all. The first time we saw him in the audience we couldn't believe that anyone with a boy in this condition would allow him to be out of the hospital, let alone the house. Our first impression was that he was either drunk or making fun of us. His head and eyes rolled around, back and forth in the manner of a wild man. His arms and legs were never still. There was a moaning, groaning sound always coming through his very broad grin. In the middle of a Broadcast (live) he was liable to get up and struggle up the aisle. You would have to see his walk in order to believe it. All fours went wildly in opposite directions. He carried, or, rather, wielded a cane. Sometimes the cane would touch the floor, other times it would be flaunted high above his head, which, incidentally, was still bobbing from one side to the other.

"You just don't know what to make of a character like that," someone said.

Soon Ray was a regular backstage visitor during rehearsals and after the broadcasts. We had gotten acquainted with him and learned that, in spite of his bodily afflictions, his mind seemed to be quite normal. His speech however was the worst as he talked only with the greatest of effort and not always in audible tones.

His only ambition was to see, hear and get to know the Western stars, Gene Autry being number one . . . who else? However, Gene did not appear to pay him any attention. Oh, he might say, "Hi Ray," or something like that, but that seemed about the extent of it.

So I thought.

One day as I entered the stage door of CBS to begin our rehearsals, I noted Ray Hodge seated in the hallway next to Studio B waiting for things to begin. Having a few minutes to spare and always curious to learn more about the poor unfortunate, I seated myself beside him where I was promptly shown a circular that he had been reading.

"That's a mighty fancy looking bicycle, Ray," I told him after observing the photographs of the impressive looking machine.

"K . . . k . . . k Quadracycle," he blurted out with much effort.

"You gonna get yourself one so you can get around Hollywood better?"

"Yeah!" The way that Ray said, "yeah" was something else. Merle Travis and I spent hours trying to duplicate the sounds and the motions that he had to go through in order to get it out.

"Looks expensive," I informed him, shaking my head. "Where you gonna get enough money together to buy all that?"

With that he clumsily produced the rest of the circular. There was the catcher. Billfolds, pocket books, purses, belts everything having to do with manufactured leather goods.

"You're going to sell these?"

Again came that word; that gesture; that production, "Y-e-o-w!"

It should be related here that Ray not only attended our broadcasts, but other shows at the CBS Studios as well, as well as those at NBC, just a couple of blocks down Sunset Boulevard. Often, we would see him displaying his wares to this entertainer and that. Regretfully, we didn't witness too many sales.

A few weeks later, while crossing the CBS parking lot headed to the stage, I spotted several of our gang gathered in a circle talking. As I approached, I saw Ray Hodge seated in his brand new Quadracycle. It was shiny and fascinating, as was the big grin on Ray's face. He was in Seventh Heaven. As our group began to break up and head for the rehearsal, I edged over to Ray who was now starting up the motor to show that it was self-propelled.

"You didn't get this by selling billfolds, did you, Ray?"

"No."

"Somebody had to buy it for you, didn't they?"

Once more came out that wild, "Y-e-o-h!"

"Who bought it and gave it to you, Ray?"

"G-G-G-Geeeeeeene did, "He blurted out.

This was my first indication of the type of charity that Gene believed in. When did they confer? None of us noticed. As far as we knew Gene had always given Ray the brush.

Now, this.

" I saw Ray's new bike," I said to Gene at the rehearsal.

"That right?" Gene answered, deep into his script.

"Nice of you to buy it."

"Didn't cost that much," he answered, walking away, obviously wishing to avoid the subject.

For the next several months Ray Hodge drove to the studio and up and down Sunset Boulevard in his new vehicle. We wondered how he managed it in traffic, but then, he managed. Then one day Ray was absent.

"Ray's late for rehearsal," Ace said, laughing.

Several weeks went by, still no Ray Hodge. We inquired about him around the studios but no one had seen him. If he had been involved in a traffic accident I think we would have learned about it, either through newspapers or some authority with whom Gene was close. The only thing that I know is that . . . Ray Hodge and his Quadracycle had vanished from the scene.

"Wonder what happened to Ray?" I asked Gene.

"Damned if I know," he answered, studying his lines.

♫   ♫   ♫

Abe Lefton was the World's Greatest Rodeo announcer. That was not only Gene Autry's opinion, but that of the rest of us as well. It was the job of the announcer to describe certain events, especially to the Eastern audiences; to give the names of the horses and riders and generally keep the show moving during lulls. For instance, while a grounded cowboy was being carried from the arena on a stretcher, Abe would fill the time relaying one of the many appropriate antidotes relating to the various events.

"Now, here comes a little doggie," he would say during the calf-roping event. "Y'all know what a dough—gie is, don't you? Well, I'll tell you. A lit-

Abe Lefton, Gene's friend and announcer.

tle doggie is a calf who doesn't have a father and whose mama has run off with another Bull."

Abe was part of the Autry gang, not just during the Rodeo season; he was conspicuously present a lot of other times as well. He and Gene were very close and it was not unusual to see them together often. Abe had appeared in Gene Autry movies as far back as 1936.

Abe was a bit older than Gene, a mite heavier and shorter. Still, when it came to Western costume, Abe held his own for he always dressed the part of the Hollywood Cowboy.

Once, I walked into the Madison Square Garden dressing room where Gene, Abe and a bunch of the boys were engaged in a poker game. Everyone was laughing except Abe, who had his eyes glued, soberly, to his cards. It was obvious that I had missed out on a story, so I began to prod them to bring me up-to-date.

"Ask Abe," they told me . . . so I asked Abe.

Abe grumbled, "Bunch of perverts. Up to their old practical jokes again."

It took only a small amount of persuasion to get the full story. It seems that sometime during the previous evening, Gene and Abe were in Autry's suite when a phone call from Ace enticed them down the hall to the latter's room. As they reached the door, Abe knocked and prepared to lead Gene inside. Instead of Ace opening the door, Abe was greeted by a shapely young lady wearing a Stetson Cowboy Hat. Nothing else!

"You should have seen Lefton's face," laughed Gene over his full house. "I never saw so many changes of color in my life."

"Trouble is," said Abe, grumbling. "That damn Autry wouldn't let me go inside."

"She was Ace's girl."

"He shouldn't be displaying her wares so openly."

"Somebody had to protect you, Abe."

"Look at him, boys," Gene pointed at the Rodeo Announcer. "That was midnight last night and he's still shaking like a leaf!"

This was only one of many practical jokes pulled on Abe or any one of the rest of us. Few people ever got as close to Autry, who's love for the announcer was no secret in rodeo or Hollywood circles. One day Abe surprised everyone by bringing in and introducing a very tall, shapely and very beautiful young lady.

"Mr. Autry and fellow hillbillies," said Abe, smiling proudly. "May I present the new boss lady, Mrs. Abe Lefton."

The announcer, at that point in his life, must have been pushing 60. The bride couldn't have been much over 25, but she proved to be a good mixer, for very soon she was one of the gang, blending into the Autry family of musicians and executive's wives. Autry teased only those that he was fond of. If he didn't like somebody, they were treated in a polite, business like manner.

"Hot-damnit, Abe," Gene would say with a broad grin. "Whatta you mean marrying up with a pretty, young thing like that? Don't you know she'll wear you down to a frazzle? Why just look at you, already you're shaking like a leaf. I told you that young bride was too much for an old man."

It was true. Abe was shaking a lot, not just occasionally, but all of the time. It is unfortunate for him that during this same time Dick Tracy was running a character in his cartoon by the name of 'Shaky.' It followed naturally that we all began applying this name to the announcer.

"Please don't do that," his wife begged us. "It's beginning to get serious." We cut it out and Gene urged Abe to see a doctor. He did, and the verdict hit us all hard . . . Abe Lefton had Parkinson's disease . . . incurable at the time.

Abe Lefton's career as a rodeo announcer lasted only a few more months as his ailment increased. Soon, he was replaced by Pete Logan.

Abe soon left the scene but we kept up with his progress through Gene. We learned that Abe was convalescing someplace where he was well cared for. Autry visited him often, but was vague in describing his condition, leaving us to guess that it was getting to the critical stage.

I was seated in Gene's office one day following a recording session when he was told that the Coliseum Committee was after him to do the Annual Sheriff's Rodeo.

"I told them that I've done it so many years in a row . . . "

"They're going to call back in a few minutes," his secretary announced.

"O.K., I'll talk to them."

When the representative called, this was Gene's proposition,

"Alright, I'll do it on one condition. You make the check out to Abe Lefton. Got that? Fine, me and the boys will all be there."

Overhearing this conversation gave me an idea. The powers at *Town Hall Party* had been asking me to use my influence to get Gene to appear as a guest, but I had begged off claiming that the budget couldn't come close to Autry's price. I went then to both Gene and Bill Wagnon, the *Town Hall Party* manager and the same sort of deal was made. Gene Autry appeared at *Town Hall Party* to a turn-away crowd. Checks were made out to Abe Lefton.

A few months later we were informed that the Parkinson's disease had finally taken it's toll. Abe Lefton, one of the great colorful figures and rodeo announcers, was gone. I have it on good authority that total, final expenses were handled by . . . guess who!

♫   ♫   ♫

When the opportunity presented itself, Gene liked to visit the local hospital and perform for the kids in the children's ward. There was the time we played for a group of kids in one big city hospital, about a dozen kids as I recall. They were happy, cheerful, laughing and all adored Gene, whom they had seen in the movies and television, and listened to him on radio and records. His "Rudolph" was hot then, so he always had them sing it with him. He sang the song whether it was close to Christmas time or not. Most times Gene would shake their hands upon leaving and say,

"Well, I gotta go now and see about Champion and Little Champ. They told me to tell you kids that they're sorry that they couldn't come along today. We'll be back in town again next year, but then, of course I hope you won't be in the hospital that long. We hope that you're all up and around again in no time at all."

With that, they all would yell out in agreement.

Upon leaving the room with the nurse in charge, Gene said to her, "They're a fine bunch of youngsters. Wish I had some of my own just like them."

"Thank you for coming, Mr. Autry," said the nurse. "This is a nice farewell for them even if they don't know."

"What do you mean by that?" asked the Cowboy.

"I mean none of them are going to live much longer."

"Why . . . you can't mean that," said Gene, obviously shaken. "Why, they all look so happy. What's wrong with them anyway?"

"Oh, didn't you know. That's our cancer ward."

"Cancer!" Gene said, looking first at the nurse, then at each of us in his musical group. His expression was one of sober, total disbelief. "But you are trying to cure them, aren't you?"

"Of course, we're doing everything we can."

"Maybe you can do it yet," Gene said. All of us looked back through the glass door at the children who were now engaged in their daily routines.

"Nobody's figured out a way to cure it yet," said the nurse, shaking her head in total defeat.

"All of them are going to die!" somebody behind me said.

"Maybe not," said Gene, slowly walking away from the door. "Maybe not."

There was total silence within the Autry group as we headed for the auditorium to start our matinee.

At least we knew how he felt.

CHAPTER TWENTY-EIGHT

Meet The Colonel

Or, Wasn't He The Boston Cowboy?
Or, Watch That First Step, Hogan, It's A Bugger!

When playing the rodeos in New York and Boston, we were accustomed to mixing backstage with dozens upon dozens of strangers in cowboy costumes. So, when I first saw the big man standing there, well over six feet tall, more than 300 pounds, cowboy boots and suit all shiny with a razor crease, Stetson hat haloed by a 5-inch brim, beet-red face flushed and full, grin that would make a Halloween pumpkin pucker, I knew full well that someone unusual had fallen into the middle of the Autry melting pot.

Everything about the big man was Western except the accent. Although he tried to imitate the deep Southwestern dialect, it always came out Back Bay, for it was there in Boston that we first set eyes upon 'the Colonel.'

Where did he come from? How did he enter the picture? Who knows? He just showed up! And where did he get the 'Colonel' bit? Here again it had to be self-invented. "Colonel Eddie Hogan, that's me, yes, su-u-u-u-u-h! Heh, heh, heh."

"What was his job with Autry? You name it. Shine the boots. Press a wrinkle out of Gene's Levi's. Drive the car. Pitch that bale. Tote that bag. As long as it didn't involve singing, picking, or flying the plane, it came under the Colonel's province.

One of the girls in Gene's fan club complained that she couldn't get in to see the singer.

"Why not?"

"I can't get around that big hippo blocking Gene's dressing room door."

"By George, you're right. A person would need a road map."

"Now he's a bodyguard!"

So, what happens? I sit down at the lunch counter with Jay Berry and Carl Cotner and whom do we see down at the other end? Colonel Hogan filling the complaining chick's ear full of steer droppings. (That's Bull!)

"Get a load of that, will you?" said Jay, shaking his head in disbelief. "The gal can't get to Gene because of the roadblock, so now she's having lunch with the roadblock!"

"That's one way to get a gal."

"Oh, he gets his share of the women. Don't sell the Colonel short."

"What's he whispering in her ear?"

"I can imagine," said Jay. "Here, watch this!"

Jay Berry arose from his seat at the counter, walked casually to a spot just behind the Colonel's right shoulder. Hogan was looking in the opposite direction, talking to the girl.

"Oh, I say, Colonel Hogan," Jay said. "Whatta you want done with them ten thousand cattle you bought yesterday?"

Without any hesitation whatsoever, the Colonel turned his head quickly to the right and said, "Ship 'em to Montana tomorrow!" After which he returned to his own special kind of 'bullshipping.'

♪   ♪   ♪

Hogan was in charge of Gene's wardrobe and dressing room. He was usually the first one in the building, seeking out Gene's private corner. It was his job to help Jay Berry drag the huge wardrobe trunks inside, and then he worked until the room looked presentable.

Every now and then certain items in the room turned up missing.

"It can't be the fans, Boss," said Hogan. The way he pronounced 'Boss' and 'Boston' was a masterpiece within itself. First he would pucker his lips, let out with a loud, long 'baugh-h-h-h,' fading it away with the lips resolving into the inevitable grin, wiping out with the 'us-s-s-s,' or as the case might be, 'baugh-h-h-h-s-s-s-tun.'

"I got me an idea it might be these local stage hands. After all, they got a key too."

"Then I think we'd better start using our own locks and keys," said our singing Baugh-h-h-h-us-s-s.

"Yes, suh-h-h-h-h. I'll get us a good one tomorrow."

The Colonel's domain. The clothes rack built for Gene at a Madison Square Garden Rodeo.

"When?"

"Right now!"

The new padlock was obtained. From that moment, only Gene and Eddie had a key. By this time it was apparent to all that Eddie was the type of servant to whom, if the boss said "Jump!" Eddie said "How high?"

Naturally, this was too good a set-up to leave lay. So before long, we were egging Gene on to get the Colonel to move faster.

Following one of Gene's stage acts, Hogan, the Boss, and several others of us were walking rapidly in the direction of Gene's dressing room in some kind of a hurry. Hogan was out front, running, puffing, straining, and carrying several articles of wardrobe in his arms. As we reached the door, Gene and the rest of us were forced to stop and wait for Hogan, who was already there, panting, cursing and fuming while fumbling through his pockets searching for his key.

"Damn it, Colonel," said Gene, winking at us where Eddie couldn't see. "I want that door opened . . . NOW!"

Without further ado, with less than a fraction of a second lost, Eddie Hogan, 'the Colonel,' reared back and, with one lunge, pushed his big frame through the door the same way that many a movie stunt man has burst through those made of balsa wood.

Hogan, now inside, turned, bowed, and said, "Come in, Baugh-h-h-h-us-s-s-s-s!"

We all entered through what was once a locked door.

♬　　♬　　♬

Later on that night, another incident on the same subject of loyalty and speed could have been fatal to Hogan. Thankfully, he suffered only a few scratches and bruises.

'One-nighters' is a term meaning just what it says. You play a town today (tonight), move on to another tomorrow. Because of the constant travel between venues, many things were strange to us, including the auditoriums in which we appeared. At one of our destinations, I entered the stage door of one such auditorium and I immediately was confronted by, of all things, a stairway.

Not thinking this unusual, I began climbing until I reached a dead end. This was not a stairway! I found myself standing on a bare platform no larger than a ping-pong table though much, much higher off the floor. With a little more momentum I might have gone on over the side where no welcome arms or fireman's net waited receptively. I looked over the edge and quickly decided that I'd better go back down the same way that I came up.

As I stood there observing this strange contraption, I came to the conclusion that it was some kind of a ramp/platform which the local stagehands used to wheel themselves from place to place while attending to their backstage chores. The thing had inadvertently been left in front of the stage door where, as it turned out, almost all of us had encountered the same experience.

"Did you climb those stairs, too?" was the question put to me by several of the gang as I joined them in our dressing room.

"Sure thing. Don't tell me you all made the same mistake."

"Doesn't everyone?" asked Jerry Scoggins, who used the phrase often.

Once the show got underway the ramp was soon forgotten.

"Got anything to eat in here, Hogan?" asked the boss.

"You name it, Boss . . . I got it.

"I think a couple of sandwiches and some soft drinks would be in order. I had so many things to do today I didn't get much time for dinner."

The Colonel was off immediately leaving the assurance that he would return 'toot sweet' (whatever that means) with the grub. After he left there was light laughter around Gene's dressing room.

"There's only one Colonel Hogan," said Gene. "He is a jewel."

Hogan's return took longer than expected. We had heard a commotion downstage, but thought nothing of it, since these disturbances were not uncommon.

When Eddie Hogan finally re-appeared, he was definitely not the same Colonel that Gene had sent out for food. He was battered, bruised, scratched, and, just a bit deflated, as was the supper that he had gone to fetch.

The local stagehands filled us in. To begin with, the Colonel does not embark on a mission as anyone else might. His is much more of a production unlike any other, except perhaps for the Bull Buffalo or the Vikings star fullback. When Hogan takes off, his head is down, his shoulders charging 'out-of-my-way,' with his strong legs digging a furrow. He must complete his mission for the Boss. Soon he is out of the building and into the small restaurant nearby where he cons the waitresses with the notion that, if they hurry with this order, he might be persuaded to return after the show and give them the pleasure of his company until dawn.

The food order is prepared and snuggly placed under the full protection of his strong arms. Once again he lowers his head, shifts into over-drive and is off for the spot where his Hero awaits.

When the Colonel entered the stage door, like everyone else, he began to scamper up those stairs. Up, across and . . . over, went the Colonel. They say that when his 300 pound frame hit the floor with a jolt that would put most of us in the hospital, he never quit plowing. He was up and going at once . . . mission completed.

"Here's your supper, Boss. Sorry it took so long," said the Colonel, mopping his brow with one hand while caressing his rump with the other.

"Better quit taking those short cuts, Colonel," Gene told him.

♬   ♬   ♬

The auditorium in Hope, Arkansas, was something less than Carnegie Hall. It resembled an Army Quonset hut more than anything. Still, it was a large one and the afternoon matinee was filled with screaming, laughing children with parents, clamoring for all of us to get on with it and 'bring on the horses.' There were no dressing rooms, so all of us had to stand around outside in back of the building, close to a doorway that led to the makeshift stage.

Fell the night. Since Autry made most of his tours in the wintertime, Hope was no exception. Hope for warmth that night was remote. When I finished my act there was no place for me to go except back outside, into the cold night. But, lo! Hope had returned to Hope. As I made my exit into the darkness, I beheld a light . . . a huge bonfire that Jay Berry, with the help of others in the troupe, and built. They dragged various types of fence posts, railroad ties, etc., up to the area of the Autry rolling stock: automobiles, station wagons and horse trailers, where the torch was lit.

The fire was blazing big and hot.

"How hot was it?" Well, let me tell you!

I mean, they had built a fire that was putting out the heat. It was at least six to seven feet in diameter, with flames rising to our shoulder heights. I rushed up to where everyone in the troupe was standing, except, of course, for those still on stage, including the Star.

The minute that I thawed out, I backed off to take note of how things stood. There was Colonel Eddie Hogan, standing directly across the flames where he could face both the source of heat and the back door of the building, just in case Gene should beckon. Carl, Frankie, Herb, and several others were there, enjoying the welcome warmth as outstretched hands rubbed themselves in the area of the leaping flames.

After a few minutes the fire simmered down to about waist high, but the heat was just as intense and the coals were just as red. From the look of Cotner and Marvin, I knew that something was in the works. After I saw Jay Berry's grinning face, I knew it. Cold silence followed. Only the crackling of the flames competed with the faint sounds of the show coming from the back door of the building about 50 feet away.

"Hey, Colonel, the Boss wants you!" yelled Jay, suddenly.

All that Eddie Hogan needed to do was to step back about two steps, take two or three steps either to his right or left and he would have a clear, open path to the back door. But Colonel Eddie Hogan didn't always take the clearest path to his ultimate destination. Upon hearing that his Boss needed him, Eddie bowed his head low threw both feet into low gear and advanced forward. Through the heat, the coals, the flames, and the roaring laughter, charged the Colonel.

When he returned to the bonfire a few minutes later with the knowledge that Gene had not beckoned, his laughter was as loud as any of ours. He loved a good joke . . . even on himself.

♫   ♫   ♫

Every time I think of Colonel Eddie Hogan I visualize him surrounded by pretty girls while running up stairways.

Eddie always was a bachelor, so when I tell about his amorous adventures I don't have to fear the wrath of wives or mother's-in-law searching for legal grounds to throw at my good and pure buddies.

We played New Orleans often, where Carl, Frankie and I would stroll through the French Quarter. After seeing the shows we would usually wind up on a street corner purchasing hot tamales from a street vendor. Anyone who hasn't experienced the thrill of peeling a steaming hot tamale on a cold, cold night along Bourbon Street has not yet lived life to the fullest.

On this particular evening in New Orleans, I declined the invitation to the Quarter; instead I went to my room at the Jung Hotel, wrote my wife a letter (I was under strict orders to write each day), then hit the sack.

The letter was no problem, but falling asleep was. I decided to get up, dress and go down to the lobby to see what was going on. The lobby was deserted. So I thought!

"Hiya, John!" came a greeting from out of the shadows. I recognized the Boston accent.

"Hiya, Colonel. What are you doing sitting here all alone? Don't you know that all the Nawleans women are waiting for you down on Bourbon Street?"

"Oh, I'd like to stroll down there alright, but I hate to go alone. Nobody around here . . . I guess they're all down there already."

Now I ask you. Could I desert my good pal, Eddie, and stand in the way of his seeing the French Quarter?

"Come on, Eddie. I'll go with you. But, I'm warning you . . . I might cut out on you early, as I'm real sleepy."

Away we went . . . tall, skinny me, and tall, big, fat, lumbering, Colonel, wide brimmed hat and all, off to see Mardi Gras land at midnight. From the way his eyes bugged out at all the strip joint's sights, I suspect that this was his first visit into the famed Southland Creole district.

We sat at a bar sipping small beers, while behind the bar the bartender, a curvaceous blonde, shucked herself like an ear of corn. Hogan would raise his beer bottle to the gal who later came over to ascertain if she could reach her small arms all the way around his bulky frame. I felt like the lone, lone ranger, but that was O.K. Hadn't I just sealed my heart in the airmail envelope? You bet cha!

On to the next joint where history repeated itself; with Hogan and the broads, that is. About the time I figured that I'd done my duty for my gigantic pal. I searched my limited vocabulary for the right words so I could tell him I was cutting out.

"Don't leave me, John" said the Colonel, trying to squeeze out some crocodile tears as if that would entice me to stick around until dawn. Dawn? The bus left at dawn and I was leaving these joints behind me now.

"Colonel, I have completed my cook's tour, showing you the exotic side of New Orleans. You've got yourself a half-a-dozen goodies staked out. All I have to say to you is, 'hang on to your pocket book and good night.'"

"Wait right here a minute, John. I'll be right back." Hogan left my side to join a few of his cuties down at the other end of the bar. They chewed the fat for a minute or two after which he returned with this message.

"Hey, John. Guess what? All these gals want us to hang around awhile longer."

"Sure they do. Didn't you buy each of them a bottle of Champagne? You're the kind they're out for."

"No, you don't understand. They're available."

"You don't say. Well, Colonel, I'll tell you what. You can have your share and mine too, I'm gone."

"Wait just one more second, John. I'll be right back," said the Colonel, returning to his anticipated all-night companions. They went into another huddle after which he returned with another communiqué.

"Hey, John, guess what? Those gals want me to stay regardless. You don't mind, do you?"

"Hogan, you're a growed-up boy, over 21. You are on your own. All that I ask you to do is to hang on to your money. You've already spent a lot on the gals and, in case you didn't know it, their companionship could get to be costly."

"No, no," said the Colonel, rummaging through his pockets. I couldn't help thinking about the time that he was looking for the key to the dressing room lock. "Here, here's all my money. They tell me they want me for free."

"I might have known." So I took all of Hogan's money and returned to my room. In spite of all my good intentions, I found that I had only about two hours until the alarm sounded.

"Here's your money, Colonel," I said to the big man at our next stop down the line, "As our Boss always says, how about a full report?"

"Heh, heh, heh," was Hogan's reply.

That was all. Just one big pumpkin grin and,

"Heh, heh, heh."

♫   ♫   ♫

The one thing about Autry's employee is that he was loyal, dedicated, eager and tireless. He aimed to please and allowed no obstacle to hinder his progress. Once, Hogan drove Gene, Ina Mae, Herb and me to our hotel. Before we could as much as get out of the station wagon, Hogan was out ahead of us and had all of the Autry's suitcases in his hands and under his arms. The fact that there were several doormen and bellboys for that very feat meant nothing to the Colonel. They had their job to do and he had his. It was his perceived duty to get to the desk first so that he could announce in a loud voice that Mistuh Awe-try had arrived.

We watched the Colonel plow his way through all of the hotel help heading toward the doors leading into the lobby. We followed him chuckling. Once inside, we discovered that the lobby was up one level and there were no stairs, only two escalators. One going up to the lobby, the other coming down. What else?

As Herb, Gene, Ina Mae and I stepped on to the up escalator for the short ride, we heard a commotion unlike anything else we had ever heard. Looking across the way we spotted Colonel Eddie Hogan, loaded with luggage, head down, wheels spinning in high gear, panting, puffing, struggling like nobody ever struggled.

The Colonel was trying to climb a set of stairs that insisted on coming down. Eddie Hogan was on a treadmill to nowhere.

"Colonel!" said Gene Autry, stifling a horselaugh. "What in the hell are you doing?"

"I gotta get up to that desk before my boss gests there," said Eddie. His wheels resembled that of the famous Roadrunner in the cartoons.

The strange part about it was . . . he beat us to the desk and completed his mission.

"Mistuh and Misses Gen AWE - tree have arrived!"

♫   ♫   ♫

"Don't give that job to Colonel Hogan," said Gene Autry to the Circus High-diver at the fairgrounds in Trenton, New Jersey, during our stand of September 1960.

"Why, he'll burn the stadium down."

In spite of the Boss's warning, the high-diver enlisted the Colonel's assistance in his act and just as Gene had predicted, the place was almost destroyed by fire. Almost, but not quite.

I made it a practice to keep my 8mm home movie camera handy and as a consequence, have a lot of great footage of my Autry years. (Come over to the house and I'll gladly show them).

I considered the high-diver's act quite colorful so I decided to film it. Here's the way the scene turned out (just in case you can't make it over in person).

As the diver began climbing the very tall pole, I started my film rolling. Up, up and away he went. The blue skies and the white clouds form a perfect background as he progresses toward the Heavens.

With my free eye I can see Eddie Hogan approaching the small tank of water at the base of the tall pole. Having caught this act before, I knew exactly what was coming next. The diver/climber reaches the small platform atop the pole and stands erect up on it . . . hands pointed upward. On cue from above, Eddie Hogan is to pour a small vial of gasoline upon the surface of the water in the tank. Then, on another cue, Hogan is to light a match, causing the entire surface of the water to become engulfed in flames.

As my camera buzzes away, I see the diver leave his lofty perch and follow him all the way down, grabbing a few frames of the flames before he hits the surface. The minute he does that, the inevitable waves devour the flames, the diver floats to the surface and waves to the crowd.

Even though the high-dive act has concluded, I kept the film rolling for I wanted to pan over to Eddie Hogan. I found him in my view-finder. He had managed to set fire, not only to the surface of the water tank, but also to the dry grass all around the base of the structure. Now he was fighting the flames with his coat and grinning at me through the viewfinder of my camera.

♫   ♫   ♫

Colonel Eddie Hogan's exit from the Autry camp is about as clouded as his entrance, at least as far as my own personal information is concerned. I do know that his leaving was on a friendly basis. He left a lot of good ol' memories.

May they never die!

CHAPTER TWENTY-NINE

Gene Autry vs the CMA

Or, Hi, Mister President
Or, The Things We Did To Get Gene To Pick Up His Award

Even though he confessed that he wasn't overly sold on the Country Music Association in its beginnings, Gene did serve as its President in 1963.

"I didn't mind doing the job." Gene told me during one of our casual meetings, probably at the Plaza bar.

"But they wanted to hold meetings all the time, in Nashville yet. Hell's fire, I can't go running down to Nashville every other day. I let the Vice-President take over most of the time. You know the toughest part about that President's job? I had to sign all those damned membership cards. Have they got a lot of members!"

I was on the Board of Directors when Gene made his final meeting with them as President. The gathering was in the old Andrew Jackson Hotel in Nashville, where the full membership was present.

Gene walked up to the speaker's platform, looked around at the huge crowd gathered from all over the US and several foreign countries, and said,

"Well, I'm glad to be here. I feel just like the young Sheik who walked into his Harem for the first time. I know what to do, I just don't know where to begin!"

Tex Ritter was elected President at that meeting and served for the next two years, during which time the Association made giant strides by re-educating the public on the subject of Country and Western Music. It was during Ritter's tenure that ground was broken for the only Hall of Fame dedicated to the business to be found anywhere. On display in the museum are many artifacts pertaining to the industry's past. Gene sent then one of his guitars which can be viewed along with Smiley Burnette's flop hat and checkered shirt.

"Oh, that danged CMA," he said, a few years later. You take (he mentioned a couple of names), why I put those guys in business, now they're in the Hall of Fame, and I'm not!"

"But, Gene," I told him. "You've been nominated to that Hall of Fame every year. I know, because I'm on the committee."

Year after year his name came up on the Hall of Fame list, and each year someone else was installed. We all knew that it was bugging him, because he was quite open about it. One fellow called me who was quite upset as he had just been in a conversation with Gene in which he detected a lot of bitterness.

"I wish Gene wasn't so teed off at the Hall of Fame," the man said. "He tells it that he's going to pull his guitar out and leave his saddles and guns to the museum in Oklahoma."

"He has to make it this year," I said. "If he doesn't, I might even start seeing things from his view."

The 1969 ballots went out. Again Autry's name was there along with several other deserving people. The results were secret, with the names of the five finalists made public. Gene Autry was in the top five.

I arrived in Nashville on October 12 and made very effort to try to find out the winner, to no avail. Carl Cotner called me from Hollywood saying that Gene was preparing to come to Nashville, but some close to him thought he should not come down for reasons of their own.

"If he doesn't win it," said Carl, "He's going to feel pretty bad sitting there with three other losers while some other guy walks up to the podium. The show is on national TV and that means a lot of prestige is on the line."

I told Carl of my efforts to find out if he was the winner. Other people in Nashville were calling us insisting that Gene must show up. We were up a tree.

"Gene's not coming to Nashville," said Carl, over the long distance telephone. "That's final."

"See if you can't get him to hang on for a couple of hours more," I told Carl, racking my brain. "I'll think of something."

"It'd better be good. You know how Gene is. Unless he's certain that he's going in, he's staying away."

I had to do something drastic. I got in touch with Tex Ritter, explained the situation to him, and the two of us put our head s together. A very few people in Nashville knew who the inductee was, but they were honor bound not to tell. When I explained the situation to Tex, he made a call and then gave me the word.

I got Carl Cotner on the phone again with the good news. He, in turn, contacted Autry who grabbed a private jet and arrived at the Nashville airport at about 6 PM. Charlie Adams went out to pick him up and brought him to the Capitol Park Inn where Jimmy Wakely and I had a suite ready for him.

"Gene," I said to the new Hall of Famer as he donned his tuxedo. "I hope you don't mind all of us taking it upon ourselves to get you down here, but we couldn't stand the idea of somebody else accepting the award for you. We just had to make certain, and you won't have to sit through the whole hour wondering what's up., No doubt about it, you're it."

"That so?" said Gene Autry, running the razor over his lathered face. "How's Wakely?"

At least we were concerned.

"He'll be here in ten minutes."

At 8 PM Central Standard Time, from the Ryman Auditorium in Nashville, *The Kraft Music Hall* presented "The 3rd Annual Country Music Awards." Johnny Cash walked off with about everything in the way of awards, and Tennessee Ernie Ford did a great job as MC.

When it came tine for the Hall of Fame Award, Tex Ritter was the presenter with only about one minute left to go. The show was running overtime. When they gave Tex the signal to mention the name of the winner, Tex was on the hot seat. Here, he had great speech planned for his friend, Gene Autry, with only a few seconds left to give it. Tex burned and later told me he was on the verge of telling off the Network, Kraft Foods and everybody else for letting a thing like this happen. Anyway, Ernie Ford broke in and announced the name and Gene just did get on the show.

"I don't deserve this," he said, nervously. "But then, I have arthritis, and I don't deserve that either."

The Kraft Music Hall came to a close and Gene Autry was the newest member of the Country Music Association Hall of Fame.

The next day, Tex Ritter, Jimmy Wakely and I left the CMA meeting early to go to the Hall of Fame to meet Gene for the official induction ceremonies. Afterwards I called him aside. I walked him over to his guitar and wardrobe displayed behind plate glass.

"There it is," I said to him softly, "Still going to pull it out?"

"Oh, hell no," he said. "I've also got two saddles. You guys here can have one of them. I'll put the other in the Cowboy Hall of Fame. I might even have something else I can send over here. I'll look around."

EPILOGUE
Recollections

Johnny Bond, circa 1970.

With the closing down of Town Hall Party and Melody Ranch, not to mention the fact that Columbia Records had dropped both Gene Autry and me from their roster, I had begun to wonder whether or not yours truly hadn't had it as far as my part in this business was concerned. Tex Ritter and I had formed our Music Publishing Company (Vidor Publishing) a few years earlier, so I made plans to try and become a big wheel, provided the executive world would move over. There was still a lot of contact with Gene even though our stage appearances were few. We worked hard to make Republic Records a success, but, as soon as the new wore off, it became obvious that Gene was more interested in baseball than being in the record business.

I accepted an invitation to join the Starday Records roster and owner/producer Don Pierce. It was here that I lucked onto another break with an on-stage rendition of "Ten Little Bottles," a number that I'd recorded twice before and had been using in my nightclub act since 1951. I was asked to perform it for an audience of music executives at the DJ Convention in Nashville and it turned out that the show was recorded. It was one of those magical nights where everything worked to perfection. It was a receptive audience and I nailed the recitation. (Tex Ritter said it was about time I got it right after all those years of practice) A few days later Don Pierce called and said they wanted to release the live recording as a single. Of all the records that I'd ever made, this is the only one that ever hit the #1 spot in the charts.

In 1963, the CMA elected Gene Autry as it's President and during the following year they let me become a member of the Board of Directors. It was both interesting and enlightening to learn how they were making headway in re-educating the Nation as a whole on the subject of Country Music and we could see much growth, especially in the way that more radio stations were beginning to program our type of music once again. It was during my stay on the Board, now under the guidance of President Tex Ritter, that the idea of a Country Music Hall Of Fame Building and Museum was conceived. What a pleasure it is to stand in front of the Foundation on 16th Ave. South and say to each passerby, "Hey! I helped build that building!" even if they do look at each other and walk on. I don't claim to have done much, but at least it's good to say, "I was there."

They say, "When it rains it pours" and, sure enough, about the same time that the 10 little bottles began to do their thing, Autry chose to resume his *Melody Ranch Show*, this time on his TV station, Channel 5 in Los Angeles. Most of the old gang was there and, here again, I was hired to write as well as to perform. Inasmuch as Gene Autry was not on the show in person, we did manage to con him into doing one show, but he begged off thereafter, saying that it was harder work than it used to be. The *Melody Ranch Show* ran each Saturday night for one hour per show and lasted from 1964 until well into 1970, when it was dropped because of rising production costs. The Program Director is supposed to have commented that The *Melody Ranch Show* was yesterday's newspaper, after which he busied himself in purchasing more old movies by W. C. Fields and Laurel and Hardy. In other words, it was the station that cancelled—not Autry.

It is said that all good things must come to an end. Indeed, I had been forewarned early in my career that the life span of an entertainer could not be expected to last forever. With the coming of the seventies I began to ask myself, "how much longer do you expect to continue at this pace?" No answer being forthcoming I sat myself down and began writing about all of my experiences with Gene Autry. At this writing (1975) I can report that the manuscript is complete. After my good buddy and business partner, Tex Ritter, passed on in 1974, his widow, Dorothy Fay, asked me to write his story. All during 1974 and 1975, that's what I've been doing and can now report that it, too, is ready. Now, let me wind this little epic up by passing on my own personal analysis of Country and Western Music and this business in general.

We've all witnessed a lot of changes in our times and there are many today asking the question, "what's happening? What's going on?"

Smiley Burnette, Rufe Davis, Gene Autry, Johnny Bond and Carl Cotner take a stroll down memory land when "The Cowboy" makes his last appearance on *The Melody Ranch Show*, over KTLA, Gene's Las Angeles television station.

Every day brings on the question, "Is Country Music as we knew it, finished? Where's it heading?"

Sorry, but I have no crystal ball and am probably the last one to come up with the answer. I was told a long time ago that the only permanent thing is change, itself. With that in mind I think we have to face the fact that the day of Uncle Dave Macon, Jimmie Rodgers, Carson J. Robison and others is gone, never to return except in historical retrospectives. While we were listening to Bob Wills and his big band in the forties, we complained that he was changing our music. Indeed, Rodgers changed it considerably with his Blue Yodels, controversial lyrics and sometimes use of big bands with trumpets, pianos and saxophones. So change is nothing new. It seems to be here to stay and I, for one, choose not to fight it or complain about it.

When I recorded "What Have You Done for Me Lately" for Starday, a certain DJ in the east refused to play it because it had a horn in the band. "What are you playing?" I asked. "Johnny Cash's "Ring of Fire" was his answer. (That record has *two* horns in the band) Jimmie Davis used a trumpet in the late thirties, as did Rodgers in the twenties. Still, if you use a horn tomorrow somebody is going to squawk.

Recently a Nashville artist complained to the CMA that the organization had gone too far, causing Country Music to lose its identity.

"You've got to keep it Country!"

Then, in the same breath he added, "but don't tell me how to record or sing my songs!"

So, what is the answer? As far as this writer is concerned, I'm not looking for answers. I'm just going to go along with the crowd—that is, as long as they'll let me.

Thanks for your time.

Sincerely,
Johnny Bond
Burbank, California 91506
July 1975

EDITORS NOTE: Johnny Bond died of heart failure June 12, 1978, in Burbank, California. He was 63 years old. He was inducted into the Country Music Hall of Fame on September 22, 1999.

CHRONOLOGY

June 1, 1915	Born Cyrus Whitfield Bond, Enville, Love County, Oklahoma, halfway between Oklahoma City and Dallas. Parents: Rufus Thomas Bond and Annie Mae Camp Bond. Grandfather, Andrew Bond of Atlanta, Georgia. Grandmother—Smith.
1917	Move from Enville to a large farm/ranch 2 miles north of Marietta, about 15 miles distance.
1920	Discovers the Victrola and phonograph records.
1923	Parents lose all in Panic of 1922. Move back into the Enville area.
1926	Move into the town of Marietta, the County Seat of Love County.
1927	'Discovers' Jimmie Rodgers and others in 'hillbilly' music.
1930	Classmates in High School participate in Brass Band.
1931	Using borrowed horn, enters school band.
1933	Still in High School. Purchases 98, Ukulele from mail order house in Fort Worth. Plays professionally in Bill Lofton's local string band. Takes up guitar and banjo.
1934	Graduates. Moves to Oklahoma City. Broadcasts on radio while playing in western dance bands.
1936	Broadcasts on radio with Jimmy Wakely—KTOK.
1937	Wakely, Bond and Scotty Harrel form Cowboy Trio; "Bell Boys", on WKY.

1937	Enters University of Oklahoma. Adopts name of 'Johnny'.
1938	Composes "Cimarron". They meet Tex Ritter.
1939	Trio travels to California to appear in a Roy Rogers Movie, "Saga of Death Valley." They meet Gene Autry.
1939	Weds Dorothy Louise Murcer of Oklahoma City.
1940	Wakely Trio moves to California joining Gene Autry's CBS *MELODY RANCH* Radio Broadcast. Trio records for Decca and begin appearing in various motion pictures.
1941	Composes "I Wonder Where You Are Tonight." Signs with Art Satherley and Okeh Records (Columbia). lst daughter, Sherry Louise, born.
1942	Begins series of Western Movies with Tex Ritter at Universal.
1943	Composes "Tomorrow Never Comes". Broadcasts on *HOLLYWOOD BARN DANCE.*
1945	Begins extensive touring with Gene Autry while still participating on *MELODY RANCH* broadcast.
1946	Second daughter, Jeannie Anne born.
1948	Makes first guest appearance on Grand Ole Opry with Red Foley.
1951	Composes "Your Old Love Letters".
1953	Joins Tex Ritter on *TOWN HALL PARTY*; Channel 11, LA; NBC Radio.
1955	Ritter and Bond establish music publishing company, Vidor Publications, Inc., Ritter bring in first song, "Remember The Alamo."
1956	Autry's CBS Radio *MELODY RANCH* Broadcast cancelled. Continues to make tours with Gene. 3rd daughter, Susan Paulette, born.
1957	Columbia Records contract cancelled after 16 years.
1958	Vidor Publications pays for membership cards for Ritter and Bond to join Country Music Association (CMA).
1960	Records "Hot Rod Lincoln" for Autrys Republic Label.
1960	*TOWN HALL PARTY* cancelled.

1962	Signs with Starday Records.
1964	Records "Ten Little Bottles" at DJ Convention in WSM Studio C. Only record to reach #1 spot.
1965	Elected to Board of Directors, CMA.
1965	Re-joins Autrys *MELODY RANCH* on Channel 5, LA.
1970	Begins writing of 30 years with Gene Autry.
1973	December 6, records two songs with Tex Ritter. December 8 the two perform "Git Off My Horse" together on *GRAND OLE OPRY*.
1974	Begins writing Tex Ritter biography.
1975	Begins writing RECOLLECTIONS.